20 00

P'ENG TE-HUAI:
THE MAN AND THE IMAGE

彭德懷評傳

杜勉著

Jürgen Domes

Peng Te-huai
The Man and the Image

Stanford University Press
Stanford, California
1985

Stanford University Press
Stanford, California 94305
© 1985 Jürgen Domes
Originating Publisher:
  C. Hurst & Co., London
First published in the U.S.A. by
  Stanford University Press, 1985
Printed in Great Britain
ISBN 0-8047-1303-0
LC 85-50942

TO THE MEMORY OF MY PARENTS
FREIA AND ALFRED DOMES

ACKNOWLEDGEMENTS

The research for this monograph was made possible by a generous grant from the Deutsche Forschungsgemeinschaft, and greatly facilitated through the granting of a visitor's fellowship by the Woodrow Wilson International Center for scholars of the Smithsonian Institution in Washington, DC, during the summer of 1981. To both institutions I am deeply grateful, as I am to the Institute for the Study of Chinese Communist Problems in Shihlin, Taipei, which provided me with many materials and with excellent research facilities during the late summers of 1981 and 1982.

My thanks go to many colleagues from different countries who have helped me with numerous suggestions, and in many fruitful discussions, particularly Chang Chen-pang, Jean-Luc Domenach, Fan Chih-yüan, Dieter Heinzig, Ellis Joffe, Roderick MacFarquhar, Thomas Robinson, Richard Thornton, Ting Wang and Ezra Vogel.

In my institute at Saarbrücken, a research team of very able and reliable assistants worked with me on the project. Susanne Stroop arranged a preliminary chronology, and Eberhard Sandschneider organized the bibliography and helped me with a number of suggestions, Christel Drawer and Uwe Grieger kept my often disorganised research notes in order, and Ch'in Ching-ying helped to screen the host of materials with great thoroughness. The whole manuscript was typed with painstaking care by Maria-Theresia Trabandt, who also made numerous apposite suggestions regarding the language and style.

While thanking all those mentioned above whose help I so greatly appreciate, I have to stress that the responsibility for this study, and particularly for any shortcomings or errors, is mine alone.

I dedicate the book to the memory of my parents, Freia and Alfred Domes. When I started the work, they followed my research with great interest, but on 4 May 1984, while I was writing the manuscript, my mother left this world. My father followed her only a week later, leaving the short time of loneliness for an early reunion after almost fifty-five years of marriage.

Saarbrücken, 15 July 1984   JÜRGEN DOMES

Peng Te-Huai

CONTENTS

ABBREVIATIONS

APC	Agricultural Production Cooperative
CB	Current Background
CCP	Chinese Communist Party
CCP/CC	Chinese Communist Party Central Committee
CFJP	*Chieh-fang-chün pao* (*Liberation Army Daily*)
CKCNP	*Chung-kuo ch'ing-nien pao* (*China Youth Daily*)
CM	Cheng-ming
CNA	*China News Analysis*
CNP	*Chi-nien P'eng Te-huai T'ung-chih* (Remember Comrade P'eng Te-huai)
CPSU	Communist Party of the Soviet Union
CRG	Central Revolutionary Group
CQ	*China Quarterly*
CS	*Current Scene*
CYCIJ	*Chih-yüan-chün i jih* (One Day with the PVA)
FA	Field Army
GRSD	General Rear Services Department
HC	*Hung-ch'i* (*Red Flag*)
HCPP	*Hung-ch'i p'iao-p'iao* (*The Red Flag Waves*)
HHLY	*Hsing-huo liao-yüan* (A single spark can start a prairie fire)
JMJP	*Jen-min jih-pao* (*People's Daily*)
KMJP	*Kuang-ming jih-pao* (*The Light Daily*)
MND	Ministry of Defence, Taipei
NCNA	New China News Agency
NFJP	*Nan-fang jih-pao* (*Southern Daily*)
NPC	National People's Congress
NRA	National Revolutionary Army
PCC	*Heng-tao li-ma P'eng chiang-chün* (General P'eng, efficient and courageous in Battle)
PLA	People's Liberation Army
PRC	People's Republic of China
PVA	People's Volunteers Army
PTHTS	*P'eng Te-huai tzu-shu* (Autobiography of P'eng Te-huai)
RoC	Republic of China
URI	Union Research Institute

'P'eng Te-huai is a great warlord, great ambitionist and great plotter who crept into our Party and our army. Since several decades, he has taken a counter-revolutionary capitalist class viewpoint. He followed a counter-revolutionary capitalist line, and he opposed our great leader Chairman Mao and Chairman Mao's revolutionary line.' — Canton Area Workers Revolutionary Committee (ed.), *Fan-ke-ming hsiu-cheng-chu-yi-fen-tzu 'jen-wu-chi'* (Collected biographies of counter-revisionists), Canton, March 1968, p. 4

'Comrade P'eng Te-huai was a proletarian revolutionary of the old generation, warmly loved by the people of our country. He was an important leader of our Party, our state, and our army. He was famous both at home and internationally as a military man and a politician.' — Peking People's Publishing House (ed.), *P'eng Te-huai tzu-shu* (Autobiography of P'eng Te-huai), Foreword, Peking, December 1981, p. II

INTRODUCTION

On 28 September 1954 General P'eng Te-huai, a member of the Polit-buro of the Chinese Communist Party (CCP) since May 1945, and Commander-in-Chief of the Chinese Communist 'People's Volunteers Army' (PVA) in Korea from October 5, 1950, to September 5, 1954, was appointed Vice-President and Minister of National Defence of the People's Republic of China's (PRC) State Council, Vice-Chairman of the National Defence Council and First Vice-Chairman of the CCP Central Committee's Military Commission. In September 1955 he, together with nine other senior CCP military leaders, received the rank of Marshal[1] and was decorated with the first class of the 'Liberation', 'August 1', and 'Liberty and Independence' orders of merit. However, when he had been in office as *de facto* Commander-in-Chief of the PRC's armed forces, the 'People's Liberation Army' (PLA), for almost exactly five years, Mao Tse-tung, as the result of an intra-élite conflict which shook the very foundations of the Chinese military, had P'eng dismissed from all his posts and criticised as the leader of an 'anti-Party clique'. From his dismissal on September 17, 1959, until late 1962, he lived in retirement, virtually isolated from his former colleagues. Then he again occasionally appeared at Politburo meetings, and with his appointment as Secretary of the Control Commission of the CCP's Southwest China Bureau in late 1965, he was partly rehabilitated. In this capacity he moved to Chengtu, the capital of the large province of Szechuan. There on December 25, 1966, he was arrested by Maoist 'Red Guards' in the high tide of the 'Cultural Revolution', and brought to Peking, where he was exposed to a series of so-called 'struggle meetings' in January and February 1967. Imprisoned in April 1967 and tortured for many days during July of that year, P'eng remained in prison until he fell seriously ill in 1974. When his sickness became worse, he was trans-ferred to a military hospital, but was discharged from there under supervision. On Mao's orders, he had no medical care. He died alone, lying in a pool of his own blood, on November 29, 1974. Only on December 22, 1978, did the Third Plenum of the Eleventh CCP Central Committee, assembled in Peking, decide to rehabilitate P'eng posthu-mously, calling him a 'great revolutionary fighter and loyal member of the Party'.[2]

During the time he was in office until September 1959, and again since his posthumous rehabilitation in late 1978, P'eng Te-huai has been pictured by the official Chinese communist media and literature as an old revolutionary who made great and important contributions to the cause of communism in China. In 1959, on the other hand, the very same media accused him of being the head of an 'anti-Party clique' and, between 1966 and 1972, a 'traitor', 'ambitionist', 'capitalist-roader', and 'anti-Party counter-revolutionary element'. The two epigraphs at the beginning of the book are examples of this extremely conflicting evaluation of P'eng by the CCP.

It was this conflicting evaluation which originally caught my attention, and persuaded me to look at his life more closely; and as I became involved in scrutinising P'eng's background and experiences, the idea of presenting his biography gradually took shape. We have attempted here to establish the facts of his life and career as clearly and accurately as possible, a particularly difficult task for the first twenty-five years of his life up till 1923, and for the circumstances of his entry into the CCP, where the hitherto available literature contains conflicting versions, but also for his experiences after 1959, for which only a few fragments of information have surfaced during the last five years. There is also disagreement among Western and Chinese authors on the quality of his generalship and his abilities as a politician. The present study may offer another reasonably informed view on these issues, and I shall try to keep it as balanced and free from normative judgements as possible.

In order to reconstruct P'eng's personal biography, I have drawn on a considerable range of source material. His revised autobiography published in the PRC in December 1981,[3] the biographical works of Huang Chen-hsia and Ssuma Lu,[4] the memoirs of P'eng's bodyguard from 1950 to 1966,[5] and a number of collections of war and revolutionary memoirs[6] have proved particularly useful, as also have some meticulously edited documentary collections in Taiwan. This study draws heavily on the newspapers, journals and magazines of the CCP before 1949 and of the PRC since then, and — last but by no means least — on material presented in Red Guard tabloids and pamphlets published during the Cultural Revolution. The generous research grant of the Deutsche Forschungsgemeinschaft already referred to enabled me to do documentary work in archives at the Harvard–Yenching Library and in Hong Kong and Taipei, and to interview a number of persons who worked under P'eng, particularly in Korea in 1950-3, both in the PRC and in the United States. A fellowship of the Smithsonian Institution's Woodrow Wilson International Center for Scholars made it possible to tap the rich resources of the Library of Congress in Washington, DC.

Each period in the life of P'eng Te-huai will be described within the historical framework of political and socio-economic developments in China. Thus in order to establish the general context, each chapter will start with a brief general review of such developments during the period in question. This study, however, is written not by an historian but by a political scientist and is therefore a political biography. Although intrigued by P'eng's personal characteristics, I attempt to contribute provisional answers to the following analytical questions:

— What does P'eng's early biography reveal for the understanding of the mechanisms whereby young rural Chinese and officers of the Kuomintang (KMT) army became Marxist-Leninists in the 1920s?

— What does his role during the Chinese civil war tell us about the formation of loyalty groups within the PLA? And what were the mechanisms of the development of his own loyalty group, if there was one?

— To what extent did P'eng's experience as commander-in-chief of the PVA in Korea influence the development of his military thought?

— What were the major elements of his mature military thought, doctrines and strategies which influenced the PLA from 1954 to 1959 — as compared to those of Mao and of P'eng's successor Marshal Lin Piao?

— What can his conflict with Mao — the P'eng Te-huai crisis of 1959 — contribute to the understanding of intra-elité conflict in the PRC?

— What were the structures of the opposition of P'eng and his group to Mao and his relations with other anti-Maoist forces in the early 1960s, and how can an understanding of these relationships sharpen our analytical tools to understand the dynamics of PRC politics?

Finally, the present study attempts to give some fresh clues to understand the structures of political communication in communist totalistic single-Party systems. From the conflicting evaluations of P'eng Te-huai by the CCP leadership and in the CCP media one has to ask the question: is a leading communist politician or general viewed as an individual, or rather as a symbol — positive or negative according to the particular attitudes required of the people by their Marxist-Leninist rulers? Are we dealing with people or with personal images that can be freely manipulated? And if with the latter, as the conflicting evaluations of P'eng strongly suggest, how do the techniques of personal image manipulation function? This political biography of a Chinese communist general and politician will certainly produce no definite answer to this central problem of Marxism, but it may bring us a small step nearer to an understanding of it.

NOTES

1. Chu Te, Ho Lung, Liu Po-ch'eng, Ch'en Yi, Lin Piao, Lo Jung-huan, Hsü Hsiang-ch'ian, Yeh Chieh-ying and Nieh Jung-chen.
2. '*Jen-min jih-pao*' (*People's Daily*), Peking (hereafter *JMJP*), Dec. 23, 1978.
3. Peking People's Publishing House (ed.), *P'eng Te-huai tzu-shu* (Autobiography of P'eng Te-huai) (Peking: People's Publishing House: December 1981, hereafter *PTHTS*).
4. Huang Chen-hsia, *Chung-kung chün-jen chih/Mao's Generals*, Hong Kong: Research Institute of Contemporary History, 1968; and Ssuma Lu (ed.), *P'eng Te-huai* (Hong Kong: Research Institute on Chinese Problems, 1969).
5. Ching Hsi-chen with Ting Lu-yen (ed.), *Tsai P'eng-tsung shen-pi Ching-wei ts'an-mo-te hui-yi* (At the side of Commander P'eng: Memoirs of a Bodyguard) (Ch'engtu: Szechwan People's Publishing House, 1979).
6. Most important: *Hung-ch'i p'iao-p'iao* (The red flag waves), 20 vols (Peking: People's Publishing House, 1957–80, hereafter *HCPP*); *Chih-yüan-chün i jih* (One day with the PVA), 4 vols (Peking: People's Publishing House, 1956, hereafter *CYCIJ*); and *Hsing-huo Liao-yüan* (A single spark can start a prairie fire), 10 vols (Peking: People's Literature Publishing House, 1958–63, hereafter *HHLY*).

1

THE MAKING OF A CHINESE
MARXIST SOLDIER, 1898–1928

The historical framework

When the onslaught of the Western powers against the Chinese empire
began in the first half of the nineteenth century, the Manchu or Ch'ing
dynasty had already entered the declining phase of its historical cycle,
which had started in 1644. Poorly trained and equipped, the Chinese
armies were no match for the British invaders who forced the opening of
China to foreign trade and foreign missions in the Opium War of
1839–42 and, together with the French, in the Lorcha or 'Arrow' War
of 1857–60. While large parts of the country were devastated as the
result of the Taiping rebellion — a large-scale popular uprising against
the dynasty in Southern China from 1850 till 1864 — the European
powers, the United States and, from 1894, Japan too pressured the
Manchu court into humiliating treaty arrangements. Chinese reactions
to the Western invasion unfolded in three consecutive steps.

At first, a number of traditionally-educated civilian and military
leaders of Han (or Chinese proper) origin attempted to remedy China's
problems by combining the restoration of Confucian values with
material modernisation, mainly through the acceptance of Western military and communications technology. After the Chinese defeat in the
first Sino-Japanese War, a number of younger scholars realised the
interdependence between technology, academic knowledge, thought
and the political system. Two of them in particular, K'ang Yu-wei and
Liang Ch'i-ch'ao, impressed by the rapid modernisation of Japan, initiated the second step of the Chinese reaction: a throughgoing reform of
the administrative and educational system. In 1898 they convinced the
young Emperor Kuang-hsü that, as in Japan, forceful action from the
throne could turn the country around. But on September 10, 1898,
ultra-conservative Manchu court circles around the Empress Dowager
Tz'u Hsi launched a *coup d'état*, put Kuang-hsü under house arrest,
and abolished all his modernising edicts. Reform had failed too.

In the eyes of a young Cantonese physician, Dr Sun Yat-sen, and
many other young foreign-trained intellectuals, only one possible course

was left to remedy the country's ills: revolution. In 1905 Sun founded a 'Revolutionary League' (*T'ung-meng-hui*) — later to be renamed the 'National People's Party' or *Kuo-min tang* (KMT) — as the major revolutionary force. After a number of abortive attempts to stage an uprising of the Han against the alien Manchu dynasty, Sun and his associates finally succeeded in forging a powerful coalition of their League with Southern Chinese secret societies, regional interest groups, and parts of the modern crack units in the Imperial Army.

On October 10, 1911, this coalition rose in revolt at Wuhan, and on January 1, 1912, in the old Ming dynasty capital of Nanking, the Republic of China was proclaimed, with Sun being appointed the first President. However, in the North a general loyal to the dynasty, Yüan Shih-k'ai, assumed control and was appointed Imperial Prime Minister. To avoid civil war, Sun entered into an agreement with Yüan. The latter forced the last Manchu Emperor to abdicate on February 12, 1912, and accepted the establishment of a republic, while Sun ceded to him the office of President. Yüan's plan was in fact merely to start a new cycle — yet another one in the series of historical cycles that had lasted more than 2,000 years — with himself as the first emperor of a new dynasty. He attempted this in 1915, but only a few months later had to step back into the position of President of a republic under mounting pressure from regional military leaders — the 'warlords' (*Chün-fa*). He died on June 6, 1916, and soon afterwards, China fell apart into between seven and thirteen regions dominated by warlords who fought each other, in ever-varying coalitions and more than thirty civil wars, for the control of taxable areas.

Under the impact of the Western onslaught, the traditional values of Confucian ideology had withered away. A young generation of intellectuals had increasingly lost confidence in the ability of Confucian ethics to promote a rebirth of the country. Iconoclastic zeal, a growing interest in the solutions offered by different schools of Western social philosophy, and rising nationalistic sentiments characterised large segments of the urban intelligentsia from 1915, exploding in the intellectual reform movement soon to be named after the anti-Japanese student demonstrations in Peking on May 4, 1919.[1]

Last, but by no means least, the living conditions of the peasants, who then made up almost 90 per cent of the Chinese populace, were deteriorating. Since the mid-seventeenth century the population had tripled while arable land had expanded by only 20 to 30 per cent.[2] Hence, the plots became ever smaller and could hardly sustain the families that tilled them. By the late 1920s, only about half of the peasants were still owner-cultivators, while about 20 per cent each were part- or full-tenants, and one-tenth worked as hired farm labourers.

Hence the mix that had spelled danger for so many rulers in Chinese history was developing again: frustrated intellectuals searching for a redistribution of power, growing discontent among the urban bour-geoisie, and a peasantry suffering from an unusually severe threat to their living conditions. Under these circumstances, the leadership of the Communist International (Comintern) in Moscow became convinced that the time had come to establish a Communist Party in China, and sent Gregory Voitinsky as its representative to China in May 1920; with his assistance an organisational network of Marxist circles was established. By the summer of 1921, Voitinskii had persuaded the different circles to come together and establish the CCP. Twelve delegates, representing a total of 57 members, assembled in Shanghai in July 1921 for the First Party Congress. A leadership core was formed with a Central Committee of three members, and Ch'en Tu-hsiu was elected Chairman of the Central Committee and Secretary-General of the new Party.[3]

The first two years after the founding of the CCP were dominated by the efforts of the young intellectuals, who formed almost the entire membership of the Party at the time, to build up an autonomous labour movement and launch severe criticism against the KMT, then to some extent its competitor in labour organisation. Yet the Comintern did not tolerate for long the fact that the CCP considered the KMT its main enemy. It applied increasing pressure on the young CCP to engage in a 'united front' with the KMT, albeit at that time in the organisational form of a 'Bloc from Without', i.e. cooperation while the two parties remained mutually independent. The KMT leader, Sun Yat-sen, was not willing to accept the offer of an organisationally independent CCP, and would only agree to CCP members joining the KMT individually while continuing their allegiance to the 'Chinese section of the Comintern', as the KMT leaders called the CCP at that time. Thus the concept of a 'Bloc from Within' was developed.

During the second half of 1922 and in 1923 an intricate pattern of co-operation started to evolve between the Soviet government, the Comintern, the CCP, and the KMT. From January 1923 the Soviet Union openly supported the attempts of the KMT to reunite China, if necessary by military force. By early 1924, the 'Bloc from Within' had started to function.[4] Sun Yat-sen died on March 12, 1925, thus bringing to an abrupt end his last desperate attempt at unifying China through negotiations with the Northern Chinese warlords, and in the summer of that year the communists' control over the organisational network of the KMT, together with a broad and fervent anti-British nationalist movement, conditioned their first major success.[5] Within eight months, membership of the CCP rose from 1,000 to 10,000. At the Second KMT Party Congress in January 1926, they secured for themselves a quarter of the seats on the 'Central Executive Committee', and soon communists dominated the Organisation, Propaganda, Peasants' and Workers' Departments of the KMT Party headquarters, the training institutes for peasants' and workers' cadres, and the political commissar network within the Party-army led by General Chiang Kai-shek. Chiang was irritated by this constantly growing influence of the communists in the KMT base, and on March 20, 1926, ventured a first blow against the CCP in Canton.[6] Several leading communists within the ranks of the Nationalist army were arrested, and the militia of the communist-led KMT labour unions were disarmed. Under the impact of these events, Ch'en Tu-hsiu and a number of other CCP leaders demanded that the communists should withdraw from the 'Bloc from Within' and only cooperate with the KMT in a loose alliance; however Stalin and the Comintern leadership forced the CCP to continue the alliance on the terms established in 1923–4.

At first Moscow's decision to adhere to the 'united front' appeared to be justified. When, in July 1926, the Nationalist army under Chiang Kai-shek's command started its all-out offensive to liberate China from the rule of the warlords, the communists were again able to strengthen their position and influence in the KMT government, taking advantage of Chiang's preoccupation with the military operations. Agitating in the countryside, the CCP significantly broadened its political base in Southern China. Moreover, it succeeded in winning the allegiance of a number of Nationalist divisional and regimental commanders, including Chu Te, Ho Lung, and, to a certain extent at least, P'eng Te-huai as well. For a few weeks in the spring of 1927, the outlook for an immediate communist takeover in China appeared bright indeed. However, the centrist and right-wing forces within the KMT struck first: on April 12, 1927, their leader Chiang Kai-shek broke with the CCP and destroyed its organisation in a swift and often brutal operation.[7] The KMT-Left soon realised that it was regarded as no more than a stooge by the communists and in July 1927 it too broke with the CCP. So the Comintern's united front strategy, which Stalin had supported up to the last moment, had completely failed.[8] In September 1927, Mao's desperate effort to turn the tide again by initiating the 'Autumn Harvest Uprising' in some areas of central Hunan failed too, but he was able to escape to the mountains with several hundred followers.[9] There Chu Te joined him, and the two leaders decided to continue the struggle for communist domination of China, forming a guerrilla army — the 'Red Army of Workers and Peasants' — in the Chingkangshan mountains on the border of Hunan and Kiangsi.[10] In the second half of 1928 they were joined by another military leader who had just openly turned communist: P'eng Te-huai.

Childhood and youth

One of the major reasons why P'eng Te-huai decided to join the CCP and the Party's guerrilla units can be found in the experiences of his childhood and youth in Hunan. There are several conflicting reports on this period of his life, but none of them casts any doubt on the considerable hardships that he went through during his first fifteen years.

Hunan province is in the very heart of Southern China, and is mainly mountainous with extremely poor soil conditions. Only the fertile valley of the Hsiang river, which opens in the north of the province to an even more fertile plain around the Tungt'ing Lake bordering the neighbouring province of Hupei, provides — in principle — very good living conditions. But this plain has been heavily overpopulated, at least since the eighteenth century, with the result that the peasants' holdings were among the smallest in China, and the proportion of tenants and landless peasants among the rural population was higher than the national average. So too were the tenancy rates. The climate of Hunan is mostly humid — very hot during the (usually) rainy summers, and uncomfortably cool in winter. The people, who amount to not quite 5.2 per cent of the population of China, are lively, hot-tempered and often rather unsophisticated. They love hot and spicy food, which has made the Hunan cuisine internationally known, and they have a long-standing tradition of rebellion.

The provincial capital, Changsha, is in the heart of the northern Hunanese plain, and about 40 km. south-southeast of there is the county (*hsien*) of Hsiangtan. Here are the village of Shaoshan, where Mao Tse-tung was born, and, not far from it, the community of Shihhsiang, birthplace of P'eng Te-huai. Although one source gives 1897 as the year of his birth,[11] most others agree that it was 1898.[12] He himself gave the date as September 10, 1898, but by the old lunar calendar;[13] this would be October 24, Western style,[14] just a month and a half after the Empress Dowager Tz'u Hsi's *coup* against the reformist policies of the emperor. Different accounts are given of his social background. Huang Chen-hsia states that his father was a 'merchant and small landlord', who also owned a beancurd shop. During the Cultural Revolution, Chinese Communist sources insisted that he was born into a 'rich peasant's family',[15] but in 1980 an official CCP publication puts his family into the 'poor peasant' bracket.[16] P'eng himself, however, gives his social background as 'lower-middle peasant', and provides detailed information on their situation. For example, they lived in a thatched-straw hut and owned nine *mu* (about 1.5 acres) of unirrigated land, on which they grew tea, vegetables, sweet potatoes, cotton and bamboo. By 1904 the family had eight members: Peng's parents, his grandmother, a great-uncle, three brothers and himself.[17] He makes no mention of the beancurd shop, but that his father did own one has been confirmed to the present author by an informant from Shihhsiang.

On most of the basic data for his childhood there is agreement in the majority of sources. However, an alternative version is given by Edgar Snow, who interviewed P'eng in Yenan in 1937. By this account his mother died in 1903, when he had just entered a private primary school which taught Confucian writings in the traditional style. Here P'eng — whose given name at that time was P'eng Te-hua — was a rather rebellious pupil, who several times hit back when beaten by the teacher. In 1906 he entered a modern-style primary school, and was soon at loggerheads with his family. In protest against bad habits he broke his grandmother's opium pipe as the result of which he was driven out of the house — at the age of nine. Thereafter he herded animals, worked in a mine, was a cobbler's apprentice and became a lumberjack over a period of more than seven years.[18] But other accounts tell a somewhat less dramatic story. All agree that his mother died in 1905, when he was seven.[19] According to P'eng's own account, he started studying in the old-style primary school in 1904, where he read the standard Confucian literature, the *San-tzu-ching*, the Analects and the *Great Learning*, among others.[20] Other accounts however, give his time in the private primary school as 1905 to 1907, when he moved to a *hsien*-administered modern primary school in his native village, staying there only a year — this is corroborated by some of his class-mates there.[21] In his posthumously published autobiography, P'eng does not mention the modern school, but goes into more detail on the period after 1908, in which he claims to have suffered severe hardship.[22]

All available information tends to the view that the family fortunes took a turn for the worse after the death of P'eng's mother. In that year his father because seriously ill for some time, and 1905 and 1906 were years of very poor harvests in Hunan, when families which could scrape a living in better times fell into poverty. This was the case in P'eng's home: his youngest brother died of hunger aged only six months, and his father was forced to sell most of his property, and to pawn away most of his modest holding of land. By early 1908 the family situation had deteriorated still further, and he and one of his brothers were forced for the first time to beg for food in their neighbourhood. This must have been the point when he finally left school and started to do various menial jobs in the village: chopping wood, fishing, and selling coal from door to door. In 1908, aged ten, he was hired to take care of two water-buffaloes owned by a richer peasant, a job which he held till late in 1910.

Two accounts say that his father died in 1911,[23] but this is obviously wrong; P'eng gives the date of his father's death (which he mentions very briefly) as the spring of 1925,[24] and describes several meetings with him in the early 1920s and the previous decade. Over this it is obvious that the two accounts in question confuse his father with his great-uncle, who indeed seems to have died in 1911. This great-uncle had a considerable influence on the formation of P'eng's views about society and politics; as a young man he had been a soldier with the army of the Taiping rebels, and between 1905 and 1908, already in his eighties, he used to tell the boy about the ideals of the Taiping rebellion: that everybody should have enough to eat, that women should no longer bind their feet, and that land ownership should be made equal.[25]

P'eng may have exaggerated his own suffering between his seventh and twelfth years, but he correctly reflects the miseries of rural life in Hunan at that time, when he must undoubtedly have led a very hard life. After his great-uncle's death he left his home village to work in a strip-coal mine in the far west of Hsiangtan *hsien*, where he pushed coal-carts for twelve to thirteen hours a day, at the very low wage of 9 Yüan a month. Yet even this was an improvement for him. However, it did not last long, because in 1912, about the time when Sun Yat-sen's KMT defeated the Manchu dynasty and the First Chinese Republic was established, the coal mine went bankrupt, the owner fled, and P'eng was left without work, and with only one year's pay for about two years' work. He returned home in the autumn of 1912, and again took a

number of odd jobs. In 1913 Hunan suffered from a bad drought, and
the village merchants started to hoard grain so as to push up the price
once the inevitable famine developed. In Shihhsiang the village poor and
also many smaller farmers staged demonstrations against the hoarding of
goods, and the fifteen-year-old P'eng joined the protest. He took part in
the storming of a grain-merchant's storehouse, and in the subsequent
distribution of this grain among the demonstrators. As a result of this,
the village police chief issued a warrant for his arrest, and he had to flee
from home. For the first time in his life, he left Hsiangtan *hsien*.[26]
Following a suggestion from a relative, he went to Hsiangyang *hsien* in
northern Hunan, where the Hsilin dam on the Tungt'ing Lake was
under construction, and signed on as a construction worker there. Again
the working conditions were poor and the pay was miserably low, but
he could just manage to keep alive. He worked there for two years till
early 1916, when the dam was completed, and — obviously no longer
in danger of arrest — he returned to Shihhsiang to look for new work.[27]

It was at this time that the warlords began their endless series of civil
wars in China. In Hunan the military governor T'an Yen-k'ai, a
member of the KMT, had just been driven to the south of the province
by an ally of the Northern Chinese warlords, T'ang Hsiang-ming —
who, fearing a counter-attack by T'an's forces, was in urgent need of
soldiers. Thus P'eng made the same choice as so many other impoverished
peasant boys during the warlord period: he became a soldier which he
was to remain — under political conditions that underwent extreme
changes — for more than forty-three years.

In warlord armies

The minimum age for entering military service in Hunan at that time
was eighteen, but P'eng, who had turned seventeen in October 1915,
cheated a little — this may be why one source has given his year of birth
as 1897 — when he went to Changsha in March 1916 and enlisted as a
private second class in the 1st company, 1st battalion, 6th regiment, 3rd
brigade of the Second Division of the 'Hunan Army'. His regimental
commander was Colonel Lu Ti-p'ing and his divisional commander
General Hu Tzu-mao, soon replaced by General Ch'en Fu-ch'u. At first
he received a monthly wage of 5.50 Yüan, just sufficient for his own
expenses and to send 2 Yüan back to the family.[28] From this moment
on, almost all sources — with the exception of Huang Chen-hsia,

according to whom P'eng joined the army in 1914 — are consistent with the account in his autobiography. He must have established a rather good military record right from the start because after only seven months, in October 1916, he was promoted private first class, which meant that his monthly pay rose to 6 Yüan, of which he could send 3 Yüan home regularly — a great help for his family in Shihhsiang of whom his grandmother, father and third brother were still alive.[29]

It was a common experience for a Southern Chinese warlord soldier at that time to find the younger officers, increasingly imbued with national-ist feelings through political education by KMT agents among the troops, turning against the Northern Chinese warlord faction and supporting military leaders who were believed to sympathise with Sun Yat-sen. P'eng's first platoon commander, Kuo Te-yün, had taken part in the 1911 revolution and was an ardent follower of Sun, 'hating corrupt officials and the landlords who bullied the peasantry.'[30] He strongly influenced the young soldier, who became increasingly inter-ested in politics and started to develop sympathies for the KMT and the national revolution which that party proclaimed to be its goal.

In the autumn of 1917, civil war again broke out between the Northern warlords associated with Wu P'ei-fu, and a number of Southern warlords in loose alliance with Sun and the KMT. The commander of the division in which P'eng was serving, Ch'en Fu-ch'u, sympathised with the North. This aroused the opposition of the younger officers in the division, who soon staged a *coup* and overthrew Ch'en, so that the division joined the anti-North forces of General T'ang Sheng-chih, who was co-operating with T'an Yen-k'ai, a follower of Sun.[31] After this turn of events, the division had to retreat from the Changsha area under pressure from the Northern forces, and was reorganised in southern Hunan. Here a KMT member Lin Po-ch'ü, who later joined the CCP, was appointed director of the administrative office of P'eng's brigade: he intensified the nationalist influence among the troops. P'eng himself, in 1918 and 1919, received advanced instruc-tion in tactics while on service, and at the same time studied classical written Chinese (*Wen-yen-wen*), which greatly improved his originally rather low standard of education.[32]

Meanwhile the civil war continued. In July 1918 P'eng went on a reconaissance expedition behind enemy lines into Changsha, where after several days he was captured and put in prison, but released after two weeks. In August he returned to his unit and was given a hero's welcome, and promoted to group leader.[33] In this new post he again distinguished himself, which led to his promotion to the rank of master-sergeant and acting platoon commander in April 1919. In March 1920 the majority of Wu P'ei-fu's troops left central and northern Hunan — the signal for the Hunan Army to rise in revolt against Wu's representative in the province, the Northern General Chang Ching-yao. In a fierce four-month campaign lasting till late July, the latter was driven out of Hunan, allowing the Hunanese troops, P'eng among them, to return to Changsha.

In the provincial capital, meanwhile, a pay dispute arose among the soldiers of the Second Division, which resulted in a mutiny. P'eng took part — he would hardly have missed any opportunity to rebel in those years. The uprising was quickly suppressed, and the rebels were soon pardoned, since the Hunan Army needed every soldier at that moment, being involved in heavy fighting with Northern troops until the autumn of 1921.[34] P'eng, particularly, suffered little for his participation in the mutiny. By late August 1921 he became an officer after more than five years of non-commissioned service: he was promoted second-lieutenant and platoon commander in the 11th company, 3rd battalion, of his old 6th regiment. A few weeks later his company commander fell ill and he became acting company commander.[35]

Under the influence of his old platoon leader, Kuo Te-yün, P'eng's political consciousness now increased further. In November 1921 his company was stationed in the village of Chu-ts'u-k'ou in the Nanhsien area of Hunan, where the landless peasantry and tenants suffered considerable exploitation at the hands of a very rough landlord, Ou Sheng-ch'in. Lieutenant P'eng, infuriated by this situation, suggested to the village people that they should organise an 'Association to help the Poor' and when they hesitated, he ordered his soldiers to arrest Ou and had him executed. Although reprimanded by his superiors for this action, he was not expelled from the army or even demoted. But the events at Chu-ts'u-k'ou seem to have convinced him that he should no longer serve in a warlord army, but consider going to Kwangtung, and joining the revolutionary forces of the KMT.[36] As the result, P'eng took extended unpaid leave — he did not burn all his boats with the Hunan Army! — and went to his home county, Hsiangtan *hsien*. There he was met by Kuo Te-yün and three others, and the five decided to establish a *Chiu-p'in-hui* in the *hsien*. Late in December they drafted a proclamation which, in spite of its rather crude formulations, reflects the influence which the KMT platform had on the minds of these young peasant officers, who were soon joined by a very close friend of P'eng, Huang Kung-lüeh, then a KMT member:

First, attack the rich, implement the equal distribution of land to the tillers (*Keng-che yu ch'i t'ien*)!

Second, attack the Westerners, abolish the unequal treaties, retrieve the maritime customs for the country, abolish the concessions and the extra-territorial jurisdiction!

Third, develop the trades and professions, improve the life of the poor!

Fourth, implement self-determination by the soldiers, open the military accounts for all to inspect![37]

In early January 1922 P'eng finally decided to go to Kwangtung, and it is obvious that at that time he seriously considered joining the forces in Kwangtung, which were then loyal to Sun Yat-sen. So he went by ship first to Heng-yang and then to Shaokuan at the Kwangtung border, and from there to Huahsien where he met his friend and former military comrade Lu Kuang-hou. Lu told him that in Canton, where the local warlord Ch'en Ch'iung-ming co-operated with Sun but would soon stage a *coup* against him, a general absolutely loyal to Sun and the KMT, Hsü Ch'ung-chih, was trying to organise an independent battalion under direct KMT control. For a while P'eng was willing to join that unit, and had he done so, he would probably have become a student at the KMT's military academy at Hwangpu two years later, and either joined the CCP earlier or developed into an ardent follower of Chiang Kai-shek. We have no information about P'eng's experiences and impressions when he reached Canton city in February 1922, because his autobiography is silent on this subject. But they can not have been very favourable. Possibly he was disappointed by the situation there, for he 'decided not to join the troops, but to return home and become a farmer'.[38] However, this was more easily said than done, since he was now about to begin a veritable odyssey. The Hunan-Kuangtung border was now very closely guarded and P'eng was obviously afraid of being arrested there as a KMT agent. So he decided to return to Hunan by ship via Shanghai and Wuhan and in March 1922 left Canton on a small coastal steamer, working his passage. After putting in at Amoy and Shanghai, he finally left the ship at Wuhan. From there he travelled on the coal-tender of a train to Changsha, and then walked to Shihhsiang, arriving at his family's home in early April.[39] This journey had shown him many parts of China he had never seen before, which again doubtless heightened his political consciousness.

But for three months after his return home, he kept to his original plan to become a farmer. With the money P'eng had sent, his father had again bought a piece of land, and this P'eng now started to work. Yet after more than five years with the troops and his journey through Southern and Central China, it seems that the poor and quiet country life in his home village failed to satisfy him. And thus in July 1922, when his friend Huang Kung-lüeh wrote to him suggesting that he should take the entrance examination for the Hunan Provincial Military Academy so that he could become a fully trained officer, he heeded the call. There are indications that he later considered this decision a turning-point in his life; from now on he would no longer serve in the army just to earn his living, but as a professional soldier trained to pursue his vocation. This may be why he now changed his personal name, and registered for the examination at the academy as P'eng Te-huai.[40] He was not convinced that he would be able to pass the entrance test, because his standard of knowledge was still rather low, but in August 1922 he passed the examination and became a student at the Hunan Provincial Military Academy on September 1. He drew 5 Yüan a month, received one free hot meal per day, and lived in a room with seven other cadets. The regular training would not begin till mid-November, and P'eng used the three months' break after the examination to continue his private studies, this time reading books on history and economics and some modern literature.[41]

After nine months of intensive training, P'eng graduated from the Academy in August 1923, and immediately afterwards returned to his old 6th regiment, where he was appointed captain and unit commander of the very same 1st company which he had joined as a recruit in 1916. Meanwhile his former regimental commander, now General Lu Ti-p'ing, had become commander of the Second Division. Already in April 1924 P'eng was promoted as acting battalion commander, but still with the rank of captain. At that time the Hunan troops had joined the Northern warlords to fight the Kwangtung troops allied with the KMT along the Hunan-Kwangtung border, and P'eng took part in these skirmishes for some months. But that did not prevent him from agitating for the KMT platform among his soldiers. When he reorganised his battalion in 1925, he started, among his troops, the educational work of the *Chiu-p'in-hui* which he and others had organised in Hsiangtan in 1921.[42]

While Chiang Kai-shek established the KMT Party-army — the National Revolutionary Army (NRA) — and succeeded in conquering the whole province of Kwangtung for the KMT by the end of 1925, starting preparations for the Northern Expedition to spread the rule of his party all over China, the Hunan military also underwent some reorganisation. In April 1926 P'eng's battalion was included in the army of General T'ang Sheng-chih, and he himself was promoted major and commander of the 1st battalion of his old 6th Hunan regiment.[43] Soon his unit was in action again. In March 1926 T'ang Sheng-chih had broken with the Northern warlords, indicated that he wanted to join the KMT forces, and occupied Changsha. But after only a few weeks, Northern troops under the direct command of Wu P'ei-fu had driven T'ang's divisions out of Changsha and into the far south of Hunan. On June 2, 1926, Chiang Kai-shek and the KMT leadership in Canton decided to employ the NRA to relieve T'ang. This heralded the start of the long-awaited Northern Expedition, when T'ang troops were included in the NRA as the 8th corps. With this decision P'eng became a KMT major and commander of the 1st battalion, 1st regiment, 1st division, 8th corps of the NRA, although he himself has stated that he did not join the KMT as a party member.[44]

Becoming a communist

From July 1926 P'eng's battalion was engaged in the Northern Expedition. As a NRA unit it was reorganised on the lines established for the KMT forces; thus political commissars, many of them CCP members, were brought into the Hunan army, and their Nationalist and incipient communist indoctrination of the troops shaped the NRA into a highly viable fighting force capable of inflicting one defeat after another on the armies of the Northern warlords between July 1926 and March 1927. P'eng was with the NRA on its march through Hunan and took part in the capture of both Changsha and Wuhan, and — after the transfer of his battalion to the 1st division of the 35th NRA corps under General Ho Chien — the battle of Fengtai in Honan, where Wu P'ei-fu's forces were thoroughly defeated. Then, however, the split between the KMT and the CCP occurred, first in April in Shanghai, and then in July in Wuhan. In the civil war which unfolded in October 1927 between the KMT factions in Wuhan and the centre/right KMT National Government in Nanking, P'eng fought with T'ang Sheng-chih's troops

against the Nanking forces. At this moment he was promoted lieuten-
ant-colonel and commander of the 1st regiment in the 1st division of Ho
Chien's troops.[45] But T'ang Sheng-chih's forces, which then included
Ho Chien's 35th corps, were soon defeated by the armies of the Nanking
government — P'eng was in command of the rearguard during the long
retreat into Hunan. Here, in February 1928, Ho Chien defected from
T'ang Sheng-shih and went over to the Nanking National Government;
so once again P'eng was included in Chiang Kai-shek's army. This time
he received his promotion to full colonel and appointment as commander
of the 1st regiment in the Independent Fifth Division of the NRA under
General Chou P'an. The 3rd battalion of the 2nd regiment in this division was commanded by P'eng's close friend Huang Kung-lüeh, who
had secretly joined the CCP as a member in 1926.[46] Meanwhile the civil
war among the KMT generals had subsided for a time, and in May 1928
P'eng's unit was stationed in P'ingchiang *hsien*, a mountainous area
about 100 km. northeast of Ch'angsha. Here he was supposed to eliminate some groups of communist guerrillas, remnants of the communist
uprisings in September 1927, who were operating in the area. But he kept
his unit passive, and refused to attack the communists. We can easily
understand this attitude when we realise that he had already secretly
become a member of the CCP. How did this political decision come
about?

According to his own account, he had first heard about the CCP in
1925,[47] and it was natural for one who had experienced such great
hardship in his childhood and youth to be impressed by the persistence
with which the communists agitated for equal distribution of land
ownership among the peasants, and the dedication they invested in their
cause. That the political developments in China in 1926–7 had further
awakened P'eng politically can, moreover, be seen from the fact that in
January 1927 he established a 'Soldiers' Committee' in his unit as a
means of airing grievances and promoting political education along the
line of the KMT programme.[48] The breakdown of the 'united front'
between the KMT and the CCP must have disappointed him, but his
experiences among the KMT units fighting each other obviously can not
have encouraged him to join the party of Chiang Kai-shek, who now
started forming alliances with the local landlords in Hunan. In August
1927 his friend Huang Kung-lüeh approached him with the suggestion
that he should try to join the CCP, in the very midst of the deep crisis
which had befallen the Party after the failure of the Comintern strategy

in China. P'eng was sympathetic, but he could not yet make up his mind.[49]

Then on October 12, 1927, when P'eng was just getting involved in the civil war between T'ang Sheng-chih and the Nanking government, a representative of the CCP named Chang K'uang visited him to sound out his attitude towards the Party. Although not an official member of the KMT, P'eng at that time considered himself a 'follower of the KMT Left Wing'; but he indicated to his visitor that he had great sympathy for the CCP. Now Tuan Te-ch'ang, the secretary of the political department of his division and a long-standing CCP member, went into action. According to his own account, P'eng had already told Tuan, a close friend of his, in January that year that he would like to join the CCP, but Tuan had then said that the Party was not willing to accept new members from the Hunan forces. It seems too that P'eng wavered for some time. But at the end of October 1927 Tuan met P'eng again and told him that he could now be accepted as a Party member depending on the approval of the CCP Hunan provincial committee. Before joining the Party, however, he was supposed to study communist theory, and for that purpose Tuan gave him two books, both brief and somewhat superficial surveys of the basic features of Marxism-Leninism that were used in political education among less well educated CCP members: *The Gist of Das Kapital* and *Proletarian Philosophy*.[50]

Sometime early in 1928 P'eng — who says nothing particular about this step — must have formally applied for CCP membership. Approval by the provincial committee, which then worked underground, seems to have come rather fast, and 'about February 15, 1928', P'eng Te-huai secretly took his oath as a member of the Party.[51] Still, there remains an element of mystery surrounding his entry into the communist movement. In the short autobiography which he wrote for the *Soviet Encyclopedia* in 1952, he gave April 1928 as the date of his entry — 'by mistake', as he insists in his posthumously published autobiography.[52] Be that as it may, he was a card-carrying though still secret communist no later than April 1928, when his unit was moved to Pingchiang to fight his Party comrades who were operating as guerrillas. And he was soon to come in to the open as a major CCP military leader in Hunan.

When, in mid-April 1928, the Independent Fifth Division was suddenly relocated to Pingchiang,[53] P'eng had just read *The Gist of Das Kapital*, Bukharin's *ABC of Communism*, and the classic Chinese novel of rebellion, *Shui-hu-chuan* (All men are brothers), and he became increasingly eager to take his troops over to the armed units of the CCP.[54]

While supposed to be fighting the communist guerrilla force in Pingchiang *hsien*, he and some of his officers who had also joined the Party started to organise CCP branches and *Chiu-p'in-hui* groups in the area. After receiving information about these activities, the CCP Hunan provincial committee on July 2, 1928, sent one of its members, T'eng Tai-yüan (Minister of Railways of the PRC, 1949–65), to Pingchiang in order to establish contact with P'eng.[55] Under T'eng's influence, the Party members in P'eng's regiment decided on July 18 to launch a *pronunciamento* in favour of the CCP.[56]

On July 22 P'eng's soldiers occupied Pingchiang and other towns in the county. The county magistrate was arrested and immediately executed, as were more than 100 landlords and leaders of the local militia organisation.[57] The next day P'eng proclaimed the establishment of a Hunan Provincial Soviet Government; his unit was renamed the 5th corps of the Chinese Workers' and Peasants' Red Army, thus indicating that it was now going to fight alongside the guerrilla forces under Mao Tse-tung and Chu Te, who had rallied at Chingkangshan in early 1928 under the named of '4th corps'. While P'eng became commander of the new unit, which then numbered 2,000 men, T'eng Tai-yüan was appointed political commissar. Yet the '5th corps' was too weak to secure its hold on Pingchiang. Already on July 29, General Ho Chien ordered his troops into a general attack against P'eng's forces, and during August and September the '5th corps' was gradually driven into the mountains in the Hunan-Hupei-Kiangsi border area, suffering severe casualties. By late October, only a few hundred Red Army fighters were left under P'eng's command, and at this moment he decided to lead the remnants of his unit to the Chingkangshan to join Mao and Chu there. By about mid-November the move was complete.[58] From this time on, P'eng fought the civil war with the main force of the Red Army against the KMT.

The peasant boy from Shihhsiang in Hunan, who in the space of only ten years had advanced from private second class to major in the Hunan warlord armies, and then from major to colonel in the NRA within only two years, was now a communist general. The history of the first thirty years of his life offers conclusive insights into the mechanism which turned so many young men from the Chinese countryside and KMT officers into Marxists and active CCP members during the 1920s. The misery of the village poor and (as in P'eng's case) of impoverished former rural middle-income-group families during the turbulent time when the Chinese empire was collapsing, sharpened the social consciousness of some of these young men very early in their lives. While quite a number of peasants became ever more fatalistic as their living conditions worsened, some, particularly in Southern China where the traditions of the Taiping rebellion were still alive, started to believe that the misery of the people could be alleviated through a new upspring. This was the message P'eng learned from his great-uncle when he was barely ten years old. Revolution came about when the KMT, led by Sun Yat-sen, over-threw Manchu imperial rule all over the South in late 1911, but politic-ally and socially this attempt at a thoroughgoing renaissance of China failed. This first disappointment left the young men in the countryside who had believed in change with three options: they could fall back into the fatalism which had became the prevailing attitude of so many of the village poor; they could leave their homes and become robbers or brigands in the forests and mountains; or they could try to find a way out of their poverty by joining the army of the warlords. P'eng had decided on the third option. Yet, unlike the majority of his army com-rades in the early years of his service but like a number of others who had gone the same way, he continued to ponder the reasons for the misery of the ordinary people and to think about how it could be alleviated.

Soldiers with such attitudes usually outshone the rest in military skill, and in addition were successful in overcoming their illiteracy or semi-literacy through self-education, so that they had the chance to start careers as commissioned officers. In their new position they were soon influenced by KMT agitators, and began to support Sun Yat-sen's continuous attempts to unify China under his party's leadership. After the 'Bloc from Within' between the KMT and the CCP had been established in early 1924, the most dedicated of the KMT agitators were often communists. With fervour they propagated the KMT platform — national sovereignty, overthrow of the warlord system, establishment of a welfare state, and equalisation of land ownership — and were soon recognised by young nationalist and socially conscious officers like P'eng as the most important revolutionaries.

What made these CCP cadres so dedicated in their work and revolu-tionary convictions? This was the question which P'eng and other military men of his kind increasingly asked themselves, and which prompted them to develop an interest in communist doctrine. Chiang Kai-shek's break with the CCP in the spring of 1927 was seen by P'eng and other officers of similar outlook as a betrayal of the revolution: in their eyes Chiang, who had started forging alliances with landlord groups in the rural areas of Southern China, was about to establish a new warlord system. Hence the CCP appeared to them as the only force which could still promote the social and political changes for which they had started fighting in 1925–6. Communist cadres skilfully used the opportunity thus presented to them for the recruitment of military leaders. This is what Huang Kung-lüeh, Tuan Te-ch'ang, Chang K'uang and finally T'eng Tai-yüan did with P'eng Te-huai.

In his conversion to Marxism-Leninism, ideological considerations and education in communist doctrine played only a very small part. After he had joined the CCP, he read only the most scanty and superficial texts on Marxist theory. It was therefore as a rebel with a populist desire for the improvement of the living conditions of the rural masses rather than as a dedicated and ideologically-trained communist that he now joined the fight for communist victory in China — which for him became synonymous with the rebirth of his country.

NOTES

1. Almost a library of studies and monographs on the 'May Fourth Movement' has been published during the last two decades, but the most comprehensive description and analysis can still be found in Chow Tse-tsung, *The May Fourth Movement: Intellectual Revolution in Modern China* (Cambridge, Mass.: Harvard University Press, 1960).

2. The figure of 20 per cent can be found in Hsiao Tseng, *T'u-ti kai-ke chih li-lun yü shih-chien* (Theory and practice of land reform), Taipei: Land Bank Press, 1953, p. 7 f.

3. Cf. Ch'en Kung-po, *The Communist Movement in China* (orig. MA thesis, Columbia University, 1924), ed. by Martin Wilbur, New York: Columbia University Press, 1960; also Wilbur/How, *op. cit.*, pp. 52–5; and Benjamin Schwartz, *Chinese Communism and the Rise of Mao*, Cambridge, Mass.: Harvard University Press, 1958, pp. 34–6.

4. Cf. Allen S. Whiting, *Soviet Policies in China* (New York: Columbia University Press, 1954); Leng Shao-ch'uan/Norman D. Palmer, *Sun Yat-sen and Communism*, New York: Praeger, 1960; and Jürgen Domes, *Vertagte Revolution:) Die Politik der Kuomintang in China, 1923–37* (Adjourned revolution: Kuomintang politics in China, 1923–37), Berlin: De Gruyter, 1969, pp. 62–89.

5. Wilbur/How, *op. cit.*, pp. 90 and 495. Cf. Teng Chung-hsia, *Chung-kuo chih-kung yün-tung chien-shih* (Short history of the Chinese labour movement), Yenan: New China Publishing House, 1949, pp. 211–17; and J. Heller, 'The Labour Movement in China', *Communist International*, Moscow, no. 17, Nov. 1925, pp. 3–5.

6. Cf. *ibid.*, pp. 148–56; T'ang, *op. cit.*, pp. 244–7; Wilbur/How, *op. cit.*, pp. 218–21; and Isaacs, *op. cit.*, pp. 113–15.

7. Cf. *ibid.*, pp. 48–85; Wilbur/How, *op. cit.*, pp. 401–3 and 460–5; Isaacs, *op. cit.*, pp. 143–5; and Domes, *Vertagte Revolution, op. cit.*, pp. 191–213.

8. *'International Press Correspondence'* (Inprecor), Moscow, no. 64, September 19, 1928. Cf. Isaacs, *op. cit.*, pp. 280–2; T'ang, *Inner History, op. cit.*, 284 f.; and Schwartz, *op. cit.*, pp. 105–70.
9. Cf. Domes, *op. cit.*, pp. 276–80.
10. *ibid.*, p. 279.
11. Canton Area Workers Revolutionary Committee (ed.), *Fan-ke-ming hsiu-cheng-chu-yi fen-tzu 'jen-wu-chi'* (Collected biographies of counter-revolutionary revisionists), Canton: March 1968 (hereafter *Canton collection*), p. 4.
12. So, e.g., Huang, *op. cit.*, p. 438.
13. *PTHTS*, p. 1.
14. Editorial Bureau for Revolutionary Heritage (ed.), *Chi-nien P'eng Te-huai t'ung-chih* (Remember Comrade P'eng Te-huai), Peking: Chinese Revolutionary Museum, 1980 (hereafter *CNP*), no pagination, 1st page of introduction.
15. *Canton collection, ibid.*
16. *CNP, ibid.*
17. *PTHTS, ibid.*
18. Edgar Snow, *Red Star over China,* New York: Grove Press, rev. edn 1956.
19. *'CNP, ibid.*; *PTHTS, ibid.*; and Ssuma Lu, *op. cit.*, p. 5.
20. *PTHTS, ibid.*
21. Huang, *ibid.*; and Office of the Vice-Chief-of-General Staff Intelligence, Republic of China (ed.), *Kung-fei chün-ch'iu: T'an chih P'eng Te-huai che-ke jen* (Military chieftains of the communist rebels: What do we know about that man P'eng Te-huai?) Taipei: Ministry of Defence, Oct. 1968 (hereafter *MND*), p. 77.
22. *PTHTS*, p. 1 f.
23. Huang, *ibid.*; and *MND, ibid.*
24. *PTHTS*, p. 40.
25. *ibid.*, p. 2 f.
26. *ibid.*, p. 3.
27. *ibid.*, p. 4 f.
28. *ibid.*, p. 6.
29. *ibid.*, p. 7.
30. *ibid.*, p. 20 f.
31. *ibid.*, p. 7.
32. *ibid.*, p. 8. Lin Po-ch'ü joined the CCP in 1921 and was a member of the CCP/CC from 1938, and of the Politburo from 1945 till his death on May 29, 1960.
33. *ibid.*, p. 10 f.
34. *ibid.*, pp. 12 ff.
35. *ibid.*, pp. 15 and 22.
36. *ibid.*, p. 20 f.
37. *ibid.*, p. 23.
38. *ibid.*, p. 25 f.
39. *ibid.*, p. 27.
40. *ibid.*, p. 33.
41. *ibid.*, pp. 34 ff.
42. *ibid.*, pp. 36–38.
43. *ibid.*, p. 40 f.
44. *ibid.*, pp. 43 and 62.

45. *ibid.*, p. 40.
46. Huang, *op. cit.*, p. 438 f.
47. *PTHTS*, p. 38.
48. *ibid.*, p. 45 f.
49. Huang *ibid.*
50. *PTHTS*, pp. 62 ff.
51. *ibid.*, p. 67.
52. *ibid.*, p. 70.
53. The account of the P'ingchiang uprising given here is mainly based on the following: Huang, *op. cit.*, p. 439; *CNP*, unpaginated, 2nd and 3rd page; *PTHTS*, pp. 71–106; *MND*, p. 12; T'eng Tai-yüan, 'The story of the P'ingchiang uprising' in *HCPP*, vol. XIX (Peking, 1980), pp. 227–47; Fang Ch'iang, 'Angry wave at P'ingchiang' in *HHLY*, vol. I/2, Peking 1958, pp. 431–6; Ch'iu Ch'uang-ch'eng, 'Attack on P'ingchiang', *ibid.*, pp. 437–440; Chung Ch'i-kuang, 'Revolutionary storm at P'ingchiang', *ibid.*, pp. 441–45; Wang Chih-hsin, 'P'eng Te-huai and the P'ingchiang uprising', *Pai-k'e chih-shih* (Encyclopaedic Knowledge), Peking, no. 3, Aug. 1979, p. 13 f.; Li Chü-k'uei, 'Comrade P'eng Te-huai at the time of the P'ingchiang uprising', Political Department of PLA unit 51034 (ed.), *Wei hsin Chung-kuo fen-tou* (Fighting for a new China), Shenyang: Ch'un-feng Literature and Arts Publishing House, 1981, pp. 1–9; also in People's Publishing House (ed.), *Heng-tao li-ma P'eng chiang-chün* (General P'eng, efficient and courageous in battle), Peking: People's Publishing House, December 1979 (hereafter *PCC*), pp. 23–32.
54. *PTHTS*, pp. 76 and 78.
55. Wang Chih-Hsin, *loc. cit.*, p. 13.
56. *PTHTS*, pp. 85 ff.
57. *MND*, p. 12.
58. *PTHTS*, pp. 113 ff. *CNP* gives December 1928 as the date of the rally, but all other sources give November.

2

FIGHTING FOR A COMMUNIST TAKEOVER
IN CHINA, 1928–1949

The historical framework

Mobile warfare, strict Party control over the troops, the establishment of a tight network of village peasant organisations, and a redistribution of farmland favouring the tenants and farmhands were the major elements of the new communist strategy for survival, and soon for expansion, which now began to characterise the politics of the guerrilla wing of the CCP. Meanwhile the official CCP leadership tried to continue underground activities, mainly in the cities, and to rally the Party's organisation again. Yet it was soon torn by factional strife.[1] A debate over revolutionary strategy developed, which kept many of the Party leaders preoccupied between 1929 and 1933. Three different concepts emerged. The first was the conviction that the Great Depression had triggered a new world-wide 'revolutionary high tide'. The second was the acceptance by the so-called '28 Bolsheviks' of Stalin's view that neither in China nor internationally did it appear that a new 'revolutionary high tide' had emerged; hence the CCP should quietly strengthen its underground network *in the cities* so as to be prepared for revolutionary action at a much later date. Thirdly, Mao Tse-tung and most leaders of the guerrilla army shared the pessimism of Stalin and his Chinese supporters regarding the imminence of a 'revolutionary high tide'. Yet, unlike the '28 Bolsheviks', they followed the strategy of gradually building up rural bases to prepare for a later seizure of power in the country.

By 1933, the guerrilla strategy seemed to be succeeding. Under Mao's influence the guerrilla army, through intensive land reform measures, secured the support of the poor peasants, particularly in Kiangsi. In the same year large areas in Kiangsi, Fukien, Anhwei, Hupei and Szechwan came under CCP control. Hence the centre of the communist movement in China had shifted gradually to the 'Soviet areas'. The CCP had left the cities and tried, in many cases successfully, to mobilise parts of the countryside against the Nationalist government. Yet with the escape of the official Party leadership to the 'Central Soviet Area' in Southern Kiangsi, Mao himself was pushed aside in early 1934, and the Central

Committee took over the leadership of the Southern Chinese guerrilla forces, reverting immediately from mobile to stationary warfare. This change in tactics had results that were detrimental to the CCP cause, for by October 1934 the KMT army had succeeded in encircling 100,000 Red Army troops — about 90 per cent of all communist guerrillas — in a narrow area in the far south of Kiangsi. The CCP army was threatened with total extinction,[2] but while Mao was still kept away from decision-making, the Party leaders decided to attempt a break-out, and succeeded in escaping to southern Hunan. Thus began the Long March, the heroic phase in the history of the communist movement in China.[3] During the march Mao Tse-tung rose to almost undisputed leadership of the movement and, as new Chairman of the Military Commission of the Central Committee, to the top of the Red Army, which at that time was, *de facto*, identical with the Party.[4]

The Red Army's retreat to northern Shensi also had the effect of temporarily relieving the KMT National government of the Second Chinese Republic (1928–49) from one of its major enemies. By the summer of 1936 the KMT government was in full control of about a quarter of Chinese territory and almost two-thirds of the population. In the eastern and central parts of the country, the National government put considerable effort into development. Remarkable progress took place in education, public finance and communications. In 1935 a new currency was introduced, which remained stable till the outbreak of war in 1937, and despite great rearmament efforts in anticipation of the expected Japanese aggression, the state budget was fully balanced in the fiscal year 1936/7 for the first time since 1911. The KMT regime also had some success in achieving international equality for China. Starting with the abolition of foreign control over the customs services on January 1, 1931, the KMT diplomats, in the course of lengthy negotiations with the powers, had finally succeeded in having all the special privileges provided by unequal treaties cancelled by October 10, 1943. Yet the KMT failed to provide solutions for the poverty and backwardness of the Chinese countryside, where more than 80 per cent of the popoulation still lived. This provided further chances for the CCP.

The communists, in urgent need of a respite after the Long March, launched a propaganda offensive, aiming at the creation of a new 'united front', this time with a specific anti-Japanese character. Under the impact of continuous Japanese advances the CCP drive was at least partly successful. Chiang Kai-shek, on the other hand, put in hand a policy of first achieving internal unity by fighting the CCP and the remaining warlords, and afterwards planning resistance to Japan. But the CCP, operating with the slogan 'Chinese do not fight Chinese!', managed to win increasing support for its programme of united action to resist the Japanese invaders. In the spring of 1937 first contacts were made between the Nationalist government and the CCP, but they did not yet result in an agreement. Rather, from late May 1937 the nationalists began to assemble new troops in order to launch another, probably final 'extermination campaign' against the communists. Yet at this moment the Japanese invasion of China saved the communist movement. On July 7, 1937, the Sino-Japanese War — and thus the Second World War — began, and immediately after open hostilities broke out, the KMT and the CCP began to co-operate once again in an 'Anti-Japanese United Front', which this time followed the pattern of a 'Bloc from Without', a federation of organisationally independent partners.[5] Within the CCP the strategies to be followed during the period of the second united front were disputed. Mao Tse-tung stood for a cautious and limited guerrilla war against the Japanese, and for diverting 70 per cent of the Party's efforts towards the stabilisation and gradual expansion of the communist base areas, so as to be ready for an all-out effort to conquer China after the end of the war. His view prevailed, and the CCP came out of the war a politically unified, dedicated and ideologically committed body under the undisputed leadership of Mao, who, at the Seventh Party Congress in May 1945, was officially elected Party leader in the capacity of Chairman of the Central Committee. Implementing a moderately reformist agrarian policy, characterised mainly by the lowering of land rents and welfare for the rural poor, the Party won the allegiance of many Northern Chinese peasants, who were then tightly organised into CCP-controlled associations.

Meanwhile the KMT troops fought a desperate defensive campaign to prevent Japan's total conquest of China south of the Hwanghe.[6] The communists, however were soon carrying on guerrilla activities, and the CCP-administered area constantly expanded behind the Japanese lines in Northern China and Manchuria.[7] When the Japanese surrender came into effect on September 3, 1945, the United States administration attempted to bring about a coalition government of the KMT, the CCP and a number of small liberal groups to take charge of post-war reconstruction in China.[8] The Soviet Union, on the other hand, violated the treaty which it had concluded with the National government in August 1945 by preventing the entry of KMT units into Manchuria until the CCP had stabilised its hold over the Manchurian countryside and the whole province of Heilungkiang. This it had done by early 1946.

In spite of American efforts to assist in the establishment of a coalition government in China, both the CCP and the KMT were aware at the end of the war that the final round in the fight for the control of China was about to begin. At the beginning of the decisive struggle, the KMT army had a 350 per cent numerical superiority over the communist troops. But the US administration, still dedicated to the idea of bringing about a coalition government, declared an arms embargo against the Chinese Nationalists which resulted in their entering a temporary armistice agreement with the communists. However, the renewed KMT-CCP negotiations, in which President Truman's special envoy General George C. Marshall acted as intermediary, brought no results. Finally, on January 7, 1947, Marshall declared that his mission had failed, and returned to Washington.[9] Open civil war now started to rage throughout China. In its incipient stage the nationalists again won victory and for more than a year afterwards, it conducted the war with varying degrees of success but with no decisive outcome. The PLA began its general military offensive in Manchuria in the summer of 1948, but in November and December 1948 the communists eliminated almost one million Nationalist crack troops in the battle of Hsüchou-Huaihai in northern Kiangsu.[10] After that, no nationalist fighting unit remained intact between Peking and the Yangtse. When in January 1949 Tientsin and Peking fell, Chiang effectively admitted defeat by resigning from his office as President of the Republic of China. Efforts to achieve peace by negotiation failed and when on April 23 Nanking surrendered, the Nationalist government escaped to Canton, from there to Chengtu, the capital of Szechuan, and finally to Taiwan. The CCP had gained control of the whole Chinese mainland, and the People's Republic of China had come into being.

Among the most important factors leading to the defeat of the KMT were the economic crisis with its runaway inflation, the decimation of the KMT's fighting forces, administrative corruption and inefficiency, and the Soviet Union's support for the CCP immediately after the Second World War. The KMT's defeat was indeed caused by political and socio-economic developments, but the reasons for the communist victory must be considered too, and these can be found in the structure and approaches of the CCP during the civil war. However, all these reasons together would not have sufficed to bring about the communist victory in China had it not been for the Japanese invasion in 1937. This invasion brought to an end five years of considerable success for KMT development policies, and probably saved the Red Army from destruction in northern Shensi. To simplify somewhat, it is possible to argue that communist rule in China emerged from the superior organisational qualities of the CCP, the weaknesses and mistakes of the Nationalists, but above all from the Japanese attack on China.

We now turn to P'eng Te-huai's role in the historical process that has just been briefly described.

In the first stage of the CCP/KMT Civil War

The arrival of the remnants of P'eng Te-huai's 'Red 5th Corps' in the Chingkangshan area marked, as we have seen, the beginning of more than thirty years of co-operation — and at times disagreement also — between him and Mao Tse-tung. In December 1928 P'eng's soldiers were included in the 'Red 4th Corps' with Chu Te as commander and P'eng himself as deputy commander. The position of political commissar was taken by Mao, and that of Director for the Political Department of the corps by Ch'en Yi. From this time those who had taken part in the Nanchang uprising, the 'Autumn Harvest' uprising, and the Pingchiang *pronunciamento* started joint or at least co-ordinated military operations.[11] Soon after the first meeting with the Chingkangshan guerrillas, P'eng had to bail out Mao when KMT units encircled a group of Red Army soldiers to which he was attached; P'eng troops broke the encirclement and drove the enemy off.[12] Not long after that, the Party Committee of the reorganised 'Red 4th Corps' met in the village of Pailu to discuss future strategies in the conduct of the civil war. The Chingkangshan area was very poor and rather cold in winter, and thus a good retreat, but it was unsuitable as a base for the gradually growing guerrilla forces. So it was decided that the troops of the old 'Red 4th Corps' under Chu and Mao should attack from the Chingkangshan into Southern Kiangsi, where only weak and poorly organised warlord units would be encountered, to enlarge the base area called the 'Soviet District'.

In January 1929 Chu and Mao moved with their guerrillas into southern Kiangsi and quickly occupied a large agricultural area around the country town of Juichin, while P'eng was left behind with his old troops to defend the Chingkangshan. Here he re-established his 'Red 5th Corps' of about 700–800 men, but soon he came under attack from about 25,000 Hunan province KMT troops and after heavy fighting was forced to evacuate the mountain area and retreat to Southern Kiangsi, where he joined Chu and Mao in March at Juichin. Thirty-eight years later, in 1967, this retreat was to be called P'eng's 'first crime' by the CCP's Cultural Revolutionary Left, and Red Guard tabloids reported, apparently with justification, that he was criticised by Mao for this retreat although he had thereby saved his units from extinction. Accepting Mao's criticism, P'eng brought the strength of his troops up to approximately 1,000 and returned to the Chingkangshan, which the Nationalists had meanwhile evacuated.[13]

Here, in mid-1928, two former bandit leaders, Wang Tso and Yüan Wen-ts'ai, had joined the Red Army and the Party with their followers, and during P'eng's retreat they had remained in the Chingkangshan area and dispersed into the forests, but after the re-established 'Red 5th Corps' returned to the mountains, a severe conflict developed between P'eng and the two local ex-bandits. The conflict was over supplies as well as over the contradiction between free-wheeling guerrilla raiding tactics and the military ethics of professional discipline in organised mobile warfare. By July 1929 the former bandit units rose in revolt against P'eng, but his troops defeated them. Yüan Wen-ts'ai was executed on P'eng's order, Wang Tso committed suicide, and their former followers were included into the 'Red 5th Corps', which thus swelled to slightly more than 2,000 men.[14] Having secured control over the Chingkangshan, P'eng fortified the base and soon started organised raids into Southern Hunan to recruit more men and acquire food and supplies. The two largest and most successful of these raids were staged in late July 1929 and in late March and early April 1930.

Between these raids, basic decisions had to be taken about the organisation of the Red Army and its future strategy. For this purpose the Party Committee of the 'Red 4th Corps' met at the village of Kut'ien in December 1929. At this 'Kut'ien Conference' Mao argued for a continuation of mobile guerrilla strategies based on classic brigand ethics and style, and for the strengthening of political indoctrination in the Red Army through the establishment of a tight network of political commissars. The professional military commanders, in particular Chu and P'eng, argued rather for strict military discipline and strategies of mobile, but organised warfare, as well as for the officers to have precedence over the commissars. After difficult negotiations a compromise was reached: in military operations professional rather than brigand ethics, style and strategy would prevail, while the generals had to accept the strengthening of political indoctrination through commissars appointed by the Party organs.[15] Thus the basic contradiction within the ranks of the Red Army was solved for the time being, but a new conflict, this time over general revolutionary strategies, was soon to evolve.

In April 1930 P'eng's troops were again reorganised. Under his command a 'Red 3rd Army' was formed, consisting of the 'Red 5th Corps', with P'eng himself as concurrent commander and T'eng Tai-yüan as political commissar, and the newly-established 'Red 8th Corps' of which Ho Ch'ang-kung was commander and Teng Ch'ien-yüan commissar.[16] It was in this formation that P'eng received new battle orders, not from Mao this time but from the official CCP leadership who had taken refuge in the French concession at Shanghai. There an honest, semi-illiterate labour leader, Hsiang Chung-fa, had officially been appointed Secretary General of the Party in 1928, but the *de facto* leadership had increasingly been taken over by the director of the Central Committee's Propaganda Department, Li Li-san, a Hunanese like Mao and P'eng. The great worldwide economic depression had convinced Li that a new 'revolutionary high tide' was evolving in China, and to take it at the flood he should instigate the Central Committee to call for a general uprising in the country. On July 13, 1930, he accordingly sent a letter to the leaders of the Southern Chinese guerrilla forces with the order to 'conquer one provincial capital' as a signal for the expected 'nationwide revolutionary storm'. While Mao and Chu were rather sceptical about Li's revolutionary enthusiasm, and so started preparations for a general offensive by their troops in a remarkably slow manner, P'eng obediently followed the orders of the Party leadership. From the most easterly part of Hunan he prepared for a large-scale attack against the provincial capital, Changsha, then occupied by KMT regular units under General Ho Chien, and the city of Yüehchou.[17]

The offensive began on July 25 with a force of almost 17,000 soldiers of P'eng's 'Red Third Army' and more than 10,000 supporting guerrillas, and at first it had shattering success. On July 27 Yüehchou was taken, the next day P'eng's troops broke through the KMT lines, and on July 30 they conquered Changsha itself, which was hastily evacuated by Ho Chien. Here on August 1, exactly three years after the Nanchang uprising, a 'Hunan Provincial Soviet Government' was established with Li Li-san — still in Shanghai — as Chairman and P'eng as Vice-Chairman. Yet the victors of Changsha waited in vain for the 'revolutionary storm' to break all over China. Even Chu and Mao moved their troops only very slowly into Eastern Hunan, and they were still too far away to give P'eng effective support when Ho Chien launched his counter-attack with 35,000 men on August 5. In heavy fighting and with a loss of about 7,500 of his men, P'eng was driven out of the provincial capital and forced to retreat to Eastern Hunan. There he was finally able to join forces with Chu and Mao. The first Changsha campaign had utterly failed, but the strategy of attacking provincial capitals continued for a while. The units of Chu, Mao and P'eng were now combined into the 'Red First Front Army' with Chu as commander, P'eng as his deputy and Mao as political commissar. After three weeks of manoeuvring, P'eng, on September 1, started a second attack on the capital of Hunan. Again Chu and Mao were very grudging in their support, and P'eng's attack, launched in a fierce open assault — at one point, in classic Chinese fashion, behind a line of wild bulls — failed in the outskirts of Changsha with heavy losses.[18] After this defeat he retreated with the 10,000 soldiers and guerrillas who remained with him into Eastern Hunan and from there he soon moved on into Kiangsi. At Hsiachiang in Kiangsi he met Mao and Chu to discuss future strategies after the failure of the two Changsha campaigns. While Chu and P'eng were still willing to try new attacks against either Nanchang or Chiuchiang, Mao argued that the time was not yet ripe for large-scale offensive, and that it was more important just now to consolidate and gradually expand the 'Soviet' base areas.[19]

For the 40,000 Red Army troops now operating in Kiangsi a decision was pre-empted by two events: a grave internal crisis in the Soviet area, immediately followed by the first large-scale KMT offensive against the Southern Kiangsi base. These forced them to accept Mao's strategy. Under the influence of Li Li-san, local Party members in Southwest Kiangsi had set up an Action Committee which opposed not only the cautious strategy promoted by Mao, but also the increasing power of Hunanese and Szechwanese cadres over the local CCP organisations in Kiangsi. In late November, some leading figures of the Action Committee, among them Li Wen-ling, Tuan Liang-pi, Hsieh Hanch'ang and Li Po-fang, were arrested by soldiers of Chu Te's corps and imprisoned in the country town of Fut'ien. When news of their arrest reached an independent local unit, the 'Red 20th Corps' — loosely connected with P'eng's 'Red 3rd Army' — 400 of its members rose in revolt at Tungku on December 7, 1930. From there they attacked Fut'ien, captured the town and freed the Action Committee leaders. After a few days they were driven out of Fut'ien, but took to the mountains and called for support from Chu Te, P'eng, and P'eng's old friend the deputy commander of the 'Red 3rd Army', Huang Kung-lüeh. The 'Fu'tien Incident' — as this event has since been called — ended with the rebellion being suppressed.[20] Mao and his supporters successfully put the blame for the uprising on a semi-secret KMT anti-communist organisation, the 'Anti-Bolshevik Corps' (which in fact had only existed in Kiangsi for less than seven months in 1927), and used it as a convenient reason for ridding the Soviet area of all intra-Party opposition. Chu, P'eng and Huang Kung-lüeh sent a letter to the rebels refusing their support, and by late January 1931 the Red Army had succeeded in defeating the insurgents; more than 4,000 people were executed in bloody reprisals.[21] In future intra-Party conflicts doubts were several times cast on P'eng's attitude during this confrontation, although he had remained loyal to Mao and Chu.

Immediately after the Fut'ien rebellion, in mid-December 1930, an external threat had to be warded off when the Kiangsi province troops of the KMT rallied about 100,000 men for a general attack on the Red Army which was soon called the First Extermination Campaign. This campaign, which lasted till January 3, 1931, ended in dismal failure with heavy losses for the KMT units; half a division were wiped out by P'eng's 'Red 3rd Army' in the battle of Tungshao, and another whole division by Huang Kung-lüeh's and Lin Piao's troops in the battle of Lungkang. A second Extermination Campaign in April and May 1931 and a third one from July to September also ended in total failure for the KMT armies.[22] In both campaigns P'eng's 'Red 3rd Army', along with the other units of the CCP armed forces, won crushing victories. Yet these victories were won in conventional mobile operations rather than by means of the guerrilla warfare which Mao had advocated. Hence they strengthened the position of professional military men like Chu and P'eng, who argued for the building-up of a well disciplined and trained regular army as the core of the communist movement, and wanted to assign only auxiliary roles to the guerrilla units which Mao regarded as the backbone of the CCP forces in the civil war.

Meanwhile, as a result of the failure in Changsha in 1930, Li Li-san had come under increasing criticism within the CCP. This was the moment of the 'Bolsheviks', who had arrived in China together with the new Comintern representative on the CCP Central Committee, Pavel Mif. Among them were Ch'en Shao-yü (Wang Ming), Ch'in Pang-hsien (Po Ku), Chang Wen-t'ien, Wang Chia-hsiang and Shen Tse-min. At the Fourth Plenum of the Sixth CCP Central Committee, which assembled in Shanghai in early January 1931, Li was accused of 'leftist adventurism', relieved of all his posts in the Party, and sent to the Soviet Union 'for study'. The official Party leadership was thus taken over by the 'internationalist', pro-Comintern group, which was soon joined by Chou En-lai, previously an ardent supporter of Li. This group now set out to establish 'Bolshevik discipline' in the Soviet area too, where some of its major leaders arrived in 1931, fleeing from the increasing persecution by the KMT political police in Shanghai.[23] This, however, meant new difficulties for Mao, whom the 'internationalists' did not trust.

The defeat of the first three KMT Extermination Campaigns had made it possible to establish a more permanent structure for the Soviet area. For that purpose the First Chinese Congress of Soviet Representatives assembled in Juichin, Kiangsi, in early November 1931 and on the anniversary of the Russian October Revolution, November 7, it proclaimed the establishment of a 'Chinese Soviet Republic' with Mao as Chairman of the Central Soviet Government and Chu Te as Chairman of the Central Military Council. P'eng became a member of the last-named, and in addition was appointed to the Central Executive Committee of the new Chinese Soviet, his first position of political leadership in the communist movement. But while Mao had thus been elevated to be official head of the newly-established communist government, he could not increase his standing in the Party organisation, and had also to give up his commissar status in the Red Army. Moreover, during 1931 and 1933 a number of professional military men who had received advanced training in Moscow returned to the Soviet area, among them Yeh Chien-ying and Liu Po-ch'eng, to be joined in October 1933 by a military representative of the Comintern, Otto Braun, who operated under the Chinese name Li Te.[24]

Under the influence of these men, and with the support of the military leaders in the Soviet area — notably Chu, P'eng and Lin Piao — it was determined 'to regularise the military by improving the curriculum [for the Red Army academy] in Juichin, standardising tactical doctrine through the use of Russian manuals, and standardising equipment and organisation'.[25] These measures appealed to the professional military man P'eng Te-huai, and he thus began to support the 'internationalists' and the military strategies which they had been suggesting since early 1932, an attitude which earned him blame as a 'supporter of the ''leftist'' opportunist Wang Ming line' from the Cultural Revolutionary Left in 1967,[26] but also abundant praise in the memoirs of Otto Braun.

The most remarkable figure among the corps commanders was P'eng Te-huai. Since he had joined the Red Army with his troops in 1928, he supported Mao, in whom he saw the charismatic leader of the revolutionary armed forces. Yet this does not mean that he agreed to everything. As active politically as militarily, he never minced his words when he thought that criticism was necessary . . . Occasional chats with him and his Soviet-trained political commissar, Yang Shang-k'un, convinced me that both were internationalist-minded and loyal friends of the Soviet Union. That may have decided their tragic fate in the 1960s.[27]

Influenced by the new strategy of conventional military attack propounded by the 'internationalists', and by Otto Braun and the officers who had returned from the Soviet Union, P'eng in February 1932 led the 5th, 7th and 8th corps, i.e. the major part of his 'Red 3rd Army', into a frontal attack on Kanchow. This city was no longer defended by KMT provincial troops but by crack units of the NRA under the command of General Ch'en Ch'eng, who inflicted a crushing defeat on P'eng's forces, forcing them to retreat after losing more than 3,000 men. After this defeat P'eng believed that although the Red Army might be able to hold its own in a conventional battle against provincial forces, it was quite another matter with the well equipped and trained 'central divisions' of the NRA, which were now increasingly involved in the campaigns against the Red Army in Kiangsi. When the leaders of the CCP convened a meeting of the Party's Military Commission under the chairmanship of Chou En-lai in Ningtu, Kiangsi, in August 1932 to plan measures against the unfolding fourth Extermination Campaign by about 400,000 KMT soldiers (July 1931-April 1933), he still sided with those who advocated conventional mobile warfare rather than roving guerrilla activity. While Mao at this conference lost his membership of the Party's Military Commission, and his ideas about 'people's war' were discarded, P'eng became Vice-Chairman of the Commission.[28] This appointment brought him for the first time into a central Party organ, and as a consequence he was co-opted about seventeen months later as an alternate member of the Sixth CCP Central Committee at that body's Fifth Plenum in Juichin in January 1934.[29] This last appointment was not only — as Cultural Revolution sources later suggested — a reward for his support of the policies of the 'internationalists', but much more for his military successes in 1933. From February 27 through March 1, his troops had annihilated the crack 52nd NRA division in the battle of Chiaohu,[30] and after the indecisive end of the fourth Extermination Campaign he had entered the province of Fukien with his 'Red 3rd Army' in August 1933, conquered Yenping, Ninghua and Chingliu for brief periods in this foray, and captured a large amount of arms and ammunition.[31]

Now, however, a grave danger loomed over the Central Soviet area in Southern Kiangsi. Starting in October 1933, the KMT government prepared for its fifth Extermination Campaign with the aim of finally annihilating the CCP base. This time Chiang Kai-shek personally took command of almost 800,000 soldiers, including most of the crack units of the NRA, to oppose altogether about 150,000 Red Army soldiers and guerrillas. To counter this threat, the active CCP military leadership — Chu Te, Chou En-lai and Chang Wen-t'ien, advised by Otto Braun — prepared for a strategy of more or less static defence, which greatly facilitated the encirclement of the 'Central Soviet' area by the NRA. In January 1934, right after the Fifth Plenum of the Sixth CCP Central Committee and the Second Soviet Congress in Juichin, the KMT Northern Army Group under Ch'en Ch'eng began to move south. It was P'eng's task to confront it with his newly organised '3rd corps' near the town of Kwangchang. He led 35,000 soldiers into this conventional resistance operation, and suffered very heavy losses, being forced to retreat with barely more than 20,000 men left.[32] Other communist commanders fared little better, and by September 1934 the Red Army in Southern Kiangsi was encircled by an ever-tightening ring of NRA troops.

This was the moment when the decision was taken that the regular troops of the CCP should evacuate the base in Southern Kiangsi and move into Hunan. P'eng's 3rd corps was reorganised in four regiments with altogether 18,000 men under his command. It formed part of the 102,000 men who, by breaking through the lines of Cantonese provincial KMT units on October 20, 1934 — started the Long March.[33] Of P'eng's 18,000 men who had left Southern Kiangsi, only about 3,000 arrived in Northern Shensi by mid-October, after a year of fighting in the main column of the March. On October 20, 1935, exactly a year after the Kiangsi breakthrough, they marched into the small Shensi town of Wayaopao, thus placing P'eng among the hard core of Long March leaders. More important, he had shifted his allegiance from the 'internationalist' group to Mao Tse-tung. The failure of the strategies suggested by the 'Twenty-eight Bolsheviks' and Otto Braun in Kiangsi during 1934 had obviously convinced him that Mao's more mobile strategy of guerrilla warfare might contribute more to the survival of this communist movement in China than the conventional ideas to which he had adhered between 1931 and 1934. Hence he was one of the major supporters of Mao at the crucial conference in Tsunyi, Kweichow, in January 1935.[34] Here Chou En-lai lost his position as Chairman of the Party's Military Commission — now the only important leadership organ in the communist movement, at least for two or three years — to Mao, and the 'internationalist' Secretary General Ch'in Pang-hsien was replaced by another of the 'Twenty-eight Bolsheviks', Chang Wen-t'ien, who however was on better terms with Mao than Ch'in. When the Maoerhkai conference of August 1935 decided against a retreat into Sinkiang and for the continuation of the Long March into the small communist base area in Northern Shensi, P'eng also supported Mao, and during the second half of the retreat operation he gradually became one of the two closest lieutenants of Mao in the Red Army, the other being Lin Piao.

After October 1935 the Red Army, now with less than 20,000 men, tried to consolidate its base in Northern Shensi, around Paoan, Wayaopao, and soon afterwards in the new capital, Yenan. Already in the spring of 1936 a new offensive was started by the newly-organised 'Red 1st Front Army' under P'eng as Commander-in-Chief, but his foray into the neighbouring province of Shansi failed, and he had to retreat to Yenan. In October he was more successful with a drive into Kansu, where he received remnants of another column of the Long March, the troops under Chang Kuo-t'ao and Hsü Hsiang-ch'ien. By early 1937 the new Soviet base around Yenan had been consolidated, and the numbers of the Red Army were already up again to about 30,000 men, but the possibility of another attack by the KMT army still presented a threat. In the reorganised Red Army, Chu Te was appointed Commander-in-Chief in April 1937, and because of P'eng's very convincing fighting record during the Long March and his strong support for Mao ever since January 1935, it was almost a foregone conclusion that he would be Vice-Commander-in-Chief, and thus the second-ranking leader of the Chinese communist forces.

Then, with the battle of Lukou Bridge near Peking on July 7, 1937, the Sino-Japanese war broke out, and with it came the establishment of the second 'united front' consisting of the two opposed Chinese parties. Once again, although this time only formally, P'eng became an officer — in fact a general — in the NRA.

Defence against the Japanese invasion

According to the 'united front' agreement between the KMT National government and the CCP, the Northern Shensi 'Soviet area' was renamed, on August 25, 1937, the Shansi-Kansu-Ninghsia Border Area with a special administrative status that secured wide-ranging autonomy, and indeed almost total independence, for the communist-ruled district. The same day, the Red Army was formally renamed the 8th Route Army of the NRA. At that time the new unit numbered altogether 32,000 regular soldiers, of whom 4,000 were attached to headquarters as guard units. Chu Te became Commander-in-Chief of the 'Eighth Route Army', P'eng was appointed Vice-Commander-in-Chief, Yeh Chien-ying Chief of Staff, Tso Ch'üan Vice-Chief of Staff, Jen Pi-shih Director and Teng Hsiao-p'ing Vice-Director of the Political Department. The former units of the Red Army were reorganised into three divisions: the 115th with 14,000 men under Lin Piao, the 120th with 6,000 men under Ho Lung, and the 129th with 8,000 men under Liu Po-ch'eng.[35]

A few days before the new KMT/CCP agreement came into force, a meeting of all major communist military and political leaders convened on August 20, 1937, at Loch'uan near Yenan.[36] Here Mao argued that during the war against the Japanese invaders the CCP in fact had a second war to fight against the KMT. Hence the Party's military units should operate cautiously in the front line against the Japanese, relying mainly on guerrilla warfare, continuously expanding their bases behind the enemy lines, and saving their military strength for future anti-KMT struggles. However, Chou En-lai, P'eng, Chang Kuo-t'ao and most of the military leaders who attended the meeting argued for an all-out war effort against Japan, and for an entirely unambiguous adherence to the 'united front' policies. For the time being Mao's strategic ideas were not accepted in full, and thus the 8th Route Army fought hard during the first three years of the war. Already in September 1937, when the Japanese army invaded Shansi and moved rapidly towards the capital of that province, Taiyuan, P'eng and Chou En-lai went there to discuss plans for a joint resistance effort with the pro-KMT Shansi warlord, Yen Hsi-shan.[37] As a result of these talks, the communist troops took part in the defence of the province, and although this could not stop the Japanese from taking Taiyuan, it did finally hold up their advance into Northern and Western Shansi. While this was mainly the operating region of Lin Piao's 115th division, P'eng stood close to the front line in the Wutai Mountains, directing the overall strategies of the communist war effort in that area. Then, although not yet a full member of the Central Committee, he was called to Yenan to attend a Politburo meeting on December 13, where he was again involved in an argument with Mao over the quantity of men and resources which the CCP should commit to the war against Japan.[38]

Yet in 1938 P'eng began to move towards Mao's positions, which he fully supported when the main promoter of an honest 'united front' policy, Chang Kuo-t'ao, broke with the CCP and fled to the KMT-held areas. Starting from the second half of 1938, P'eng set up headquarters in the T'aihang Mountains in eastern Shansi, close to the Hopei border, from which he directed the fight against the Japanese in both provinces, committing to it about two-thirds of the 'Eighth Route Army', now already numbering approximately 150,000 soldiers. A former communist cadet Ssuma Lu, who lived in the communist-held areas in the late 1930s, later recorded this impression about P'eng's military role: 'In 1938–9 . . . Chu Te was rather often in the rear, in Yenan. At the front line the real responsibility of leading the war rested with P'eng Te-huai and the frontline chief-of-staff, Tso Ch'üan.'[39] From 1938 to the summer of 1940 the communist troops confined the Japanese in Northern China to cities and communication lines, ever expanding their areas and gaining a considerable number of new recruits. P'eng was mostly in the T'aihang Mountain base, from which conventional forays were frequently made into Japanese-held territory. Then in July 1940 Chu Te, from Yenan, ordered the '8th Route Army' to undertake an all-out offensive with the aim of destroying as much of Japanese communication lines and posts as possible: the 'Hundred Regiments Campaign', the largest communist effort of the whole war, in the making.[40] To this campaign the different units of the communist army committed altogether 105 regiments with at least 200,000 regular soldiers and about 200,000 guerrillas, mostly from the 129th division of Liu Po-ch'eng, the 120th division of Ho Lung, and the newly-established 'Independent Brigade' under Nieh Jung-chen, while Lin Piao's troops were only marginally involved. P'eng, who had had no units under his direct leadership since his appointment as Vice-Commander-in-Chief of the Red Army early in 1937, was given overall command.

The campaign, which lasted from August 20 to December 5, 1940, started with a very successful assault in late August and early September, in which large numbers of bridges, tunnels and railway tracks were destroyed, and comparatively heavy losses were inflicted on the enemy. The second stage of the campaign, from mid-September to early October, brought destruction of numerous Japanese outposts, but also heavy losses for the communist troops. Then the Japanese army counter-attacked, and from October 6 till December 5, 1940, the communist regular units were involved in large-scale defence operations, which were mainly successful in so far as the Japanese attempts to break up the communist bases were repelled. In all, the 'Hundred Regiments Campaign' can be called a limited success, although later Cultural Revolutionary critics of P'eng called it a 'strategic mistake which brought great losses for our army',[41] and P'eng's 'second crime'. As a result of the campaign, the Japanese had large parts of their forces tied down in Northern China for large parts of 1940 and 1941, and had to work until well into 1942 to restore their communication network in the area. But this price was high too: the '8th Route Army' lost more than 22,000 men, while Japanese losses were between 4,000 and 6,000. After this campaign, the communist commanders became much more cautious, and increasingly adopted the strategies which Mao had suggested in late 1937: to save manpower, establish and consolidate bases, and fight only when attacked. In early 1941, the Japanese army started a counter-attack with the main objective of driving P'eng's headquarters out of the Taihang Mountains, where the main force of the 1940 campaign had retreated. After protracted and fierce fighting, P'eng finally decided to move his headquarters and the major base away from the T'aihang area to save manpower. He returned to Yenan in late 1941.[42]

From early 1942 until the end of the war in September 1945, P'eng's tasks were increasingly political rather than military, and he seems to have moved closer to Mao during that time. His political career in the CCP started with his appointment as an alternate member of the Sixth Central Committee in January 1934. From then on he also participated occasionally in meetings of the Politburo, although he is not listed as a member before 1945.[43] As usual with communists who have reached the higher circles of decision-making, he also began to publish articles and booklets; the first came out in November 1937 and was a small pamphlet discussing strategic problems of the war against Japan. In it P'eng still took the attitude that the war effort of the CCP should have been full-blooded and without reservations.[44] This was followed by a newspaper interview in January 1938 in which, for the first time in a publication, he praised the role of the guerrillas,[45] another interview in June 1939, and an article the following month, where the views he expressed were almost entirely those of Mao.[46] With two further booklets published in his name, in 1940 and 1943 and thus authorised by him even if he did not actually write them — P'eng supported Mao's strategic views in strong words, praising the 'mass line' and the contribution of mobile and guerrilla warfare to the survival and expansion of the communist-held base areas.[47] However, this no longer required great courage because already in 1938 Mao had defeated his intra-Party rival Chang Kuo-t'ao, and by 1940 even the remnants of the 'internationalist' group were no longer able to challenge his leadership. When Chang was expelled from the Party, at the Sixth Plenum of the Sixth CCP Central Committee in Yenan (September 29 to November 11, 1938), P'eng was co-opted as a full member of the Central Committee,[48] and in August 1942 he became Acting Secretary of the CCP North China Bureau, temporarily replacing Liu Shao-ch'i who was deeply involved in the 'Cheng-feng' movement. From 1942 to 1944 P'eng also played a quite important part in this movement; in 1980 a PRC source stated that he 'led the Cheng-feng movement in the base area of Northern China' and also the 'great production mass movement'.[49] On November 23, 1943, he addressed a meeting of cadres and Party intellectuals in Yenan whom, in a rather commanding style, he exhorted to 'reform themselves', 'become one with the masses', and submit themselves to party discipline.[50]

The years of war against Japan were crucial in the formation of the political ideas to which P'eng adhered in the next decade. He never gave up his professional military ethics, but he had now accepted that Mao's strategies would be more successful in preparing for the final victory of the Party, to which he had developed an unswerving loyalty. His knowledge of Marxist and Leninist doctrines was still not very profound, but he agreed to the iron Stalinist discipline which was inculcated into the CCP members during the 'Cheng-feng' period. Otherwise he projected an image of simplicity, straightforwardness and care for his subordinates. Ssuma Lu recollects that he was 'very kind to the soldiers'[51] — a feature which frequently recurs in stories about P'eng — , and even P.P. Vladimirov, a Soviet adviser in Yenan from 1942 to 1945, in an otherwise highly critical account of CCP leaders, awards him high marks:

P'eng Te-huai is well-versed in military affairs, and is popular in the army. He dresses simply, even in Yenan terms. The most significant trait of his character is modesty. He has a deep, coarse voice, his movements are slow. This man has a rare sense of personal dignity. He holds Mao Tse-tung in respect as the leader of the CCP.[52]

The war years from 1937 to 1945 not only further shaped P'eng's personality and brought his views close to those of Mao at the time, but they also changed his personal life. Some sources mention that P'eng was married in 1926, but it is difficult to assess what significance this had for him. In 1938, however, he was married again, this time — like several other CCP leaders — to one of the young intellectuals who had come to Yenan for patriotic reasons and joined the Party. His new wife, P'u An-hsiu, was twenty-five years old at the time of the marriage. She and her elder sister who married Lo Lung-ch'i, a liberal intellectual, were born in the province of Kiangsu, having received their college education in Peking in the turbulent years of student activism between 1932 and 1936. From now on P'u An-hsiu assisted him with his reading and writing.[53]

Thus suitably equipped on both the personal and political levels, P'eng was about to move officially into the very centre of decision-making. Between April 23 and June 11, 1945, the Seventh Party Congress of the CCP took place in Yenan, the first such meeting for seventeen years. Here P'eng was one of the six major speakers — the others being Mao Tse-tung, Liu Shao-ch'i, Chou En-lai, Ch'en Yi and Kao Kang — and on June 10 he was elected a full member of the new Seventh Central Committee, a Vice-Chairman and the Chief-of-Staff of the Party's Military Commission, and — even more important — either an alternate member (according to one source)[54] or even a full member (according to several other sources) of the new Politburo.[55] It was in this capacity that he entered the decisive period of the second Civil War against the KMT.

Towards victory in the Civil War

On September 3, 1945, Japan's unconditional surrender became effective, and the Second World War was at an end. However, in China this was only the sign for the beginning of the final showdown between the CCP and the KMT. Already in October 1945, despite all the negotiations that were in progress, armed clashes between the communist troops and the NRA were occurring almost throughout Northern China. It was during this month that P'eng was given command of units of the CCP which, in a combined operation with Soviet and Outer Mongolian troops, occupied most of Inner Mongolia and accepted the surrender of the Japanese troops stationed there.[56] And only a few months later, for the first time in nine years, he was again in direct command of an army unit. In March 1946 the regular military forces of the CCP, now already numbering some 1.1 million, were reorganised under the new name of 'Chinese People's Liberation Army' (PLA), and divided into a number of 'Field Armies'. P'eng himself became Commander-in-Chief of the Northwest Field Army of approximately 175,000 men, which consisted mostly of troops who for many years had served under the leadership of Ho Lung. Ho was consequently appointed Vice-Commander-in-Chief, but he spent most of his time at the Party Centre headquarters. P'eng brought with him the new Political Commissar for his unit, Hsi Chung-hsün, but his subordinates included very few who had been under his direct command before. The Northwest Field Army (NWFA) was divided into seven 'columns', of which four were led by generals with long periods of service under Ho Lung — Chang Tsung-hsün, Hsü Kuang-ta, P'eng Shao-hui and Yao Che — while the other three 'column' commanders — Wang Chen, Chang Ta-chih and Lo Yüan-fa — had previously led independent smaller units.[57]

In its major field of operation in the incipient Civil War — the provinces of Shensi, Ninghsia and parts of western Shansi — the NWFA had to face a dangerous enemy indeed: crack units of the NRA commanded by a first-class military leader and brilliant strategist, one of the best minds in the KMT army, General Hu Tsung-nan. Moreover, it was the most poorly equipped of all the newly-organised PLA Field Armies. When, after ten months of negotiation between the KMT and the CCP during which there was continuous fighting, the last stage of the Civil War broke out openly, the NWFA was given the difficult task of defending the communist capital at Yenan against the offensive which Hu Tsung-nan launched with a force of 260,000 in early March 1947. Despite stiff resistance, P'eng had to fall back and abandon Yenan to the enemy, who celebrated the capture of the CCP's capital as the beginning of the end for the 'communist rebellion'. But before his troops evacuated the city, their resistance made it possible for Mao and the Party Centre to move further north.[58] Pushed back towards the Inner Mongolian border, P'eng managed to stop the attack of Hu's army in early August in the fierce battle of Shachiatien, now often considered to have been the turning-point of the Civil War.[59] During this battle his forces saved Mao and the personnel of the CCP Central Committee organs from being taken prisoner by the NRA, an event which caused the Party Leader to dedicate this poem to his general:

> The mountains are high, the road is long and full of potholes,
> Many soldiers are moving to and fro.
> Who is the courageous one, striking from his horse in all
>   directions?
> None other than our great General P'eng! [60]

After Hu's advance had been stalled, the NWFA spent the rest of 1947 and January-February 1948 in further defence movements, gradually increasing its fighting strength to close on 200,000 men, and holding its own in the northern Shensi/Inner Mongolia border area. By March 1948 P'eng's forces were ready for a counter-attack. By late March they encircled an isolated KMT garrison at Watzuchieh near Yich'uan in order to lure stronger NRA units into a reinforcement operation. And indeed in this way they were able to ambush a whole NRA corps in the battle of Yich'uan, where the enemy was decisively beaten and forced into a disorderly retreat. [61] In hot pursuit P'eng recovered Yenan on April 22, 1948, but his further offensive towards the west with the aim of taking the town of Paochi found Hu's troops reorganised and with their morale recovered. In two days of fighting at Chingchuan in May the NWFA was defeated and driven back to its operational base in the Huanglung (Yellow Dragon) Mountains. From there P'eng attacked the enemy again in August, and defeated a KMT division in the battle of Fengyuanchen, thus saving Yenan from a second attack by Hu's troops. However, another offensive which he launched on October 5, 1948, against the town of Tali resulted in another defeat and forced him to withdraw to his base area for the winter of 1948/9. [62]

Meanwhile, the armies of Liu Po-ch'eng and Ch'en Yi had won the decisive battle of Hsüchou-Huaihai, and Lin Piao had forced the surrender of the NRA in Manchuria. Tientsin fell to Lin's and Nieh Jung-chen's forces in January 1949, and a few days later the PLA entered Peking. All over North China the Nationalist lines were crumbling, but this was still not the case in P'eng area of operations. Here Hu Tsung-nan's troops were putting up a strong and successful defence effort. In February 1949 the whole PLA was reorganised into five large Field Armies. P'eng's NWFA now became the First Field Army, with himself as Commander-in-Chief, with Ho Lung, Chang Tsung-hsün and later

Chao Shou-shan too as Vice-Commanders-in-Chief, and Hsi Chung-hsün as Political Commissar. The First Field Army now had a strength of approximately 260,000 men, divided into two armies with four corps each: the 1st under General Wang Chen and the 2nd under General Hsü Kuang-ta.[63] In this structure the First FA was supposed to launch the final offensive against the NRA in Northwestern China by May 1949, but P'eng, who had visited Peking in April and again in May to discuss the plans for his last campaign in the Civil War with Mao and Chou En-lai,[64] was still not blessed with an easy victory. While the forces of Liu Po-ch'eng, Ch'en Yi and Lin Piao swept through all of Southern China, the First FA just managed to capture the city of Sian in late May with difficulty after strong resistance from Hu's force. The further events of the last months in the Northwestern campaign have been succinctly described by William Whitson and Huang Chen-hsia:

In a plan to draw P'eng into a trap, Hu Tsung-nan fell back to the west along the Wei River and ordered Ma Pu-fang, commander of the Ninghsia army [a Chinese Muslim], to concentrate on P'eng's northern flank. On June 12, 1949, the battle was joined in the Kuanchung River valley, where P'eng discovered, too late, that he had fallen into a trap. After suffering heavy losses, his six corps fell back to the east. Fortunately for P'eng, Nieh Jung-chen's victory at T'aiyüan [Shansi] in April had released forces for commitment elsewhere. Nieh dispatched the 18th and 19th Armies [commanded by Hsü Hsian-ch'ien and Yang Te-chih respectively], as a strategic reserve for P'eng. When these forces were committed to P'eng's support in mid-July, the Nationalists were forced to withdraw, permitting the First Field Army to occupy Poach'i on July 14.

There, the First Army, supported by the 18th and 19th armies of the North China Field Army, continued its attack to the northwest, seizing Lanchou [the capital of Kansu] on August 25 and Hsining [the capital of Tsinghai] on September 5. In the *Kansu Daily* (August 1, 1957), 'Chang Ta-chih [in 1949 commander of the 4th corps, 2nd army] wrote that the six-day battle of Lanchou was one of the bloodiest engagements of the Civil War. Attacking with three corps on line and one in reserve, Hsü Kuang-ta's 2nd Army suffered nearly 10,000 losses. Approximately 50,000 Muslim defenders under Ma Pu-fang 'fought like devils'.[65]

And even after Lanchou and Hsining had fallen — and by September 22, 1949, all of Kansu, Ninghsia and Tsinghai was in the hands of the PLA — P'eng could not totally destroy the forces of Hu Tsung-nan and Ma Pu-fang. They made an orderly retreat through the mountains to Szechwan, from which some of Hu's best units were soon evacuated to

Taiwan. The vast region of Sinkiang still remained to be conquered, and here P'eng's First FA had a much easier task. The commander of the NRA in Sinkiang, General T'ao Chih-yüeh, realised that, trapped between the PLA and the borders of Outer Mongolia and Soviet territory, it made no sense to fight on. On September 29, the day on which the proclamation of the PRC was being prepared in Peking, he declared an armistice and in early October surrendered to Wang Chen and his Political Commissar, Wang En-mao. His forces were now included in the First FA as the new 22nd army.[66] During the ensuing winter, PLA troops under P'eng's command gradually occupied most of Sinkiang, and then moved into the Pamir Mountains. There, in September 1951, one of its cavalry regiments reached Ladakh and so completed the CCP's takeover of the Chinese mainland.[67]

Right after the establishment of the PRC on October 1, 1949, P'eng was appointed Chairman of the Northwest China Military and Administrative Commission and concurrently Commander-in-Chief and Political Commissar of the new Sinkiang Military Area, with Wang Chen as his deputy. In this capacity, he was in charge of political, administrative and also military affairs for the vast north western part of the country, including the provinces of Shensi, Kansu, Ninghsia, Tsinghai and Sinkiang, an area of almost 3 million square km., but at that time with less than 30 million inhabitants. The NRA colonel who, together with all his comrades, had joined the fight for communist rule in China at P'ingchiang in Hunan on July 22, 1928, had at last reached his goal after more than twenty-one years of incessant war.

To evaluate P'eng's merits as a military commander during these twenty-one years is not easy. All available sources indicate that he easily won the loyalty of his subordinate officers and troops, and this was a matter of his personal character: he led a simple, frugal life and worked hard. Most sources — excluding the inimical attacks during the Cultural Revolution — praise his straightforward way of dealing with superiors and his kindness towards his subordinates. He could be bitingly critical of errors, but because he never cringed to the Party leaders, including Mao, this was not held against him. In battle he was always courageous, but often made quick and unpremeditated decisions. Hence his record as a commander up till 1949 remains a mixed one. Of twenty-nine major battles which he personally directed, fifteen were victories and fourteen resulted in defeat for his units. He was always ready to take high risks, and his most outstanding achievements were when he was fighting for survival, as at the time of the rebellion of former bandit troops in the Chingkangshan (June 1929), during the storming of Huichou in January 1932, the defence of Yenan in March 1947, and the battle of Shachiatien in August the same year. However, his offensives often failed, as at Kanchow in February 1932, in the battle of Kwangchang in January 1934, in the Tali campaign in October 1948, and again in the battle of the Kwanchung valley in June 1949, which turned out to be the last major defeat of PLA forces in the Civil War on the Chinese mainland. In particular, P'eng had difficulties holding his own when confronted by enemy commanders who were either moderately or exceptionally good strategists, like Ch'en Ch'eng in Southern Kiangsi in 1932–4 and, especially, Hu Tsung-nan in the northwest in 1947–9. In sum, the evidence of P'eng's military performance in the Civil War and the Sino-Japanese war suggest that he was extremely brave, a good campaigner and tactician, but at best a fair if not a mediocre strategist, never attaining the brilliance of Liu Po-ch'eng and Ch'en Yi, or even the astuteness of Lin Piao.

As a corollary, one finds a certain naivety in P'eng's political attitudes during the several intra-Party disputes in the 1930s and early 1940s, probably the result of his straightforward nature. Hence an almost blind loyalty to the Party meant that he usually followed the dominant line in CCP politics and strategies at any given period. This was not due to opportunism but because he respected the Party leaders provided that they did not work openly against his few rather simple basic convictions. These convictions included the idea that the CCP's major task was to strive for the improvement in the living conditions of the ordinary people, particularly the peasants and the village poor. In military matters, the major trait was his belief in professional military ethics as opposed to the classic brigand ethics of the guerrilla. Within the limits of these professional ethics and the military style that went with it, he promoted mobile warfare but was mostly against the roving tactics of guerrillas. Also, he had no particular liking for excessive political indoctrination, especially if it impeded professional military training. Last but by no means least, he was firmly convinced that political commissars should be under the command of professional officers, and his personal relations were best with those of his commissars who respected his position — T'eng Tai-yüan, Yang Shang-k'un, and Hsi Chung-hsün.

These basic convictions were mostly not in accord with those of Mao. Hence the two men not infrequently clashed, especially during the operations of 1929, in the Changsha campaign of 1930, in 1933–4, and again in the early years of the Sino-Japanese war. In the summer of 1930

P'eng clearly supported the strategy promoted by Li Li-san, and thus later accusations that he was 'following the Li Li-san line' were well substantiated. Li's idea that an attack on a provincial capital should be the signal for a general uprising in China appealed to his courage and to his temperament which made him believe more in offensive and mobility than in defence and caution. However, he had no personal connection with Li, and thus no special loyalty to him. After Li's failure had become obvious, P'eng, therefore had no difficulty in changing his allegiance to the 'Twenty-eight 'Bolsheviks' early in 1931. But again he had few personal ties with this faction. He was pleased by Ch'en Shao-yü's, Chang Wen-t'ien's and Otto Braun's emphasis on a professional military style, on thorough training, and on the importance of conventional warfare. Yet when the strategies of the 'internationalists' brought the Red Army to the brink of extinction in the second half of 1934, P'eng realised that Mao's prescriptions might make more sense if the survival of the communist movement was at stake. This was apparently his major reason for switching his allegiance to Mao and his followers during the Long March, which became instrumental in bringing about Mao's victory at the Tsunyi conference.

P'eng nevertheless parted ways with Mao again in the early stage of the Sino-Japanese war. In the Loch'uan and December conferences of 1937, he supported the strategy of an all-out military effort against Japan, and honest and close co-operation with the KMT in the second 'united front' — promoted by Chang Kuo-t'ao and the remnants of the 'internationalist' faction — against Mao's strategic concept of waging the war against the Japanese invaders with limited efforts and goals, while simultaneously preparing for a final showdown with the KMT after the end of the Sino-Japanese war. The reasons for this attitude are difficult to assess since P'eng had no particularly close personal ties with either Chang Kuo-t'ao or the 'internationalists', but it can be argued that Mao's concept appeared too tricky to his plain and simple mind, and to his basic conviction that the CCP, once the 'united front' agreement had been concluded, was bound to execute it faithfully.

With the beginning of the 'Cheng-feng' movement, P'eng had finally found himself ranged on Mao's side, although he was still criticised severely for his 'mistakes' in 1937–40 on the eve of the Seventh CCP Party Congress in March and April 1945.[68] But despite later accusations by the Cultural Revolutionary Left, there is no solid evidence that P'eng engaged in further conflicts with Mao after the Seventh Congress. He had already accepted Mao as the undisputed Leader, and he admired him as well for his success in the communist movement. By 1945, and for a number of years afterwards, Mao became the object of P'eng's almost unswerving loyalty.

But who could be considered a loyal follower of P'eng? Since the early days of the Red Army, and right through the Civil War and the Sino-Japanese war, a distinct type of primary group formation developed within the ranks of the Chinese communist armed forces: the 'Field Army' networks or loyalty groups formed on the lines of the traditional fighting units in the PLA. There was a 'Second FA system' which rallied around Liu Po-ch'eng and Teng Hsiao-p'ing, a 'Third FA system' around Ch'en Yi, and a 'North China FA system' around Nieh Jung-chen, and a large number of 'Fourth FA' military leaders, though not all, were loyal followers of Lin Piao. P'eng did not have a large group of followers tied to him by many years of joint fighting. His closest followers were probably those who had joined in the P'ingchiang uprising of July 1928 — among them Huang K'e-ch'eng, T'eng Tai-yüan, Fang Ch'iang, Yao Che, P'eng Shao-hui and Liao Han-sheng — and who had survived the wars. But many of his P'ingchiang comrades had been killed in action. By 1966 only nineteen major participants in the P'ingchiang *pronunciamento* were still alive.[69] Of these nineteen, eleven were purged and persecuted in the 'Cultural Revolution', seven survived it in office, and the fate of one — Chou Yü-ch'eng — is unknown. However, a number of the P'inchiang rebels moved to other units of the Red Army as early as 1930–1. In fact, those military men and commissars who served under him in the 'Red 5th Corps' and the 'Red 3rd Army', and of whom most were with his units on the Long March, had a much longer history of personal ties to P'eng. Ten of them were to hold important positions in the PLA or in the Party and state administrative machine after 1949: Huang K'e-ch'eng, Hung Hsüeh-chih, Yang Shang-k'un, Hsü Hai-tung, Ch'eng Tzu-hua, T'eng Tai-yüan, Liu Chen, Fang Ch'iang, P'eng Shao-hui, and Yao Che. This group can be considered as P'eng's oldest and most personal network, and it is note worthy that all but the last two of these ten cadres were purged and persecuted in the Cultural Revolution.

In his overall command position as Vice-Commander-in-Chief of the Red Army and the '8th Route Army' from 1937 till 1946, P'eng had no troops under his direct command, except during a few campaigns like that of August-December 1940. This seems to be the major reason why, at the end of the Civil War, he could not rally such a tightly-knit network as the other major PLA commanders. When he took charge of the NWFA in 1946, which became the First FA in February 1949, most of it's units had a very long record of service under Ho Lung, and some came from independent Northwest Chinese units under Wang Chen, Hsiao K'e and Chang Ta-chih. Hence there was a 'First FA system', and P'eng obviously won the sympathy of most of its major cadres during 1946–9, but this network was much more the loyalty group of Ho Lung, to whom twenty-three of the thirty-five major commanders and commissars of the First FA had developed close allegiance in joint fighting over more than fifteen years up till 1945. As we shall see, this fact became of great importance when P'eng clashed openly with Mao in 1959. But in late 1949 the Marxist-Leninist general was setting out with his comrades to consolidate communist rule in China — at first as the undisputed overlord of the wide Northwest.

NOTES

1. Cf. Hsiao Tso-liang, *Power Relations within the Chinese Communists Movement, 1930–1934: A Study of Documents* (Seattle: University of Washington Press, 1961).
2. Documents in *Ke-ming wen-hsien, op. cit.*, vol. XXV, pp. 90–2; and Wu Hsiang-shuang (ed.), *Chung-kuo kung-ch'an-tang chih t'ou shih* (Behind-the-scenes history of the CCP), Taipei: Wen-hsin Publishers, 2nd edn, 1962), pp. 156–8. Cf. Charles B. McLane, *Soviet Policy and the Chinese Communists, 1932–1946* (New York: Columbia University Press, 1958), pp. 54–6; and Robert C. North, *Moscow and the Chinese Communists* (Stanford University Press, 2nd edn, 1968), pp. 166–8.
3. For CCP accounts of the Long March, see Peking People's Publishing House (ed.), *Stories of the Long March* (Peking: Foreign Languages Press, 1958).
4. Dieter Heinzig, *Mao Tse-tung's Weg zur Macht und die Otto-Braun Memoiren* (Mao Tse-tung's road to power and the Otto Braun memoirs), Berichte des Bundesinstituts für Ostwissenschaftliche und Internationale Studien, Cologne, no. 52, 1970, pp. 28–33.
5. Cf. Domes, *Vertagte Revolution, op. cit.*, pp. 674–6.
6. Cf. Lily Abegg, *China's Erneuerung: Der Raum als Waffe* (China's renewal: Territory as a weapon) (Frankfurt/Main: S. Fischer, 1940; Jack Belden, *China Shakes the World* (New York: Random House, 1949); Tong, *op. cit.*, pp. 237–9; and Gottfried-Karl Kindermann, *Der Ferne Osten in der Weltpolitik des industriellen Zeitalters* (The Far East in world politics in the industrial age) (Munich: DTV, 1970), pp. 384–6 and 389–91.
7. Cf. Chalmers A. Johnson, *Peasant Nationalism and Communist Power: The Emergence of Revolutionary China 1937–1945* (Stanford University Press, 1962); and Jacques Guillermaz, *Histoire du parti communiste Chinoise, 1921–1949* (History of the CCP, 1921–1949) (Paris, 1968), pp. 302–4.
8. *United States Relations with China: With Special Reference to the Period 1944–1949* (Washington, DC: US Government Printing Office, 1949), pp. 127–255; Vidya

Prakash Dutt (ed.), *East Asia: China, Korea, Japan 1947–1950* (Oxford University Press, 1958), pp. 197–201 (Wedemeyer Report). Cf. Tsou Tang, *America's Failure in China, 1941–1950* (Chicago University Press, 1963).

9. Dutt, *op. cit.*, pp. 197–199.
10. Cf. James Pinckney Harrison, *The Long March to Power* (New York: Praeger 1973), pp. 630 f.
11. For the events of early 1929: *PTHTS, pp. 113–328; Huang, op. cit.*, p. 439; and Capital Red Guard Congress, Ch'inghua University Chingkangshan Corps (ed.), *Ta yin-mou-chia, ta yeh-hsin-chia, ta chün-fa P'eng Te-huai tsui-e shih* (The wicked history of the big plotter, big ambitionist, big warlord P'eng Te-huai) (Peking, November 1967), also in Ssuma Lu, *op. cit.*, pp. 116–40 (hereafter quoted from there; here p. 119).
12. *MND*, p. 36.
13. *PTHTS*, pp. 117 and 126 f., and Ssuma Lu, *op. cit.*, p. 119.
14. *ibid.* P'eng Te-huai mistakenly places this event in 1930 (*PTHTS*, pp. 141 ff.).
15. For a very succinct account of the Kut'ien conference, cf. John A. Rue, *Mao Tse-tung in Opposition, 1927–1935* (Stanford University Press, 1966), pp. 171–89.
16. Huang, *op. cit.*, p. 441. *CNP*, unpaginated, places this event in June 1930.
17. For the attack on Changsha and other events of the summer of 1930: *PTHTS*, pp. 149–59; Ssuma Lu, *op. cit.*, p. 120, and *HHLY*, vol. I (Peking 1958), pp. 548–57. Cf. William W. Whitson/Huang Chen-hsia, *The Chinese High Command: A History of Communist Military Politics, 1927–1971* (New York: Praeger, 1973), pp. 46 ff.
18. *PTHTS*, pp. 157–9, and Ssuma Lu, *ibid.*
19. *ibid.*
20. For the Fut'ien incident, cf. Cheng Hsüeh-chia, *Chung-kung Fut'ien shih-pien chen-hsiang* (The real story of the Chinese Communist Fut'ien incident) (Taipei: Institute for the Study of International Communism, October 1976); Wang Chien-min, *Chung-kuo kung-ch'an-tang shih-kao* (Draft history of the CCP), 3 vols (Taipei: Reprint Institute on Mainland Problems, Chinese Cultural University, 1983), vol. II, pp. 528–41; and Whitson/Huang, *op. cit.*, p. 49.
21. Huang, *op. cit.*, p. 439 f. Cf. Cheng, *op. cit.*, pp. 89 ff. Ssuma Lu (*op. cit.*, p. 2) even gives a figure of 'more than 10,000' executions.
22. For the first three 'Extermination Campaigns', cf. Whitson/Huang, *op. cit.*, pp. 268–74.
23. The best treatment of these events currently available, albeit a short one, can be found in Richard C. Thornton, *China: A Political History, 1917–1980* (Boulder, Colo.: Westview Press, 1982), pp. 44–8.
24. Otto Braun, *Chinesische Aufzeichnungen, 1932–1939* (Chinese notes, 1932–1939) (East Berlin: Dietz, 1973), pp. 46–9. (English transl. by Jeanne Moore: *A Comintern Agent in China, 1932–1939*, London: C. Hurst/Stanford University Press, 1982).
25. Whitson/Huang, *op. cit.*, p. 275.
26. Ssuma Lu, *op. cit.*, p. 120 f.
27. Braun, *op. cit.*, p. 85 f.
28. Ssuma Lu, *op. cit.*, p. 121.
29. *CNP*, unpaginated. Huang Chen-hsia mistakenly states that P'eng Te-huai had already become a full member of the CCP/CC at that time.
30. Whitson/Huang, *op. cit.*, p. 277.

31. *ibid.*, p. 280.
32. Huang, *op. cit.*, p. 440.
33. Whitson/Huang, *op. cit.*, p. 281.
34. *PTHTS*, p. 195 f.
35. *ibid.*, p. 220 and footnote 56 on p. 296 f.
36. For the Loch'uan meeting, cf. Chang Kuo-t'ao, *Wo-te hui-yi* (My memoirs), 3 vols (Hong/Kong: Ming-pao Monthly Press, 1972–4), vol. III (1974), pp. 1287–1302, and Whitson/Huang, *op. cit.*, p. 67 f.
37. *PTHTS*, p. 221.
38. *ibid.*, pp. 224 ff; and: *CNP*, photograph no. 27.
39. Ssuma Lu, *op. cit.*, p. 1.
40. Discussions of the 'Hundred Regiments Campaign' can be found in People's Publishing House (ed.), *K'ang-jih chan-cheng shih-ch'i te Chung-kuo jen-min chieh-fang-chün* (The Chinese PLA in the period of the Anti-Japanese War) (Peking: People's Publishing House, July 1953), pp. 108–18; *PTHTS*, pp. 234–241; Ssuma Lu, *op. cit.*, p. 124 f.; and Whitson/Huang, *op. cit.*, p. 70.
41. Ssuma Lu, *ibid.*, p. 125.
42. Huang, *op. cit.*, p. 441.
43. *CNP, ibid.*
44. P'eng Te-huai, *Cheng-ch'ü t'e-chiu k'ang-chan sheng-li-te hsien-chüeh wen-t'i* (Grasp the problems of securing victory in the protracted war of resistance) (Yenan: no publisher, Nov. 1937).
45. 'Hsin-hua jih-pao', *New China Daily*, Yenan, Jan. 13, 1938.
46. 'Commander P'eng talks about how to grasp the war of resistance in Hopei and how to strengthen unity'; in *Ch'ien-hsien* (Front Yenan, no. 8/9, 1939, pp. 2–6; and P'eng Te-huai, 'Strengthen the Anti-Japanese bases in the enemy's rear', *Ch'ün-chung chou-pao* (The Masses Weekly), Yenan, July 6, 1939, p. 230.
47. P'eng Te-huai, *San nien k'ang-chan yü pa-lu-chün* (Three years war of resistance and the Eighth Route Army) (Yenan: New China Publishing House, 1940), and P'eng Te-huai, *Wo-men tsen-yang chien-ch'ih Huapei liu nien-te K'ang-chan* (How did we stand through six years of resistance in Northern China?) (Yenan: New China Publishing House, 1943).
48. *CNP*, photograph no. 41. Significantly, the caption of this picture does not mention K'ang Sheng, who is clearly recognisable.
49. *ibid.*, unpaginated.
50. 'On the Reform of Intellectuals' in New China Publishing House (ed.), *Cheng-feng ts'an-k'ao wen-chien* (Reference documents of the *Cheng-feng*) (Yenan: New China Publishing House, 1944), pp. 63–8.
51. Ssuma Lu, *op. cit.*, p. 3.
52. P.P. Wladimirow, *Das Sondergebiet Chinas 1942–1945* (The special area of China, 1942–1945) (German edition East Berlin: Dietz, 1976), p. 262 f.
53. She became an NPC deputy in 1959, and CCP secretary of Peking Normal University in 1965. During the Cultural Revolution she was purged and severely persecuted. Since 1978 she has been a member of the Central Disciplinary Investigation Committee of the CCP, and was appointed as such in 1982.
54. Thus, among others, Huang, *op. cit.*, p. 441.
55. So, e.g., *CNP*, unpaginated.
56. Huang, *ibid.*

57. Whitson/Huang, *op. cit.*, Chart A between pp. 102 and 103.

58. *ibid.*, p. 112; and: Huang, *op. cit.*, p. 441.

59. Shuai Che, 'Eminent Marshal, brilliant example: Remembering Comrade P'eng Te-huai', *HCPP*, vol. XVII (Peking 1979), pp. 146 ff., and Hsi Chung-hsün, 'Commander P'eng on the North-western battlefield', *JMJP*, Jan. 25, 26, and 28, 1980.

60. Huang K'e-ch'eng, 'An honest man of eternally straightforward character: Mourning for the outstanding leader of our Party, our country and our army, Comrade P'eng Te-huai', *Hung-ch'i* (Red Flag), Peking (hereafter *HC*), no. 1/1979, p. 41; also in *PCC*, p. 13.

61. War History Bureau, Ministry of National Defence, RoC (ed.), *K'an-luan chiang-lieh chan-shih: Yich'uan chan-tou* (History of heroic generals of the civil war: The battle of Yich'uan) (Taipei, Ministry of National Defence, 1959).

62. Huang, *op. cit.*, p. 441; and Whitson/Huang, *op. cit.*, p. 112 f.

63. *ibid.*, Chart B opposite p. 114.

64. Shuai Che, *loc. cit.*, p. 149 f.

65. Whitson/Huang, *op. cit.*, p. 113.

66. Ho K'e-hsieh *et al.*, *Chiang-chia wang-ch'ao-te fu-mi eh* (The downfall of the Chiang dynasty) (Peking: PLA Cultural Publishing House, 1961), pp. 55–64.

67. Whitson/Huang, *ibid.*

68. Ssuma Lu, *op. cit.*, p. 126.

69. Namelist in Huang, *op. cit.*, p. 758.

3

IN CHARGE OF THE 'PEOPLE'S VOLUNTEERS' IN KOREA AND OF CHINA'S ARMED FORCES, 1950–1959

The historical framework[1]

The CCP did not consider its victory over the KMT and the establishment of the People's Republic on October 1, 1949, as the triumph of a 'communist' or even only as that of a 'socialist' revolution, but rather as the successful conclusion of a 'new democratic' one, albeit under the leadership of communists. Such an understanding of the events of 1949 coincided with the Marxist-Leninist doctrine of the stages of revolution in the version proposed by Mao Tse-tung since 1940. According to this doctrine, the first task of the CCP was to establish a 'New Democracy' in China.[2] In the 'new democratic' stage of the revolutionary process, the 'petty bourgeoisie' and the 'national bourgeoisie' — meaning liberal intellectuals and capitalists with an anti-KMT orientation — were still considered 'revolutionary classes', and hence entitled to participate in the affairs of the country through political parties of their own in a 'united front' with the CCP. Eight such parties had decided to co-operate with the communists during the last stage of the Civil War from early 1948 onward.[3] In addition, the CCP invited a number of so-called 'democratic personalities', mostly elderly non-partisan scholars and representatives of overseas communities, to participate in the new government of the PRC.

Thus the Chinese People's Political Consultative Conference, the provisional parliament which convened in Peking on September 21, 1949, and ten days later proclaimed the establishment of the PRC, included 76 members of the non-communist 'united front' parties and 74 'democratic personalities', while 434 or 74.3 per cent of its delegates were members of the CCP or represented communist-led mass organisations. In the Central People's Government Council, the official supreme organ of the state machine chaired by Mao Tse-tung, there were 22 communist and 21 non-communist members. The very influential Revolutionary Council, also under the leadership of Mao, derived its importance mainly from the fact that up till 1953/4 the PLA played a vital role in the country's regional administration. Here the armed forces were entrusted with the task of establishing civilian administrative structures in six large regions, which enjoyed considerable autonomy in the areas of planning, economic organisation and public health services.[4]

With the aid of the structures thus established, the new regime set out, in the winter of 1949/50, to accomplish three major tasks: first, to consolidate and stabilise the rule by the CCP all over the Chinese mainland; secondly, to reconstruct the economy which had been badly damaged after the eight years of the Sino-Japanese and a further four years of civil war; and thirdly, to enact thoroughgoing social reforms, particularly in the countryside. The consolidation of communist rule was initiated by a wave of executions of former KMT members and other supporters of the *ancien régime*, which began immediately after the PRC was established. Starting in February 1951, this wave of physical liquidations assumed the features of a systematically organised mass movement, called the 'Campaign for the Suppression of Counter-Revolutionaries.'[5] In the context of this campaign, which lasted till the autumn of 1952, altogether 2 million 'counter-revolutionaries' lost their lives.[6] Two additional mass movements served to strengthen communist control over respectively, the groups of administrative officials and the urban business circles. The wide-ranging application of physical terror during the first four years of communist rule consolidated the Party's tight and efficient control over China's cities. The few remaining non-partisan cadres were frightened into obedience.

The Party's efforts to complete the second task — economic reconstruction — were at least as successful as those directed towards the consolidation of its rule. Already in early 1950, the runaway inflation, which had been so damaging to the KMT, was brought under control, and in 1952 most sectors of the economy had once again reached the production levels of the time before the Sino-Japanese war. The speedy recovery of the Chinese economy between 1949 and 1952/3 may thus be considered one of the greatest achievements of CCP rule.

As for as the third task — the initiation of social reform — two measures, both enacted between 1950 and 1953 in the form of large-scale mass movements, were of lasting importance: land reform and marriage reform. The land reform, which began in late June 1950 and lasted till early 1953, aimed at three goals:[7] first, the equalisation of land ownership; secondly, the elimination of potential pockets of resistance to CCP rule; and thirdly, the mobilisation and structured organisation of the peasant masses under the Party's leadership. All three goals were achieved. With the marriage reform of 1950/1, the Party attacked the traditional Chinese lineage system and the rampant abuses which had been tolerated within it. Polygamy and child marriages were almost entirely abolished, but arranged marriages persisted in many areas, as they still do today.[8]

Between 1950 and 1953 the new leaders of China not only stabilised their rule, promoted economic recovery and initiated social reforms, but during the same period they also engaged in a major foreign political and military enterprise by taking part in the Korean war.[9] After the withdrawal of Soviet troops from the North of Korea by December 1948, and that of American troops from the South by June 1949, the conflict between the two Korean systems escalated, with the communist-ruled North steadily increasing its military strength. On June 25, 1950, the North launched an all-out surprise attack on the South. Two days later, on June 27, President Harry S. Truman ordered United States naval, air and soon ground forces to support the South Koreans. By the end of August the American and South Korean troops, now operating under a mandate of the United Nations, had been thrown back by the North Koreans to a small bridgehead round the port city of Pusan in southeast Korea, but an audacious amphibious operation of the 'United Nations' army far behind the enemy lines, together with their counter-attack from the Pusan bridgehead, turned the tide of the war. When the total defeat of the North Korean armed forces became evident in the second half of September, Stalin began to prod the CCP leadership into a PRC intervention to save communist rule in the North. Mao Tse-tung seems also to have feared that a breakdown of the North Korean political system would destabilise communist rule in China, and on October 4, 1950, he obtained approval for a Chinese intervention into the war from the Politburo in Peking.

Under P'eng Te-huai as Commander-in-Chief, the People's Volunteer Army (PVA) was established, consisting of more than 400,000 Chinese 'people's volunteers'. In mid-November the PVA launched its first major offensive, which drove the American and South Korean troops out of North Korea, over the 38th parallel, and down to a line south of Seoul, before the Chinese attack ground to a halt in the face of American reinforcements. General Matthew B. Ridgeway, who succeeded General MacArthur as commander of the UN forces, succeeded in driving the PVA back over the 38th parallel, and by mid-July 1951 the war had died down, approximately along the old demarcation line. Armistice negotiations had gone on for two years when finally, on July 27,

1953, the Panmunjom armistice agreement was concluded, recognising — more or less — the territorial *status quo* before the North Korean attack of June 25, 1950.

With the PVA effort, the PRC had succeeded in saving North Korea, and — at least in the eyes of the CCP leadership — fending off the attack by the major world power of that time. By the second half of 1953, after the Korean armistice, the CCP had fully consolidated its control over the Chinese mainland. At the fourth anniversary of the establishment of the PRC, on October 1, 1953, the ruling élite proclaimed the start of a new policy, the General Line of Socialist Transformation — the second stage of revolution according to Marxist-Leninist doctrine. The model for this period of transition was the Soviet Union, with which at that time the PRC was working in close alliance. One of the major preconditions was a tight centralisation of the state administrative machine. On September 20, 1954, the first official Constitution of the PRC was promulgated, very similar to the Soviet constitution of 1936 but with an important difference in that there was an individual head of state, the 'Chairman of the PRC', a post now taken over by Mao Tse-tung. From that time until 1966–7 the PLA and the state administrative machine, directed by a State Council, which had been closely linked with each other in the large regions until 1954, were separated and developed into viable sub-systems of their own under the Party's leadership. The state organs were now preoccupied with economic problems, and a systematic development of the national economy began with the First Five-Year-Plan, covering the years 1953–7. Supported by the Soviet Union with loans as well as a large number of Soviet advisers,[10] China's First Plan became a remarkable success. Soviet concepts also provided for the collectivisation of agriculture, the nationalisation of private industry, and the compulsory transfer of handicrafts and retail trade into co-operatives.

The collectivisation of agriculture began on December 16, 1953, and was accelerated after the summer of 1955, following a decision which Mao himself had carried through against considerable opposition in the Party. At the end of 1957, already 97.4 per cent of all peasant households in the PRC had been collectivised in 'fully socialist' Agricultural Production Co-operatives (APCs),[11] thus practically concluding the collectivisation of agriculture in production units, very similar to the Soviet *kolkhoz*. In the cities the 'socialist transformation of the modes of production', i.e. the nationalisation of private industries, began with initial experiments in 1954, and were in full swing by the winter of

1955/6.[12] China's intimidated industrialists gave way with little resistance, and ceded their shares in their firms 'voluntarily' to the state, not only because of considerable pressure but also because many of them were appointed managers of their former plants. By the end of January 1956 the nationalisation drive was already successfully concluded.[13] At the same time, handicrafts and the retail trade were collectivised.[14] Individual enterprise in the PRC was now confined to a small number of street vendors, photographers and drivers of pedicabs. Yet the objective economic success and the triumphs of 'Socialist Transformation' were accompanied by the first serious conflict within the leadership since 1949, and also by severe persecution of the very same nationalist and liberal intellectuals who had supported the CCP in the last years of the Civil War.

The major result of this conflict and the purge was a further centralisation of the Party's organisation, leading to a new campaign to discipline the intelligentsia. This began in December 1954 under the name the 'Campaign to Purge Counter-Revolutionaries' (*Su-fan*).[15] By the end of 1955, fear and uncertainty among intellectuals were widespread, and universities and research institutes, even including those involved in vital scientific and technological work, became increasingly paralysed. These results of the *Su-fan* campaign began to affect the development of the economy and of science and education, and to overcome such adverse affects the Party leadership decided in early January 1956 to discontinue the campaign. For a year and a half the atmosphere in the country was relaxed, and this culminated in the Hundred Flowers Campaign promoted by Mao Tse-tung. After cautious and hesitant beginnings in March and April, the campaign unfolded to full vigour in the cities and universities.[16] The wave of criticism it let loose did not — as Mao had hoped and expected — remain confined to bureaucratic failures and the mistakes of basic- and middle-level cadres, but soon turned towards matters of principle and high-ranking targets. Criticism escalated even more, being directed against Marxist-Leninist doctrines, against members of the inner core of the Party leadership, and against the system of totalitarian single-Party rule itself. It was obvious that the Chairman had overestimated the level of support for communist rule among the people, and around July 1957 the CCP made its counter-attack with the 'Campaign against Rightist Deviationists', which dominated the country throughout the second half of that year.

The CCP thus weathered the storm, and the opposition of the non-communist intellectuals was suppressed again. But Mao Tse-tung's prestige had, in the process, suffered its first blow since 1949. This was the beginning of the long-drawn-out erosion of his charisma. The Chairman tried to stave this off with a turn towards radicalism, and it was this turn which brought him and P'eng Te-huai into head-on collision.

The Korean command

When P'eng Te-huai took over the military and administrative responsibility for the Northwest China region in October 1949, he had severe problems to solve. A pro-communist guerrilla army was operating in the Kulja-Ili area of Sinkiang, which had been established with Soviet support and was under strong Soviet influence: the 'East Turkestan People's Army' under the leadership of Ishhak Beg Saifuddin, a Uighur and a member of the CPSU since the late 1930s. This organisation had fought for an independent 'East Turkestan' in close alliance with the Soviet Union, and it was not easy for its leaders to accept Chinese rule, albeit communist. Only after protracted negotiations with P'eng and his delegate Wang En-mao, and under heavy Soviet pressure, Saifuddin agreed in December 1949 to transfer his Party membership from the CPSU to the CCP and to have his units included in the PLA's First FA as the new 5th corps.[17] This, however, did not end the difficulties in the Northwest. In Sinkiang Uighur, Turkmen, Kazakh, Kirgiz and Uzbek tribes were in continuous conflict with the Han Chinese invaders of P'eng's First FA, while in Kansu and Ningsia, Chinese Muslim (Hui) groups continued to wage guerrilla warfare. P'eng, who commuted between Sian, Lanchow, and Urumchi but mostly worked in his headquarters in Urumchi, the capital of Sinkiang, tried with some success to make agreements with a number of these splintered forces. Yet he had to leave the Northwest before Sinkiang could finally be brought under control. This was only achieved by his subordinate, General Wang En-mao, in a fierce campaign between November 1950 and May 1951 to 'suppress counter-revolutionaries'. In this context, at least 7,500 former KMT officers and national minority leaders were executed, including the NRA generals Li Tsu-t'ang and T'ang Ching-jan, the Kazakh leaders Osman Batur and Enni Batur, the Uighur leader Masud Sabri, the Uighur intellectuals and writers Janmu Khan, Nivad, Ulambai and Utkür, and the Muslim leaders Ma Sheng-shan and Ma Sheng-jung.[18]

At the time of Wang En-mao's wholesale killings in Sinkiang, P'eng had already begun a new stage in his career. On October 5, 1950, he was appointed Commander-in-Chief (*Ssu-ling-yüan*) and concurrently Political Commissar of the PVA, soon to become engaged in the Korean war.[19] Already in August, P'eng had been called to Peking, where in long talks with the Chief of Staff of the Soviet Army, Marshal Shtemenko, the Commander-in-Chief of the Soviet Far East Military Area, Marshal Malinovsky, the Soviet Air Force commander in the Far East, Klazovsky, and the Soviet Anti-Aircraft Forces commander in the Far East, Bilizov,[20] he discussed the possiblity of participation in the war by the PRC, and the conditions for all-out Soviet support with military hardware and advisers. As a result, a Joint General Staff was established in Shenyang by mid-September, with the Soviet Lieutenant-General Kuzman Derevyanko as Chief and the commander of the PLA's 40th Corps, General Han Hsien-ch'u, as Deputy Chief.[21] Yet these were, for the moment, mainly defence preparations in case the United Nations forces under General MacArthur should attack either the Chinese or Soviet territory; the decision that Chinese troops should participate directly in the war was taken somewhat later. In early October a joint meeting of the CCP/CC's Politburo and Military Commission convened in Peking, and it was there that Mao suggested the intervention of the PLA in the form of so-called 'volunteer' units in the Korean war. This suggestion met with opposition from some CCP leaders. Carsun Chang, who at that time still had viable channels of information from the PRC's ruling élite, has suggested that, in particular, Tung Pi-wu and other older leading Party members opposed China's entry into the war, with the argument that the PLA was not yet sufficiently trained, armed or organised to fight against American forces, and that the 'liberation of the whole country' should first be completed by the conquest of Taiwan.[22] This is indirectly confirmed by P'eng, who reported in his autobiography that 'almost everybody' had argued that this was not the time to join a foreign war (he himself kept quiet), but that Mao had then said: 'What you say makes sense, but if somebody else is in an extremely dangerous situation with his country, and we stand aside as onlookers and do not know what to say, we shall feel very bad too.'[23] Mao was finally able to convince most of the leaders, and the decision to intervene was taken, probably on October 4. P'eng was called on that very day, about noon, to fly immediately to Peking to attend the meeting, which had already started. He does not relate where he was when he received the call, but since he arrived at the seat of the

Party Centre, the Chungnanhai in Peking, at 'about 4 p.m.', given that he was flown in a propellor-driven plane, it must have been Sian. On October 5 he received his appointment, and 'during the first ten days of October', probably between the 7th and 10th, he set up his headquarters in Shenyang, the capital of Liaoning province. Here he immediately discussed the requirement of the war effort with the commanders of the units now placed under his command at a 'PVA High-Ranking Cadres' Conference'.[24]

This answers a historical question which remained obscure until very recently: as to whether P'eng really commanded the PVA from the very beginning, or whether, as Whitson and Huang suggest in their other-wise succinct and correct account of the Korean war,[25] he replaced Lin Piao in that position at the end of February 1951. There is no documen-tary evidence for the assumption that Lin was the first commander of the PVA, and all sources available to the present author state that P'eng led the PVA from the first day of the war to the last. The notion expressed by Whitson and Huang may originate from the fact that the first troops to engage American and South Korean forces belonged to the 13th Army under General Li T'ien-yu who, before becoming involved in the war, had held a command in Lin Piao's 4th FA. Most probably prisoners and deserters from this unit named Lin as their commander.

P'eng crossed the Yalu into North Korea with vanguard units on October 18, 1950,[26] and seven days later his troops had the first engagement with units of the American 1st Corps at Unsan. At the beginning of the war, P'eng had at his disposal the 13th Army with four corps from the Fourth FA under Li T'ien-yu, and the 9th Army with four corps from the Third FA under General Sung Shih-lun, both consisting of some of the best trained and most battle-hardened units of the PLA. They were joined on November 11 by the Fourth FA Special Army with five infantry and two artillery corps under the command of Han Hsien-ch'u. With this fighting force of more than 400,000 men, P'eng attacked the UN army along the whole coast-to-coast line through the length of North Korea. In three major campaigns — the first from October 25 to November 1, the second from mid-November to December 12, and the third from December 30 to January 11, 1951 — the PVA drove the American and South Korean forces out of North Korea, crossing the 38th parallel on December 31, and recaptured Seoul. However, these victories exacted a very high price from the Chinese armies. Soviet hardware and logistic support arrived only slowly, most of the supplies had to be moved from Manchuria by a support force of almost 700,000 coolies under the leadership of General Fu Ch'iu-t'ao, and the Allied forces had decided air superiority. Bitterly cold weather also took its toll: for example, between November 27 and December 12, Sung Shih-lun's 9th Army lost 45,000 men who froze to death in the unsuccessful attempt to block the retreat of the American 1st Division in the Wonsan area on the east coast.[27] Most costly of all were the tactics of the 'human sea', which P'eng applied until the summer of 1951: bayonet charges by between ten and twenty waves of soldiers (who were often made drunk on strong Kaoliang brandy) in the face of concentrated enemy fire, with insufficient artillery and tank support and virtually no air cover.

Still, the PVA had succeeded in regaining North Korea for communist rule in the form of the Stalinist dictatorship of Kim Il Sung. But the fourth campaign, which started on January 25, 1951, and lasted till mid-March, broke down before the Allied lines south and southeast of Seoul. Attacked by American and South Korean troops with very strong fire power, Li T'ien-yu's 13th Army had to evacuate Seoul on March 14 with extremely heavy losses. Yet P'eng, again displaying the stubborness which so often characterised his military exploits, did not yet relinquish his hope of leading the PVA to full victory by capturing all or at least most of South Korea. With the 16th Corps he launched a fifth campaign on April 22 with the aim retaking Seoul, and breaking through the enemy lines in the central sector of the front. But his offensive was broken by the US forces under General Van Fleet north of Seoul and by South Korean, Australian, American and Turkish forces in central Korea. On May 21 the front line came to a virtual standstill almost exactly along the 38th parallel.

Attacks on P'eng by the Cultural Revolutionary Left in 1967 insisted that the first three campaigns — the successful ones — had been fought according to 'Chairman Mao's instructions', while the fourth and the fifth were organised by P'eng in a way of which Mao was critical. But all CCP reports and accounts published before 1959, and again after 1979, state clearly that P'eng himself was in unchallenged command of all operations, so that both the success of the first three campaigns and the failure of the fourth and fifth ones must be attributed to his leadership. According to Red Guard sources of 1967, Mao's son, Mao An-ying, who served as a Russian-language interpreter at P'eng's headquarters, died during the fifth campaign because P'eng had failed to protect him.[28] But in fact he had already died in late November or early December 1950 in an American air-raid on the PVA headquarters, and indeed P'eng blamed himself for 'not having taken good care of Mao An-ying'.[29]

By early June 1951, the war had become almost entirely static and in July the armistice negotiations between the Chinese and North Korean representatives and the representatives of the UN Korean command began at the front line village of Kaesong (later they were moved to Panmunjom). Whitson and Huang give the following apt description of the last part of the war:

With the beginning of negotiations at Kaesong in July, 1951, the long, costly, but (for the Communists) educational Korean stalemate began.

Symbolic of the new emphasis on modernization [of tactics, supply, and equipment] during this stalemate, about 700,000 Manchurian coolies were gradually replaced by a logistical system that employed some 7,000 trucks and 300 anti-aircraft guns along the main supply route. The construction of an 'underground Great Wall' — a system of deep underground fortifications across the waist of the Korean peninsula — and the provision of a regimental artillery unit under each regular regiment in Korea further confirmed the new dedication to position warfare. Training in position defense tactics proceeded simultaneously. With the continuing buildup of heavy Soviet artillery and the 1952 arrival of Yang Ch'eng-wu's Twentieth army, P'eng Te-huai was able to deploy five armies in a horseshoe configuration — three armies on the front and one on each flank — to secure North Korea against UN amphibious attack.

In 1952, the combat-training function of Korea for the PLA was reflected in the return to China of the 20th, 26th, and 27th Corps, which were replaced by other Third Field Army units (the 21st, 23rd, and 24th Corps). Between July and September, 1952, the CPV [PVA] received its second armored division, which was organized and trained under the supervision of Hsü Kuang-ta. Now ready to challenge the United Nations tactically, the PLA launched a series of tactical offensives, which brought heavy UN and Communist casualties at Sniper Bridge and Triangle Hill, in battles that sometimes involved entire divisions on both sides [. . .] By April, 1953, . . . P'eng had twenty-one regular corps with organic artillery, nine artillery divisions, two armored divisions [altogether a little more than 1 million men] and a supporting air force of around 1,800 aircraft.

Employing this force to present an image of strength from which to negotiate between May and July, 1953, P'eng launched a series of offensives against such famous targets as 'Old Baldy', 'Porkshop Hill', and the 'Vegas' and 'Berlin' outposts. On July 11, a massive five corps offensive . . . against the ROK [South Korean] 2nd Corps actually effected penetration, under the impact of more than 250,000 rounds of Communist artillery. The counterattack by the American 3rd Division, plus heavy air attacks, stemmed this breach and permitted General Mark Clark to block a CPV advance. This was the end of major Communist hostilities in the Korean War. Yet the bulk of the Communist (Chinese) forces in Korea were not evacuated until four years later.[30]

On July 27, 1953, P'eng personally signed the armistice agreement at Panmunjom for the PVA and a few days later, on July 31, Kim Il Sung, at a mass rally in Pyongyang, awarded him the North Korean 'National Flag' Order of Merit, First Class, which he had already once received in 1951, and conferred on him the title 'Hero of the Korean Democratic People's Republic'.[31] On August 11 P'eng left North Korea for Peking, and returned to a hero's welcome at the T'ienanmen Square in the centre of the capital.[32] There are differing accounts of his whereabouts during the next 5 months. According to some, he spent September 1953 in Sinkiang, having returned to his position as military and administrative leader of Northwest China, and was then called to Peking in November to run the daily affairs of the CCP/CC's Military Commission. Red Guard sources in 1967 say that he had already been given this new assignment — which meant the *de facto* supreme command of the PLA — in July 1953,[33] while Roderick MacFarquhar argues that he appeared in Peking on January 20, 1954 — his first visit since late August 1953 — to attend a ceremony commemorating the thirtieth anniversary of Lenin's death.[34] However, there is confirmation of his presence in Peking from official CCP media for September 12, September 16–18, November 12, November 23, December 8 and December 9, 1953,[35] which leads the present author to suggest that he probably went to the Northwest, if at all, to wind up his affairs there at some time between late September and early November, and that he took over his position in charge of the Military Commission's day-to-day affairs during the first half of November. Be that as it may, he officially remained Commander-in-Chief of the PVA until he resigned that position on September 5, 1954.[36] General Teng Hua, who had stood in for P'eng from August 1953 up till that date, succeeded him for just a month. Then from October 1954 to March 1955 the PVA was commanded by General Yang Te-chih, and thereafter until the last Chinese soldiers withdrew from North Korea in 1958 by General Yang Yung.

The Korean experience strongly influenced P'eng's military thinking. The high losses of manpower during the first year of the Chinese military engagement apparently convinced him that the PLA needed a thoroughgoing modernisation of its equipment, a strong drive towards professionalism, and the development of new techniques for modern combined operations. The propensity for conventional rather than guerrilla warfare, which he had constantly shown from the early 1930s till the end of the Civil War, was again confirmed. He had once more realised — this time with deepened conviction — that military training of the troops should never be reduced in favour of political indoctrination, that professional commanders would have to take priority over commissars, and that the PRC needed armed forces prepared for modern technical warfare, following the only model then available to the PLA — that of the Soviet Red Army. It was armed with such doctrines that he now took over the leadership of the Chinese Communist military.

In supreme command of China's armed forces

Already at some time in the spring of 1954 P'eng had been confirmed as the First Vice-Chairman of the CCP/CC's Military Commission, whose Chairman was Mao himself. It was in this capacity that P'eng Te-huai had now become, for all practical purposes, the supreme commander of the PLA. On September 28, 1954, the First National People's Congress confirmed this position by appointing him Minister of National Defence as well as the highest-ranking Vice-Chairman of the National Defence Council, and concurrently one of the ten Vice-Premiers of the State Council. In the latter capacity, however, he ranked behind Lin Piao, who had only joined the Politburo of the CCP in January of that year.

In his new command position, P'eng was aided by a team of highly competent military leaders. Generals Hsiao K'e and T'an Cheng served as his first Vice-Ministers; General Su Yü, a leader from the Third FA with an excellent fighting record, became Chief of the General Staff; his old friend General Huang K'e-ch'eng became Director of the General Rear Services Department, and a long-term associate of Lin Piao, Lo Jung-huan, became Director of the General Political Department with T'an Cheng as his deputy. Also of great importance was the appointment of the former Commander-in-Chief of the Second FA, the Soviet-trained strategist Liu Po-ch'eng, as Director of the Training and Inspection Department of the PLA. Only three days after his official appointment, P'eng set the tone for the planned revamping of the PRC's armed forces with his 'Order No. 1', published on October 1, 1954:

The whole army must sincerely study the advanced experience of the Soviet army, grasp the art of modern warfare, bring to the fore revolutionary heroism, strictly obey orders, and honour discipline. Struggle to grasp and guarantee the victorious conclusion of each and every military task![37]

But for the addition of the adjective 'revolutionary' (*Ke-ming*) to 'heroism', this edict could have come from any general in any professional military system in the world. Hence the signal for the PLA was now one that pointed in the direction of strict professionalism, with the Soviet Army held up as a model to be emulated.

This professionalism dictated the form of the very first military operation of which P'eng took personal charge after his appointment as minister: the Ichiangshan-Tachen campaign in January and February 1955. The island of Ichiangshan and the Tachen Archipelago, off the coast of Chekiang province, had been held by KMT troops since the Civil War had ended on the Chinese mainland. From there the Nationalists occasionally staged commando raids into Chekiang and even as far as the area around Shanghai. Around New Year 1955, P'eng rallied crack units of the Third FA, strong elements of air cover and a large number of warships, under his direct command, to stage the first combined amphibious operation in the PLA's history, aimed at driving the Nationalists off the archipelago. On January 18 his units started to attack the small Ichiangshan island, which was seized on January 20 after its 720 defenders, facing a PLA force of almost 12,000, had been completely wiped out. In view of the long and hazardous supply lines from Taiwan, and under pressure from the Americans, Chiang Kai-shek decided to evacuate his remaining troops from the Tachen Archipelago. The Nationalist retreat began on February 7, and by the end of the month the PLA had occupied the islands. This, up to the present time, is the only victory the PLA has won over the armed forces of the Republic if China,[38] but it provided, in military terms, a good start for P'eng's period as head of the Chinese armed forces. It also prompted decisions by the United States which would make it difficult for the PRC in future to launch attacks on Nationalist-held territory: on January 26 the US House of Representatives, by a vote of 409 to 3, approved a resolution authorising President Eisenhower to employ American forces to defend Taiwan, the Penghu Archipelago (Pescadores) 'and related positions and territories'. This was the 'Taiwan Straits Resolution', which protected the refuge of the KMT until the early 1970s, and was applied to counter the last major effort of the PRC against the Republic of China in the late summer of 1958.

P'eng's new position as Minister of National Defence soon occasioned his first experience of travel outside China and North Korea. After he had visited the Soviet naval base at Lüshun (formerly Port Arthur) with a delegation of twenty PLA leaders on February 22, 1955, in preparation for a return visit by the Soviet naval commanders to the PRC on May 1 — at which he again officiated —, he went on his first extensive tour abroad. Between May 6 and 28, he visited East Germany, Poland and the Soviet Union, meeting among others Wilhelm Pieck, Josif Cyrankiewicz, Nikita Krushchev and the Soviet Marshals Rokossovsky and Zhukov. In the following years he made further trips, usually accompanied by large delegations: to Poland and the Soviet Union in September 1955 for the signing of the Warsaw Pact, which he attended as an observer; accompanying Mao when he paid his second visit to the Soviet Union, the 'great fraternal country', from November 2 till December 3, 1957; and finally, from April 24 to June 13, 1959, on the fateful 'Military Goodwill Mission' to Poland, East Germany, Czechoslovakia, Hungary, Romania, Bulgaria, Albania, the Soviet Union and the Mongolian People's Republic.[39]

P'eng's first visit to East Germany, Poland and the Soviet Union in the spring of 1955 must have strengthened his resolution to modernise the PLA, because in early June, immediately after his return, he accelerated his professionalisation drive. He now started to enact what soon became known as the 'Four Great Systems' (*Ssu ta chih-tu*: the Compulsory Military Service System, the System of Military Ranks, the Salary System, and the Order of Merit System).[40] These reforms, which were intended to bring about an almost total change in the character of the PLA, were approved — probably by the CCP/CC's Military Commission — in the latter part of September 1955,[41] and soon implemented.

Following a decision of the Standing Committee of the National People's Congress on September 23, P'eng was appointed, on September 27, as one of the ten Marshals of the PLA. At the same time, a large number of PLA leaders became generals, colonel-generals, lieutenant-generals or major-generals. Many of them received the newly-established military orders of merit. On P'eng himself were conferred the First Class of the Order of August 1 (for his achievements during the first period of the anti-KMT Civil War in 1927–37), the First Class of the Order of Independence and Freedom (for the Sino-Japanese war), and the First Class of the Order of Liberation (for the second period of the Civil War).[42] At the same time, rank insignia were introduced in the PLA, and new uniforms modelled on those of the Soviet Red Army were issued to the men. Starting from January 1, 1956, compulsory military service was substituted for the old would-be 'volunteer' system, and the career soldiers now received regular salaries, differentiated on a scale of eighteen grades from Private second-class to Marshal. These were just the outward signs of an escalating campaign in the course of which the PLA, which P'eng had taken over as a force of more than 5 million men with a strong sprinkling of guerrilla traditions, became a professionalised military establishment of about 3 million regulars.

To encourage the reforms, which continued with the introduction in May 1956 of a clear priority in rank for the commanders over the political commissars,[43] P'eng himself made numerous inspection tours all over the country, everywhere encouraging professional military training and ethics.[44] At the Eighth CCP Party Congress in September 1956, his doctrine of professionalism, strict training, discipline and the use of modern equipment seemed to have triumphed. On September 18 he addressed the congress with a report on 'army building' (*Chien-chün*) in which he gave a detailed elaboration of the general ideas enshrined in his 'order No. 1' in 1954, culminating in the guiding principle:

We need a regularised military system. . . . A regularised [or 'professionalised'] military system is an important condition for a modern army. In particular, because in the past our army was spread over many different areas, the military system of all the different units was not unified. For this reason, in the course of modernisation, it is of extreme importance that we stress regularisation![45]

Such doctrines entirely contradicted the military thought of Mao who, throughout all the war years from 1927 through to 1950, had stressed that men were more important than weapons, that political indoctrination had to take priority over technical training, that the guerrilla tradition of the PLA should be emulated, and that good political commissars were at least as important as good professional officers. The first remarks critical of P'eng's doctrines seem to have been aired at a meeting of the CCP/CC's Military Commission in October 1957 by Lin Piao, who expressed his doubts that P'eng's 'Line of army building' would enable the PLA to withstand the test of a major military confrontation.[46] In November 1957 the ardent promoter of professionalism, Marshal Liu Po-ch'eng, lost his position as Director of the Training and Inspection Department of the PLA to the somewhat more — though not entirely — guerrilla-oriented General Hsiao K'e. However, Liu, by being transferred to the presidency of the Supreme Staff and Command College in Nanking, kept at least some of his influence on the shaping of the PRC's armed forces.[47] It seems that P'eng was able to weather the crisis which his doctrines encountered during the autumn of 1957, and by late that year the proponents of Mao's theory of 'people's war', most prominent among them being Marshal Lin Piao, but also including Marshal Yeh Chien-ying and at that time to a certain extent even Marshal Ho Lung, had once again relapsed into silence. It was only in 1967 that P'eng was finally accused, in a comprehensive broadside, of three major 'crimes' committed during the time when he was in command of the PLA:

First, he rejected Chairman Mao's line of army building by wholesale copying of the style of the Soviet revisionists. He prepared to abolish the system of Party committees [in the PLA], and to substitute it with the single-commander system. He also prepared to abolish the political commissars, and introduced the System of Military Ranks. This was straight against Chairman Mao's line of army building, which follows the principle of 'revolutionization first, modernization second'!

Second, he rejected Chairman Mao's line of army building by opposing the doctrine of people's war. He was firmly against the large-scale organization of people's militia. Like bald-headed Khrushchev, he opined that 'militia is just a heap of flesh', and he followed the Soviet revisionists wholesale.

Third, at the front line of national defence [meaning the Fukien front towards Taiwan] he established defences in the style of warlords of the old army. Thus he wasted very much money, and the damage was enormous.[48]

The last of these accusations already pointed towards the last campaign in which P'eng was directly involved, and which indeed gave reason to doubt the success of his drive towards professionalisation: the bombardment of Chinmen (Quemoy) and Matsu in the late summer and autumn of 1958. On August 23, PLA artillery started heavy shelling of these offshore islands held by Nationalist troops. The strategy of this campaign, for which the Chief of General Staff, General Su Yü, was directly responsible, involved planning a massive attempt to cut off the enemy's air and sea supply lines, and saturation shelling using about half of the modern artillery available to the PLA, massed along the coast facing the two groups of islands. The aim was to demoralise the KMT troops on the islands and force them into surrender, as a first step leading to an attack on Taiwan. But the Soviet Union did not give its whole-hearted support to this Chinese communist effort, while the United

States provided naval and air cover to Nationalist supply ships up to within 3 nautical miles from the PRC coastline, and the forces of the Republic of China put up a successful resistance: 37 PLA jet fighters were shot down in dogfights as against three Nationalist air force planes, and Nationalist artillery and naval fire destroyed fourteen PRC navy vessels. On October 6 P'eng declared a week's cease-fire, later extended by another week. Shelling was resumed on October 20, only to falter on October 25 when P'eng announced a further cease-fire for at least every alternate day. With this the shelling subsided, and the campaign had in fact ended in dismal failure for the PLA.

The first consequences of the Chinmen-Matsu defeat occurred already on October 12: Su Yü was dismissed as Chief of the General Staff. This did not yet effect P'eng's position; his old associate from P'ingchiang days, General Huang K'e-ch'eng, became the new Chief of the General Staff and was succeeded as Director of the General Rear Services Department by General Hung Hsüeh-chih, with whom P'eng had established good relations in Korea. However P'eng's showdown with Mao and his first purge came about in the context not so much of his actions as the leader of the PLA in the Chinmen-Matsu debacle as of his activities as a CCP politician.

Getting involved in CCP politics

As an alternate member of the CCP/CC since 1934, a full member since 1938 and a member of the Politburo since May 1945, P'eng Te-huai had already been participating officially in the political decision-making process for almost twenty years before he took over the leadership of the PLA in late 1953. However, it appears reasonably safe to assume that for most of these years — with the possible exception of the *Cheng-feng* movement in 1942–4 — he was occupied mainly with military affairs and left policy making, at least in domestic matters, to the civilian Party leaders at the centre. Yet this situation must have changed when he became permanently resident in Peking around November 1953, and was thus able to attend Politburo meetings regularly. Nevertheless, only limited information is available concerning his attitudes to the major political decisions between 1953 and the autumn of 1957, and much of that comes only from the publications of the Cultural Revolutionary Left in 1967 and 1968, which were self-evidently hostile.

These sources blame him for having 'worked in alliance with Kao

Kang and Jao Shuh-shih' in 1954, and claim that 'the Kao-Jao anti-Party clique was in fact a P'eng Te-huai/Kao Kang/Jao Shu-shih anti-Party clique'.[49] However, the evidence given for this accusation is scanty: P'eng was supposed to have said in 1953 that 'Kao Kang is a very able man', and that Kao was the only Politburo member who supported Mao Tse-tung from the very beginning on the PRC's intervention in the Korean war.[50] At the same time, P'eng apparently once stated that 'the credit for the resist-America aid-Korea struggle should be given to two pockmarked persons [*Liang-ke ma-tzu*]: 50 percent to pockmarked Kao [Kao Kang] and 50 percent to pockmarked Hung [Hung Hsüeh-chih].'[51] But even his Red Guard persecutors in 1967–8 could not provide any evidence of collusion with Jao Shuh-shih, and one should not overlook the fact that at the time when P'eng said such friendly words about Kao Kang, Kao was still a Politburo member in good standing. When the purge of Kao and Jao occurred, P'eng was thoroughly in line with their enemies; he attended the CCP National Delegates Conference on March 21-31, 1955, which expelled the two from the Party, taking the eleventh rank in the pecking order of the Politburo, and made a speech at the meeting attacking Kao.[52]

However, even the attacks on P'eng during the Cultural Revolution, with one exception, do not accuse him of having opposed Mao on the decision to accelerate the collectivisation drive in the villages of China in the summer of 1955. It seems that here, as during the Kao-Jao affair, he remained loyal to Mao, and joined the majority of the decision-making bodies which the Party Leader had brought into being. Yet only a few months later, probably for the first time since late 1937, he turned against the Chairman and thus became the initiator of an important decision which reduced Mao's standing. P'eng's propensity for modesty and simplicity had imbued him with a thorough distaste for any cult of personalities. Hence he definitely opposed attempts to elevate Mao to the position of a flawless hero. Sometime in 1955 the draft of the preface for a book entitled *The War History of the PVA* (*Chih-yüan-chün chan-shih*), which he had to authorise, was submitted to him, and in the draft it was stated that the 'victories of the PVA' had been won 'under the correct leadership of the CCP and of Comrade Mao Tse-tung'. He authorised the text — after having the words 'and of Comrade Mao Tse-tung' cut out.[53] During the first half of 1956 P'eng's distaste for the personality cult grew into what can only be called a personal campaign. Probably in early 1956, a 'counter-revolutionary revisionist' — who was not named in the Red Guard source which recounted this affair

— wrote a letter in which he condemned the display of Mao portraits and the singing of songs in his praise. P'eng immediately passed this letter on to Huang K'e-ch'eng for further distribution, and moreover he would not allow a bronze statue of Mao to be erected in the Peking Military Museum. His comment at the time was, as we know now, prophetic: 'Why take the trouble to put it up? What is put up now will be removed in the future.'[54]

He is also credited with some other rather caustic remarks during this period on different features of the personality cult surrounding Mao. Once, in 1956, he addressed soldiers who had greeted him at an inspection with the shouts of 'Long live Chairman Mao!' or '10,000 years for Chairman Mao!': 'You shout "10,000 years for Chairman Mao!" — does he, then, live for 10,000 years? He will not even live for 100 years! This is personality cult!' And when a political commissar suggested that a song in praise of Mao — 'The East is Red' (*Tung-fang hung*), which was later sung in place of the national anthem during the Cultural Revolution — should be taught to the troops, he commented: 'That is personality cult, that is idealism!' Again in 1956, a delegation of soldiers who had come to Peking asked P'eng whether he could arrange for them to see the Chairman. He retorted: 'He is an old man, what is so beautiful about him? [*Lao-t'ou-tzu-le, yu shen-mo hao-k'an-te*?]'[55]

In view of this it was only to be expected that P'eng should become the CCP leader who initiated a move of considerable importance on the eve of the Eighth CCP Party Congress. When a committee of the Politburo examined the draft of the new Party Statute, which was scheduled to be passed by the Congress, he suggested deleting the reference to the 'Thought of Mao Tse-tung' from the preamble, where it had been taken over from the CCP Statute of 1945.[56] Liu Shao-ch'i, Teng Hsiao-p'ing, P'eng Chen and other major CCP leaders immediately accepted P'eng's suggestion, and so the 1956 Statute, in its final version, no longer contained this reference. The decision to eliminate it was later considered to be evidence of major hostility to Mao by the Cultural Revolutionary Left. At this Congress P'eng was re-appointed a full member of the CCP/CC, and at the First Plenum of that body on September 28, 1956, he again became a member of the Politburo. In this capacity he was doubtless involved in the debates concerning Mao's turn towards cultural and political liberalisation, i.e. the launching of the Hundred Flowers Campaign. But there is little evidence from which one can establish exactly what was his attitude towards Mao's drive. When the Party Leader gave the speech which opened the floodgates for the campaign on February 27, 1957, P'eng was one of the six Politburo members who did not attend the meeting at which the speech was given, the other absentees being Liu Shao-ch'i, Marshal Chu Te, Marshal Lin Piao (at that time in opposition to Mao's policy of liberalisation), Lin Po-ch'ü, and Marshal Lo Jung-huan.[57] Whether P'eng's absence was to make clear his disapproval of the campaign is not entirely clear. But it is certain that, although he had a high degree of visibility during the whole period February 28-June 8, 1957, with sixteen public appearances, he did not utter one word in support of Mao's policy of liberalisation. Thus, we may conclude that he probably joined Liu, Teng, P'eng, Chen and the majority of the military leaders in opposing it. If one accepts this suggestion, he must also have been among those who took an 'I-told-you-so' attitude when it became clear that the campaign had grown into a severe threat to the political system and had to be stopped. So it is also very likely that P'eng supported the CCP's decision to make a devastating counterattack on the intellectual critics, starting in mid-June 1957.

As a result of P'eng's disagreement with Mao's military doctrine, his distaste for the developing personality cult, and possibly his opposition to the Party Leader's experiment in liberalisation, it would seem that his relations with Mao must have cooled significantly since late 1953. His wife, P'u An-hsiu, in the 'confession' extracted from her at a kangaroo court set up by the Red Guards in 1967, spoke of his frequent complaints:

'[He had said] "I am old. The Chairman doesn't like me, neither does he hold me in esteem. The young men have come up. I do not want to be in charge any more. I defeated Chiang Kai-shek and imperialism. My wishes have been fulfilled. Now I can go home and till the land. I don't care whether he likes me or not." '[58]

P'eng obviously also disapproved of the luxurious way of life of many of the Party leaders, particularly Mao himself, in the capital. P'u An-hsiu 'confessed' to her interrogators:

'Sometimes, when the central leaders gathered to have a group picture taken, he [P'eng] was unwilling to go if Chairman Mao was also present. [. . .] There was a very nicely-built place in the suburbs of Peking. There Chairman Mao and other central leaders took rests. On Sundays, I suggested to go there for recreation. He was reluctant to go, saying: "That's where the Chairman lives. You may go there if you want to. That place is too luxuriously furnished for my taste." '[59]

Yet although one can conclude from these and other indications that by 1956–7 P'eng's relations with Mao were no longer very close, they were not decidedly inimical either. P'eng still held the Party Leader in considerable respect for his role in the communist takeover of China, and his political views around the time when the Hundred Flowers crisis had been weathered by the CCP can best be described as those of an ardent and loyal Bolshevik. He believed in discipline, in the rightness of the Party, and in the necessity of supporting the Party's policies once they had been decided. But he also believed in the wisdom of collective leadership, and therefore disapproved of the elevation of one person over the Party's decision-making organs. As a result of his Bolshevik convictions, P'eng did not support any attempt at an intellectual, cultural or, even less, political liberalisation. However, he was also not a man to accept a change of direction towards economic and social adventures. It was this position which soon brought him into open opposition against Mao's political concepts and style.

NOTES

1. Because the major conflict between P'eng Te-huai and Mao Tse-tung (the subject of Chapter 4 of the present work) developed gradually from the late autumn of 1957, this section covers the general political developments in the PRC only until that time. The dates in this chapter's title have been used because P'eng remained officially 'in charge of China's armed forces' until Sept. 17, 1959, and practically until mid-August, 1959.
2. Mao Tse-tung, 'On New Democracy' in *Mao Tse-tung hsüan-chi* (Selected Works of Mao Tse-tung), vol. II (Peking: People's Publishing House, 2nd edn, 1969), pp. 623–70.
3. Cf. Lyman P. Van Slyke, *Enemies and Friends: The United Front in Chinese Communist History* (Stanford University Press, 1967), pp. 208–19.
4. *China Digest*, Hong Kong, Dec. 14, 1949.
5. *Chieh-fang jih-pao* (Liberation Daily), Shanghai (hereafter *CFJP* Shanghai), July 23, 1953; *JMJP*, July 12, 1951; and *Nan-fang jih-pao* (Southern Daily), Canton (hereafter *NFJP*) Sept. 18, 1951.
6. This figure is quoted in Georg Paloczi-Horvath, *Mao Tse-tung* (Frankfurt/Main: S. Fischer, 1962), p. 249.
7. For the Land Reform Campaign, cf. Jürgen Domes, *Socialism in the Chinese Countryside: Rural societal policies in the People's Republic of China, 1949–1979* (London: C. Hurst & Co., 1980), pp. 4–12.
8. Cf. *China News Analysis*, Hong Kong (hereafter *CNA*), no. 5 September 25, 1953; Tang/Maloney, *op. cit.*, pp. 499–501; Christopher Lucas, *Women of China* (Hong Kong: Dragonfly Press, 1965), pp. 43–87; and Jürgen Domes, *The Internal Politics of China 1949–1972* (London: C. Hurst & Co., 1973), p. 39 f.

9. For the following paragraph, cf. Robert Leckie, *Conflict: The History of the Korean War* (New York: G.P. Putnam's Sons, 1962); C. Turner Joy, *How Communists Negotiate* (New York: Macmillan, 1955); William C. Bradbury, *Mass Behaviour in Battle and Captivity: The Communist Soldier in the Korean War* (Chicago University Press, 1968); Allen S. Whiting, *China Crosses the Yalu* (New York: Macmillan, 1960); Wang Chien-kuo, *Jen-hai ta tsui-hsi* (The criminal game of the human ocean) (Hong Kong: Asia Publishing House, 1956); Resist-America Aid-Korea Association General Chapter (ed.), *Wei-ta-te K'ang-Mei Yüan-Ch'ao Yün-tung* (The great Resist-America aid-Korea movement) (Peking: People's Publishing House, 1954); *CYCTJ, op. cit.*; and Whitson/Huang, *op. cit.*, pp. 93–7 and 247–9.

10. Mikhail Kapitsa, 'An important date in the life of two nations' in *Kraznaia Sviezda (Red Star)*, Moscow, Feb. 14, 1964.

11. Yang *loc. cit.*, p. 156.

12. Cf. Cao I-neng, 'Industries' in URI, *op. cit.*, vol. II, pp. 150–6; and *CNA*, no. 118, Feb. 3, 1956.

13. Chao, *ibid.*, p. 156.

14. *ibid.*, p. 161.

15. Cf. Douwe W. Fokkema, *Literary Dissent in China and the Soviet Influence* (The Hague: Mouton, 1965); and Domes, *Politics, op. cit.*, pp. 53–5.

16. For the Hundred Flowers Campaign, cf. *ibid.*, pp. 200–57; Fokkema, *op. cit.*, 82–146; Domes, *Politics, op. cit.*, pp. 58–62; Merle Goldman, *Literary Dissent in Communist China* (Cambridge, Mass.: Harvard University Press, 1967), pp. 158–202; René Goldman, 'The Rectification Campaign at Peking University, May–June 1957', *CQ*, no. 12, Oct.–Dec. 1962, pp. 138–153; and *CNA*, nos. 185, 187, 189 and 195, June 26, July 6 and 19, and Sept. 6, 1957, respectively.

17. Whitson/Huang, *op. cit.*, p. 113 f; and: Huang, *op. cit.*, p. 749 f.

18. *ibid.*, p. 28.

19. P'eng's activities during the Korean war have been reconstructed here mainly on the basis of the following sources: *PTHTS*, pp. 257–64; Ching/Ting, *op. cit.*, pp. 1–32; Ssuma Lu, *op. cit.*, pp. 128–30; Han Hsien-ch'u/Chieh Fang, 'Commander P'eng in the resist-America aid-Korea war', *Hsin-hua wen-chai (New China Digest)*, Peking, no. 1/1981, Jan. 25, 1981, pp. 166–70; and a number of articles and reports in *CYCIJ, op. cit.*

20. Huang, *op. cit.*, p. 44.1

21. *ibid.*, p. 687.

22. Carsun Chang, *op. cit.*, p. 186.

23. *PTHTS*, p. 257 f.

24. Han/Chieh, *loc. cit.*, p. 166.

25. Whitson/Huang, *op. cit.*, p. 95.

26. *PTHTS*, p. 259.

27. Whitson/Huang, *op. cit.*, p. 96.

28. Ssuma Lu, *op. cit.*, p. 128 f.

29. Ching/Ting, *op. cit.*, p. 5.

30. Whitson/Huang, *op. cit.*, p. 97.

31. This date is given in URI (ed.), *The Case of Peng Te-huai* (Hong Kong: URI, 1968) (hereafter URI, Peng), p. 355. Han end Chieh (*loc. cit.*, p. 169) give July 13, which may be a printing terror.

32. Han/Chieh, *ibid.*

33. Ssuma Lu, *op. cit.*, p. 130.
34. MacFarquhar, *Origins 1, op. cit.*, note 56 on p. 340.
35. *JMJP*, Sept. 13 and 19, Nov. 12 and 23, Dec. 9 and 10, 1952, respectively.
36. Huang, *op. cit.*, p. 442.
37. *Chieh-fang-chün pao (Liberation Army Daily)*, Peking (hereafter *CFCP*), Oct. 1, 1954.
38. Huang, *ibid.*
39. *URI, Peng*, pp. 358 f., 376 f., and 387–9. For P'eng's trip abroad, see below, pp. 87 f.
40. *CFCP*, June 11 and 18, and July 24, 1955, Cf. Huang, *op. cit.*, p. 443.
41. *CFCP*, Sept. 21, 1955.
42. *JMJP*, Sept. 28, 1955.
43. *CFCP*, May 18, 1956.
44. Some of these inspection tours are vividly described in Ching/Ting, *op. cit.*, pp. 38–46.
45. Ssuma Lu, *op. cit.*, p. 28. Text of the speech *ibid.*, pp. 17–39.
46. Information provided to the present author by a former aide of P'eng in Peking, Sept. 1980.
47. Huang, *op. cit.*, p. 611.
48. Ssuma Lu, *op. cit.*, p. 131.
49. *Canton collection*, p. 5.
50. *Huang-ch'i t'ung-hsün (Red Flag Bulletin)*, Chiangmen (Kuangtung) no. 10, Jan. 25, 1968.
51. Ssuma Lu, *op. cit.*, p. 130.
52. *JMJP*, April 5, 1955.
53. *Ta-p'i-p'an t'ung-hsün (Great Criticism Bulletin)*, Canton, Oct. 5, 1967, p. 5.
54. URI, *Peng*, p. 201.
55. *Ta-p'i-p'an t'ung-hsün, ibid.*
56. URI, *Peng*, p. 445; and Ssuma Lu, *op. cit.*, p. 134.
57. MacFarquhar, *Origins 1, op. cit.*, p. 251.
58. URI, Peng, p. 447.
59. *ibid.*

4

OPPOSING THE CHAIRMAN, 1958–1959

Historical preconditions

Each of the preceding chapters has begun with an attempt to describe the general historical framework within which the story of P'eng te-huai's life progressed. However, for some nine months between late November 1958 and mid-August 1959 P'eng stood at the very centre of political decision-making; and the conflict between him and Mao Tse-tung which now developed became, in a way, the essence of PRC politics. Hence the present chapter does not begin with the overall historical framework for P'eng's experiences during these nine months, but with an overview of political and social developments in the year preceding the autumn of 1958, while subsequent developments up till the summer of 1959 have to be included in the account of his activities.[1]

The course of the Hundred Flowers Campaign and its results between March and June 1957 were a severe shock for Mao. The influence of external 'reality' had not been able to change people's inner 'consciousness': after years of economic success, and after a remarkable improvement in standards of living, the intellectuals and other urban groups still had not absorbed the Party's doctrines, but instead had risen against CCP rule and offered a substantial threat to the political system. This experience seems to have led Mao to conclude that it was necessary for 'consciousness' to be changed first so as to bring about changes in the 'reality' later. Moreover, emulation of the Soviet model in the First Five-Year Plan (1953–7), while quantitatively producing impressive results, had also led to an economic imbalance: progress in the capital-intensive sector of basic and heavy industry was accompanied by the continuing underdevelopment of light industry and by an extraordinarily backward agriculture.

So Mao and his closest associates decided, against the opposition of a strong minority within the central CCP leadership around Premier Chou En-lai and the leading cadres of the economic machine, to solve the political and economic problems by means of an enormous effort of collective willpower. The Party Leader replaced the Soviet concept of development by a 'Chinese' one, i.e. by the genuinely Maoist platform of a permanent mobilisation of the production forces. He presumed that, supported by the 'revolutionary enthusiasm' of the masses, a whirlwind of development in both heavy industry and agriculture could be instigated, all at the same time. The PRC entered upon the period of the 'Three Red Banners' policy. In a 'Great Leap Forward' Mao wanted to expand heavy industrial production so as to 'catch up with and overtake' the *per capita* production of Great Britain in coal and steel by 1972.[2] The 'General Line of Socialist Construction', officially proclaimed at the Second Plenum of the Eighth CCP Party Congress in May 1958, provided for the simultaneous and balanced development of heavy industries and agriculture through simultaneous application of 'modern and traditional' methods of production. The third of the 'Three Red Banners' — indeed the central plank of Mao's new platform — was the movement to establish People's Communes: large rural collectives, in which the collectivisation of agricultural production should be brought to completion, and a collectivisation of the peasant's whole life should be initiated as well.

During the autumn of 1957 Mao began to suggest the amalgamation of a number of the Agricultural Production Cooperatives (APCs) into larger production units. While the central decision-making organs of the Party were still reluctant to follow this concept, he succeeded in inspiring provincial and local cadres to start experiments based on his ideas. By mid-April 1958 the local cadres in some areas of Honan province began to establish large rural collectives — the first were in Suip'ing and P'ingyü *hsien*.[3] About the same time the First Secretary of the Shanghai Municipal CCP Committee, K'e Ch'ing-shih, started a drive for 'mass steel production' — in fact, poor-quality cast iron — in small backyard furnaces. By the end of May large rural collectives were established in a number of other provinces, and on July 1 the alternate member of the Politburo and former private secretary of Mao, Ch'en Po-ta, used for the first time the term 'commune' as the name of these collectives.[4] By mid-July 1958, at least some 'Communes' had been set up in almost every region of the country, and only a month later they included about 20 per cent of all peasant households on the Chinese mainland. At an enlarged meeting of the CCP Politburo, held in the northern Chinese seaside resort of Peitaihe on August 17-29, the establishment of 'people's communes' was proclaimed as official Party policy and therefore mandatory for the whole country.[5]

After the decision of the Peitaihe conference, the new wave of escalated collectivisation reached almost every Chinese village without exception. In late September the central CCP media reported that 90.4 per cent of all peasants had been organised into 23,390 communes,[6] and on November 15 they announced the organisation of 99 per cent of the peasantry into 26,578 communes, with an average of 4,637 households in each commune.[7] At this moment, it appeared that the Party had succeeded in establishing the communes even faster and more effectively than agriculture had been collectivised in the APCs between 1955 and 1957.

The CCP used the terms 'large' (*ta*) and 'general' (*kung*) to characterise the new type of rural collectives. 'Large', in this context, meant the amalgamation of all the APCs in a township (*hsiang*) into one commune, which would now unite administration and production under consolidated leadership. The meaning of 'general' was that the rural communes were to be not only production units, 'in which agriculture, forestry, animal husbandry, peripheral occupations and fisheries are combined', but also 'organisational units which combine farmers, workers, commercial personnel, students and soldiers' with the task of 'implementing not only collective production, but also collective living'.[8] This meant in practice a far-reaching regimentation of the peasants' personal lives by the collective. In the second half of 1958, the peasants in most communes had to work for twelve hours a day and at harvest time for as much as sixteen or eighteen hours. Except for breakfast, the meals were taken — 'voluntarily', according to the CCP media — in mess-halls. Children and babies often stayed for the whole week in kindergartens or nurseries, and old people were concentrated in so-called 'houses of happiness' (*Hsing-fu chih chia*), where they were given light manual work. According to concepts that were quite widespread in the PRC in the autumn of 1958, the communes were to be basic units for the 'transition to communism', and thus could begin experimenting with a remuneration system 'according to need'. As a rule, 70 per cent of all remuneration was distributed equally according to the number of members in a family, and 30 per cent according to work performance.[9] The labour force was organised on military lines into 'work platoons', 'work companies' and 'work brigades'. In some villages the peasants had to muster in military formations every morning to march together to the fields.[10]

As the fervent and stormy campaign developed, manifold variations occurred in the organisational structure of the communes. Some were just loose federations of APCs, and there was no great change in reality; however, at others the collectivisation of life went so far that men and women were garrisoned in different living quarters, and thus families were broken up. Yet, in spite of all these differences, the overwhelming majority of communes had five common characteristics:

1. State administration and the leadership of production had been unified at the *hsiang* level.

2. All arable land, forests, water, houses, trees and bushes, animals, machines and larger tools had been transferred into commune property. The peasants could keep their clothes, some household implements, and a few domestic animals and fowls as their personal property, but individual ownership of houses and individual agricultural production had ceased to exist.

3. The life of the individual peasant became increasingly collectivised.

4. The remuneration of the commune members combined the elements of distribution according to work performance and of equal distribution 'according to need'.

5. Of great importance was the introduction of the system of 'production guarantees' (*Pao-ch'an*), which regulated the relations between the commune and state procurement for foodstuffs. Before the harvest, the communes were supposed to guarantee a fixed production quota to the state. If after the harvest the guaranteed amount could not be met, the communes had to reduce their members' remuneration in order to reach the procurement quota — or at least get as close to it as possible. This system gave the communes the power of decision over planning and administration for the entire agricultural production. The lower echelons of production units — the 'production brigade' (*Sheng-ch'an ta-tui*) and the 'production team' (at that time *Sheng-ch'an hsiao-tui*) — were little more than mere units of work organisation.

These five common characteristics of the communes in their original form began to undergo revisions, which the Party leadership has gradually implemented since December 1958. This happened because it soon became obvious that Mao and his associates had overplayed their hand. The speed of the campaign in the summer and autumn of 1958 resulted in dangerous structural deficiencies. The simplest preconditions for the efficient working of the communies were lacking almost everywhere. There were no adequate premises for mess-halls, nurseries, kindergartens and old-age homes. Regular accounting could not be introduced, because the leadership personnel of the communes — mostly retired soldiers — had not been trained in book-keeping. Hence there was increasing disorder, which in a number of provinces developed into veritable chaos.[11] Moreover, the arbitrary actions of the local Party cadres, organisational inefficiency and the general disorder resulted in the opposition of the peasantry to the new collectives; this had not been particularly strong at the start of the campaign, but it increased rapidly and soon began to turn into open resistance.

From mid-October 1958 this open resistance took on, in many regions, the character of a general though entirely uncoordinated movement.[12] The peasants refused to march to their work in the fields in military formation and they secretly continued cooking food at home despite orders from the cadres to the contrary. Parents took their children out of the nurseries and kindergartens in large numbers, and the elderly people left the 'houses of happiness' and returned to their families, often over great distances. Grain was not delivered to the state granaries because the labour units in the villages divided it among their members. In some villages the peasants even started to poison wells, and slaughtered animals at night in the fields. Occasionally they stormed the commune storehouses and beat up the cadres. During November and December 1958, according to reports in the CCP provincial media, these activities escalated in the provinces of Kwangtung, Hupei, Hunan, Kiangsi, Szechwan and Tsinghai into local rebellions, which began to pose a serious threat to the structures of political and economic control.[13] As the result a majority of the Party leadership decided in late November or early December 1958 to beat a strategic retreat from Mao's developmental concept of the Three Red Banners, even if this meant overruling the will of the Chairman. This decision was supported by P'eng Te-huai, who soon became one of the most outspoken critics of Mao's policies.

Investigating and formulating critical thoughts

P'eng's opposition to Mao's mobilisatory policies was not evident at first during the winter of 1957–8, but developed slowly from the spring of 1958, and took definite shape in the following winter.[14] However, a deterioration of P'eng's relations with Mao had been noticeable since February 1958, when P'eng, in a speech at the celebrations for the fortieth anniversary of the Soviet Red Army, suggested closer military co-operation between the Soviet Union and the PRC — an idea of which the Chairman did not approve. Roderick MacFarquhar has suggested that Mao decided about this time to groom a rival and possible substitute for P'eng in the person of Marshal Lin Piao.[15] There is also some evidence, though it is not conclusive, that P'eng opposed the shelling of Chinmen and Matsu in August 1958,[16] which had taken place on Mao's direct order. It was undoubtedly P'eng who initiated the cessation of the Chinmen/Matsu campaign in October.

Furthermore, the Minister of Defence was not among the promoters of the militia (*Min-ping*) movement, which Mao launched in September 1958 in order to mobilise the Chinese masses for some basic military training. In the context of this movement tens if not hundreds of millions of people were organised into militia units with the aim that 'everybody should become a soldier'. Even if only a limited number of so-called 'core militiamen' (*Ku-kan min-ping*) were issued with rifles and live ammunition, a second armed force besides the PLA seemed to develop, controlled by the local Party committees.[17] This could not be welcomed by the *de facto* Commander-in-Chief of the regular forces, and the 'people's war' doctrine propagated in the militia movement at Mao's behest went directly counter to P'eng's professional military convictions. Thus large rifts were growing between P'eng and the Party Leader in the realm of military doctrine, strategies and style. Over the Three Red Banners policy it took P'eng some time to reach a more definite formulation of his views, but it was clear that his lack of support for the new Maoist developmental concept dated back to the very beginning. In April 1958, on an inspection tour to Canton, he made some disrespectful comments: 'The Chairman talks all the time about more, faster, better, and more economical results. That is annoying. What does he want with chanting these liturgies all the time?'[18] During the summer and autumn of 1958, P'eng did not once come out openly in support of the Three Red Banners, and in particular there is no record of his having praised the communes, at least not before the decisions of the Peitaihe conference. However, even in the attacks made on him during the Cultural Revolution, he was not blamed for having openly opposed Mao before the last months of 1958, with the exception of the above-quoted remark in Canton in April.

There is every indication that P'eng's awareness of the dangers which the Great Leap and the communes had brought to the country was significantly sharpened during an inspection tour which he made to the province of Kansu in October 1958. He had originally thought that the campaign for backyard 'steel' furnaces had brought positive results for the peasantry, and possibly even resulted in the production of primitive land-mines and bombs.[19] One day, however, he saw by the road a large quantity of ripe crops lying unattended on the ground. When he asked an old peasant what it meant, he received the answer that 'unless the centre sends down a great cadre, one cannot stand up against this storm'. On the same tour, P'eng was also confronted with complaints from some officers at an infantry school that in their home villages cooking utensils had been confiscated as raw materials for the 'steel' campaign, and wooden houses and even orchards had been ripped down to serve as fuel for the backyard furnaces. As he travelled through the province of Honan during the night on his way to Kansu, he saw the lights of the myriad steel furnaces in the countryside, and remarked to his bodyguard: 'This won't work. We may be able to burn up our household utensils this way, but we certainly did not use our brains when we devised this!'[20] This may have been the night — we do not know the exact date — when P'eng summarised his impressions in the following poem:

> Grain scattered on the ground, potato leaves withered;
> Strong young people have left to make steel.
> Only children and old women reap the crops,
> How can they pass the coming year?
> Allow me to raise my voice for the people![21]

Yet there is no record that he did raise his voice at the first conference in Chengchow or the conference in Wuhan, both of which discussed the problems of the people's communes, and which preceded the crucial Sixth Plenum of the Eighth CCP/CC, also convened in Wuhan, between November 28 and December 10, 1958. By his own account, he attended the first Chengchow conference only on November 10 and, since he was in Peking until December 6, he could not have been at the Sixth Plenum for more than its last four days.[22]

The plenum in Wuhan marked the beginning of the retreat for the communes, and of the first revisions concerning the Three Red Banners in general. In a 'Resolution on Some Problems concerning the People's Communes', the CCP/CC, although starting with ritualistic praise for the commune as a 'new social organisation', significantly watered down the concept that had been current during that summer. 'For the time being' the movement to establish communes in the cities as well was interrupted, and a general investigation of the rural communes was ordered to decide what further readjustment might prove to be necessary. Accommodating peasants by sexes, each sex in separate barracks, was now forbidden, and the resolution guaranteed that peasants would retain the private ownership of their houses, vegetable gardens and small animals 'for all time' (*Yung-yüan*), as well as having eight hours' sleep and four hours' leisure every day. Working time was to be restricted to eight hours. Wages should once more mostly be paid in cash. The use of nurseries, kindergartens and mess-halls would now be entirely voluntary for commune members, and it was strictly forbidden to seize and destroy household utensils. Moreover, the plenum no longer made a connection between the communes and a 'Great Leap' in agriculture, but contented itself with declaring that they constituted a 'step forward'.[23] The leaders of the CCP apparently assumed at the time that these revisions would be sufficient to win back the consent of the peasantry to the new collectives. This assumption was soon proved wrong.

Of equal importance for the future course of politics in the PRC was the decision taken by the plenum on December 10 to 'approve of the wish of Comrade Mao Tse-tung not to run again as a candidate for the position of the Chairman of the People's Republic after the end of his term in office'.[24] This meant that Mao was resigning from the position of head of state right in the middle of a mounting crisis over the very policies he had so fervently propagated throughout most of 1958. Nevertheless, there is no evidence that the majority of the Party leadership had forced him into resignation. Even the election of Liu Shao-ch'i as Mao's successor as head of state at the First Plenum of the Second National People's Congress on April 27, 1959, should not be over-interpreted in the light of later developments during the Cultural Revolution. Mao's intensive activity during the first half of 1959 rather suggests that he himself wanted to be rid of the many representative duties he had to shoulder as head of state. He had to concede some revision of his developmental concept in Wuhan, but he now wanted to reaffirm his grasp over the Party organisation so as to prevent the unfolding 'investigation' of the communes from turning into their *de facto* liquidation; this required his whole attention and a great investment of time. Finally, the choice of Liu as his successor could possibly win for Mao the support of Liu's large clientele within the civilian Party machine, and Liu, who had begun to doubt the validity of Mao's concept, was at that time obviously not yet fully opposed to it. There are many indications that Liu wanted to slow down the pace of the Three Red Banners around the turn of 1958–9, — as shown by his speech to delegates of agricultural machinery co-operatives on December 26, 1958 — but that he and his supporter were not yet willing to initiate a fundamental revision of the policies of 1958.

Despite the many and varied problems that had arisen as a consequence of the 'Great Leap' and the establishment of the communes, the
CCP leadership began 1959 on an optimistic note. On January 1 the
Minister of Agriculture, Liao Lu-yen, confirmed that in 1958, 375
million tons of grain, or 92.3 per cent above 1957, had been harvested,
and that the people need not expect any shortage of food or clothes.[25]
However, in the first months of the new year there were no signs of a
successful solution to the problems which had arisen in the communes.
On the contrary: the mess-halls, in particular, were the subject of an
escalating crisis. Peasant resistance to them spread still further, and
became more violent, with some open fights between the peasants and
security forces. Yet while the world hardly noticed such resistance in the
Chinese villages, the uprising in Tibet in March 1959, which was caused
not by opposition to the policy of the Three Red Banners but by the
desire for national self-determination and independence, received considerable attention in the world at large.[26] It also absorbed the attention of P'eng as Minister of National Defence in the second half of
March.

At the end of 1958, between 25,000 and 30,000 guerrillas of the
Tibetan Khampa tribe, which had fought against Chinese colonialism
ever since 1954, moved into the region of the country's capital, Lhasa,
and on March 10 the city rose in revolt with Khampa support against the
Chinese occupation forces. The secular and religious leader of the
Tibetans, the Dalai Lama, joined the movement, and with the exception
of the PLA barrack area, Lhasa fell quickly into the hands of the Tibetan
national revolutionaries. Negotiations with the PLA commander in
Lhasa, General Chang Kuo-hua, for a greater degree of autonomy
remained unsuccessful, and soon the Dalai Lama escaped over the
Himalayas to India at the behest of the movement's leaders. In Lhasa
35,000 PLA soldiers regained control of the city in two days of fierce
street battles with more than 20,000 rebels between March 19 and 21. In
the countryside scattered fighting and guerrilla activity continued for a
number of years but the PLA, this time under direct orders from P'eng
in Peking, had succeeded in suppressing the major thrust of the revolt.

Yet before and after the Tibetan uprising, the Minister of National
Defence continued his inspection tours throughout the countryside.
Right after the Wuhan plenum, he visited Hunan, and returned to his
native township of Shihhsiang for the first time in thirty years. There he
saw at first hand the deteriorating conditions of the peasants' life:

serious food shortages, hungry babies and children, embittered elders and the boasting of cadres. The peasants, some of them his relatives, complained that the basic-level cadres lied about production figures and the successes of the Great Leap to the higher echelons in the Party organisation; they also voiced their bitter resentment at collective living and the militarisation of life. Obviously deeply impressed, P'eng exhorted the First Secretary of the Hunan CCP Provincial Party Committee, Chou Hsiao-chou, who accompanied him, to curb the excesses of the Leap in the province.[27] And he promised that he would 'report to the Chairman' on the situation.[28] In early March, and again in April 1959, he also visited Kiangsi, Anhwei and some villages in Hopei where his impressions were the same or, in some cases, stirred him even more than those he had had during his tours in Kansu and Hunan.[29] By late March 1959 P'eng was definitely convinced that the whole developmental approach of the Three Red Banners needed revision.

P'eng was by no means the only CCP leader who had developed such a conviction. Already in February 1959 the Secretary-General of the CCP/CC, Teng Hsiao-p'ing, demanded that the State Planning Commission and the State Economic Commission should prepare proposals for further 'improvements' in the commune system, and that in order for such proposals to be based on solid documentation, the New China News Agency (NCNA) should gather information through its regional and local branches on the state of the new collectives throughout the whole country.[30] Soon the Chairman of the State Economic Commission, Po I-po, sent an investigation group headed by the Vice-Chairman of the State Planning Commission, the economist Hsüeh Mu-ch'iao, and the Director of the Academy of Science's Institute of Economics, Sun Yeh-fang, to a number of communes to gather material on planning mistakes.[31] The report of this group trenchantly criticised the disorder and misallocations in the communal mess-halls and concluded that these mess-halls should be abolished.[32] Even one of the staunchest promoters of the communes in 1958, the Minister of Finance Li Hsien-nien, now argued that the establishment of these collectives had 'undermined the national economy'.[33]

The initial results of the 'investigation' launched at the Wuhan plenum prompted the calling of an enlarged meeting of the Politburo at Chengchow in Honan, from February 27 to March 5, 1959. This meeting, later called the 'second Chengchow conference', initiated further revisions in the commune structure. It decided that the ownership of arable land, local industrial workshops, larger agricultural tools, livestock and seedgrains, which had previously been reserved for the communes, was to be distributed over three levels — the commune, the production brigade, and the production team — with land, workshops and seedgrains remaining for the time being in the hands of the communes.[34] The Chengchow decisions were then confirmed by a second enlarged Politburo meeting in Shanghai, held from March 25 till April 1, and finally by the Seventh Plenum of the Eighth CCP/CC, also held in Shanghai on April 2–5, 1959.[35] It was at the enlarged Politburo session in Shanghai that P'eng first openly criticised Mao in the Chairman's very presence, blaming him for 'taking personal command' (*Ch'in-tzu kua-shuai*), and thus disregarding the collective leadership exercised by the Politburo's Standing Committee. When Mao retorted with — unspecified — criticism of P'eng, the Minister of Defence countered that this criticism was 'provocative' (*t'iao-po*).[36]

Soon after this Seventh Plenum, P'eng had to leave China to go on a long trip through all of Eastern Europe, leading a goodwill military mission. He left Peking on April 24 and returned seven weeks later on June 13.[37] It was during this journey, on May 28, that he had an extended conversation with Khrushchev in Tirana, the capital of Albania. During the Cultural Revolution P'eng was accused of having 'informed bald-headed Khrushchev' about the shortcomings of the Great Leap Forward, and it was alleged that the Soviet leader had 'encouraged P'eng to oppose Chairman Mao after coming home'.[38] In an article in 1961 the pseudonymous 'David A. Charles' argued that at their meeting P'eng had handed Khrushchev a letter criticising the Three Red Banners policy, and that his ensuing attack on Mao 'had been made with the knowledge of the Russians'.[39] This article resulted in a broad stream of Western analytical opinion which, over a long period, connected P'eng's confrontation with Mao in July 1959, of which more will be said shortly, with the incipient attacks of the CPSU leadership against Mao and the CCP. Roderick MacFarquhar, however, doubts a 'Soviet connection',[40] and I tend to agree with the analysts at the Union Research Institute in Hong Kong who in 1968 made the following rebuttal of the arguments of David A. Charles:

There is of course no secrecy about Peng Te-huai's itinerary in 1959. He did meet Khrushchev; but whether he wrote a letter as described in Mr Charles' article seems to be questionable. What could have been his motive in sending such a letter criticizing the policies of the Chinese Party in front of the Soviet Party? It is conceivable that he would honestly voice his own views when and if Khrushchev asked him about them; but it is rather difficult to believe that he would voluntarily write a letter about the subject, especially when he was to meet Khrushchev in person. If he had indeed written such a letter, the incident surely would have been brought up when the Maoists most viciously 'settled accounts' with him from August to November 1967. However, all that was said about P'eng's contact with Khrushchev was: 'To meet the needs of the class enemy at home and abroad, P'eng Te-huai, who had gathered around him a few anti-Party elements, could wait no longer and came out with an even more ferocious attack on the Party at the Lushan Meeting in 1959. In this, they were actively encouraged by the Soviet revisionist clique and had the direct support of China's Khrushchev [Liu Shao-ch'i].[41]

Even excerpts of a letter of P'eng to the CPSU were not quoted at the time when the most violent attacks were being made on him by the Cultural Revolutionary Left. Moreover, Mao did not mention any collusion with the Soviet Union when he made a counter-attack on P'eng at the Lushan conference. Finally, we have to take account of the fact that P'eng's opposition to the Great Leap and the communes had already begun in April 1958 and had taken definite shape during his Hunan trip in December that year. Before he left for the Soviet Union and Eastern Europe, he had already attacked Mao directly for the first time in Shanghai in March 1959. His conflict with the Chairman, which emerged fully during the Lushan conference on July 2–30, and reached its climax with his purge by the Eighth Plenum of the Eighth CCP/CC which was convened on August 2–16, also at Lushan, had developed mainly for domestic political reasons even if not entirely so. The allegation of collaboration between P'eng and the Soviet leadership was definitely raised *ex post facto*. Nevertheless, one can agree with Roderick MacFarquhar that P'eng's meeting with Khrushchev in Tirana enabled Mao 'to feed doubts and perhaps inspire rumours to discredit the Marshal'.[42]

To sum up the experiences with the Three Red Banners policy on the basis of the investigation of the communes (concluded by late June) and prepare for the Eighth Plenum of the Eighth CCP/CC, an enlarged Politburo meeting was convened at Lushan, Kiangsi, on July 2, 1959, in which many CCP/CC members and alternates as well as some provincial Party leaders took part.[43] It seems that P'eng, tired after the strain of his seven-week journey through Eastern Europe, wanted to be excused from attending the conference. But Mao personally phoned him and asked him to come. Obeying this call, P'eng went by train to Wuhan, and from there by ship to Chiuchiang, where a car took him up to the Lushan resort — right into open confrontation with the Party Leader.[44]

Confrontation

The resort area of Lushan in Kiangsi has been described by the American journalist Ross H. Munro as a place of 'special beauty where mountains of rocks and evergreens rise abruptly from the flat Yangtse River plain' with a 'huge chalet-like building' and 'dozens of summer homes built of stone . . . for some Chinese who are more equal than others'.[45] In fact, it is one of the many retreats for high-ranking cadres in the PRC — thoroughly sealed off by PLA sentries so that the Chinese 'masses' may not disturb their leaders while they take their vacation or engage in caucus activity there. For the Lushan conference in July 1959 the resort was guarded by the PLA Unit 8341, which is code for the so-called Central Guard Division, distinguished for its absolute loyalty to Mao. Its tasks were not only to protect the central CCP leadership but also occasionally to act as secret police. This it obviously did during the conference, because during the Cultural Revolution Maoist Red Guards accused Marshal Ho Lung of having brought to the Lushan meeting in his luggage only classical novels and no writings of the Chairman — something that could only have come to light if (as had obviously been the case) his room had been secretly searched.

The conference was opened on July 2 with a brief address from Mao. The Party Leader exhorted the audience to 'criticise and offer opinions' on the 'mistakes and shortcomings' which 'still exist in our Party's work', and at the same time promised that he would not 'put a hat' on anybody for any criticism. This meant that nobody should be branded as, for example, a 'rightist' or a 'counter-revolutionary' owing to opinions expressed during the meeting.[46] For the first three weeks the conference mostly met in discussion groups organised according to the six large regions of the country. These regions, though already officially disbanded as administrative units five years earlier, still had some importance in 1959.

As the former political and military leader of the Northwest China region, P'eng was involved in the discussion of the 'Northwestern Group'. Obviously encouraged by Mao's opening remarks of July 2, he attacked the Three Red Banners policies in the discussion group at the very first meeting, on the morning of July 3. Because of its great successes in 1957, he said, the Party had 'got a fever in the brains'.[47] In the same statement P'eng plainly accused Mao of lying:

'The commune of Chairman Mao's native village [Shaoshan] increased production last year, but its figures of increase, in fact, were not as high as reported. I went there to find out the truth, which was only an increase of 16 per cent. I also asked comrade Chou Hsiao-chou. He told me that this commune had increased its production only by 14 per cent, with much assistance and loans from the state. The Chairman has also visited this commune. I asked the Chairman what was his finding. He said he had not talked about the matter. In my opinion, he had.'[48]

In six further interventions during the group discussions, P'eng reiterated and intensified his criticism of the excesses of the Great Leap and the communes, saying that 'everybody is responsible for the mistakes committed during the campaign. Everybody had a share of the responsibility, including Comrade Mao Tse-tung.'[49] In particular, he addressed himself to the period of the collectivist storm in the late summer and autumn of 1958:

'After the Peitaihe meeting, something "leftist" was done. This slogan "Let the whole people make steel" — is it really correct or not? In the program of running industries by the whole people, over 13,000 small-scale projects were launched. What are we going to do now? To set up an industrial system in every region or province is not a matter of one or two plans.'[50]

In his often blunt way, he also attacked other leading members of the Party for their fear, even insinuating cowardice:

'That we suspended supplies of edible oil to the villages for four months was an impossible act [*Pan-pu-tao*]. This was entirely subjectivism. As soon as I returned to the country and saw the telegram, I immediately uttered my opinion over the telephone. Did you utter your opinion, too? (Comrades from different provinces: "The centre already issued a document to change the original regulation!") Have you opposed it or not?'[51]

The group discussions during the first week of the conference must have convinced P'eng that now was the time to advance his opinion more systematically. In this he may have been encouraged and even assisted, as MacFarquhar suggests, by Chang Wen-t'ien, Vice-Minister of Foreign Affairs and alternate member of the Politburo, with whom he was consistently in touch during the Lushan conference.[52] The ideas he put forward were most probably his own. He formulated them in a 'letter of opinion' (*I-chien-shu*) addressed to Mao Tse-tung, which he wrote mostly during the night of July 13–14.[53] On the morning of the 14th, he had the letter delivered to Mao's residence, but Mao only read it for the first time on July 17. According to a later statement by P'eng, the letter was not meant for circulation among the conference participants, and when the conference secretariat began circulating copies on July 17, he claims that he even requested its withdrawal.[54] That may, however, have been said to protect himself.

P'eng's 'letter of opinion', although most of it was expressed in polite terminology, was in fact an all-out attack on the policies promoted by Mao. Never since he had assumed the unchallenged leadership of the Party between 1938 and 1940 had Mao been confronted with such scathing criticism within the limited circle of the ruling élite. At the beginning of the letter, P'eng compared himself with Chang Fei, a courageous but uncouth general of the period of the Three Kingdoms (221–64 AD), who had taken a stand against the cunning and malign tyrant Ts'ao Ts'ao.[55] The parallel between the latter and the Chairman must have been obvious to all who read the letter because, since the spring of 1959, Party propaganda had made a sustained attempt to improve the historical image of Ts'ao Ts'ao, probably in order to answer comparisons of the ancient tyrant with Mao among the populace.[56] After this introduction, the Marshal launched on a detailed criticism of what he saw as mistakes committed in 1958:

It now seems that some projects for capital construction in 1958 were too hasty or excessive, with the result that a portion of capital was tied up and some essential projects were delayed. . . . The formation of rural communes in 1958 was of great significance. This will not only enable our peasants to free themselves completely from poverty, but it provides the correct way to speed up the building of socialism and the transition to communism [obviously a polite concession to Mao's views]. Nevertheless, there has been a period of confusion regarding the question of the ownership system, and in our concrete work some shortcomings and mistakes appeared. This is, of course, a serious phenomenon.[57]

Discussing the Great Leap, P'eng turned to irony:

In the course of refining steel by the whole people, a number of small blast furnaces were unnecessarily built, and thus a certain amount of resources (material, financial, and in terms of manpower) was wasted. This is of course a relatively big loss. But a preliminary geological survey was carried out on a large scale all over the country, and many technicians were trained. The broad masses of cadres have tempered and improved themselves in this movement. Although a tuition fee was spent (in the amount of two billion *Yüan*), even in this respect there have been *losses and gains*.[58]

Here, the Marshal had deliberately reversed the usual order. In the esoteric language of communication within the CCP, it was the rule to refer to '*gains and losses*', thus indicating an optimistic note. P'eng plainly refused to copy this feature.

The more devastating criticism was reserved for the second part of his letter. At the beginning of this part he disputed a privilege enjoyed by Mao: the Chairman had always been the only member of the inner leader-ship core who was allowed, after discussions, to 'sum up [*Tsung-chieh*]'. Now P'eng began the second part with the phrase 'How to sum up the lessons of working experience'. And this he did very frankly and at times caustically:

We have not sufficiently understood the socialist laws of planned and pro-portionate development, nor have we implemented the policy of walking on two legs in practical work in a number of fields. We have not handled the problems of economic construction in so successful a way as we dealt with the political problems of shelling Chinmen, and of quelling the Tibetan revolt. On the other hand, the objective situation is that our country is poor and blank (there are still a number of people who do not have enough to eat. Last year, there was an average of only 18 feet of cotton cloth per person, enough for a shirt and two pairs of pants). The people urgently demand a change of the present condition.[59]

Finally, P'eng turned to what he called 'problems in our way of thinking and style of work', of which he considered two as the most important:

First, the habit to exaggerate spread rather universally. Last year, at the time of the Peitaihe conference, a higher estimate of grain production was made than was warranted. This created a false impression: everybody felt that the problem of food had been solved, and that our hands were free to engage in industry. . . . At that time, from reports sent in from all directions, it would seem that communism was just around the corner. This caused not a few comrades to become hot in their brain. In the wave of high grain and cotton production and the doubling of iron and steel production, extravagance and waste developed. . . .

Second, petty-bourgeois fanaticism [*Hsiao tzu-ch'an-chieh-chi-te k'uang-je-hsing*] renders us liable to commit 'left' mistakes. In the course of the Great Leap Forward of 1958, like many comrades, I myself was also bewitched by the achievements of the Great Leap Forward and the passion of mass movement . . . Our minds swayed by the idea of taking the lead, *we forgot the mass-line and the style of seeking the truth from the facts* which the Party had developed over a long period of time. As far as our method of thinking was concerned, we often confused strategic planning with concrete measures, long-term policies with immediate steps, the whole with the part, and the big collective with the small collective.

Then he directly attacked the slogan which had been advanced by Mao and his closest supporters:

In the view of some comrades, *putting politics in command* [*Cheng-chih kua-shuai*] could be a substitute for everything. . . . Putting politics in command is no substitute for economic principles, much less for concrete measures in economic work. Equal importance must be attached to putting politics in command and to effective measures in economic work; neither should be overstressed or neglected.[60]

P'eng's letter hit the assembled ruling élite like a bombshell. Supplemented by an equally devastating speech by Chang Wen-t'ien on July 21 — probably given in the East China group, which may explain why P'eng did not hear it[61] — amounted to a head-on assault on Mao's authority and prestige. The attacks were greeted with obvious agreement by many conference participants. Nineteen years later, Huang K'e-ch'eng recalled that 'The opinion of commander P'eng was warmly welcomed by the comrades attending the meeting.'[62] In one way or another, possibly with a vote or a straw vote taken among all those who participated in the Lushan conference on July 21 or 22, the majority of the assembled ruling élite expressed their appreciation of P'eng's arguments, probably by making his letter an official conference document.[63]

What prompted the Minister of Defence to oppose Mao openly? It is possible to deduce three motives from his experience in 1958–9 and from the context of the first two weeks at Lushan. First, P'eng the former peasant boy had been deeply moved by what he had seen on his inspection tours, particularly in Kansu and in his home village in Hunan, and he felt emotionally compelled to act as spokesman for the suffering Chinese peasantry. Secondly, P'eng the Defence Minister had realised that a continuation of the Three Red Banner policies would lower the morale of the men serving in the army, since most of them came from the villages. This was a situation which P'eng wanted to avoid by all possible means. And thirdly, P'eng the Politburo member was convinced that he spoke for many, if not the majority, of his colleagues, and that Mao himself wanted open criticism in order to ameliorate the crisis of the PRC which became ever more obvious.

Yet, over the last consideration at least, P'eng was wrong. The Chairman, whose charisma had undergone a process of gradual erosion ever since the failure of the Hundred Flowers Campaign in 1957, could not tolerate the loss of authority which was developing in Lushan. He decided to strike back, and his counter-attack took the form of a very emphatic and angry speech to the plenum of the conference on July 23, 1959.[64] From the start Mao's tone was aggressive:

'You gentlemen who are present here, you have your ears. Just listen! There are only complaints about the mess. Now, listen to what is unpleasant to hear. Welcome! When you think in this way, it would not be unpleasant any more. Why should people be allowed to say such things? The reason is that China will never sink into the water, and the sky will never tumble down.[65]

He then attempted to analyse the attitudes with which the populace had responded, albeit in very broad terms, and turned this immediately into an attack on P'eng:

'The cadres [meaning the members of the ruling élite] are leading several hundred million people. At least 30 per cent of these people are activists, another 30 per cent are pessimists and landlords, rich peasants, counter-revolutionaries, bad elements, bureaucrats, middle peasants, and a group of poor peasants. The remaining 40 per cent are followers of the main stream. How many are 30 per cent? This is 150 million people. They want to run communes and mess-halls, establish large-scale co-operation, they are very activist. They are willing to do all this. Can you say that this is petty-bourgeois fanaticism? They are not petty bourgeois, they are poor peasants, lower-middle peasants, they are proletarians and semi-proletarians.'[66]

Mao defended the mess-halls and went on to suggest that 'until now, not a single commune has collapsed'. Here he became even more threatening:

'Some people will not give up their views. It will go on for one year, two years, three to five years. It won't do if you cannot listen to strange talks. You must get accustomed to them. I myself always listen to them with a stiffened scalp. They cannot do more than throw dirt at your past three generations. Don't blame them . . . I never attack others if I am not attacked. If others attack me, I always strike back. Others attack me first, I attack them later. I have never given up this principle until this very day. Now, I have learned to listen, listen with a stiffened scalp, for one or two weeks, before I launch my counter-attack'.

This 'counter-attack' followed immediately with unmistakeably clear insinuations:

'Historically, there have been four [revisionist] lines: the [Li] Li-san line, the Wang Ming line, the Kao-Jao line, and now again this line. . . . These people [meaning P'eng Te-huai] do not mention adventurism, but they just smell opposition to adventurism. For instance, they say that 'there have been losses and gains'. To place 'gains' in the second position is obviously done after much deliberation. . . . Under the pressure of imperialists and the bourgeoisie, they tend to become rightists'.[67]

Then, in what may be considered one of the vital passages of his speech — if not the vital one — Mao gave the conference a plain ulti-matum:

'If we have done ten things, nine of which have been bad, and are reported in the papers, we must perish. And if we deserve to perish, then I shall go. I shall then go to the countryside *to lead the peasants to overthrow the government. If you from the PLA do not follow me, I shall find myself a Red Army.*'[68]

This meant nothing less than that if the conference accepted P'eng's views, Mao would split the Party. The confrontation was now no longer over the Three Red Banners policies alone; it even threatened the consensus on procedures, which had hitherto been preserved despite the obvious breakdown of the consensus on issues in the latter part of 1958. The men in charge of the Party organisation and state administration, led by Liu Shao-ch'i and Chou En-lai, were definitely not willing to risk the split threatened by Mao, even if they fully or at least partly agreed with P'eng's criticism. Thus they left P'eng out in the cold, and Mao won his personal fight with the Marshal.

The defeat of P'eng

In 1978 Huang K'e-ch'eng, who had supported P'eng during the Lushan conference, recollected that Mao's speech 'turned the tide of the meeting. Having initially been anti-leftist, it all of a sudden turned into an anti-rightist one.'[69] We still have no reliable information on how this dramatic change came about, but from circumstantial evidence as well as from a host of accounts and data advanced first during the Cultural Revolution, and then after 1978, we are able to make a number of reasoned, though admittedly speculative, suggestions about the course of events which finally led to P'eng's removal from office.

On July 30, 1959, a week after Mao's speech, the enlarged meeting of the Politburo came to an end, and only three days later, on August 2, the Eighth Plenum of the Eighth CCP/CC was convened — also at Lushan and, according to Huang K'e-ch'eng, 'in a hectic way'.[70] Since plenary meetings of the CCP/CC are hardly ever opened without the issues having been previously decided by the Politburo, it can safely be assumed that the Politburo members present at Lushan had decided the contest and hence the fate of P'eng and his closest supporters, either during the last days of the July conference or in a special caucus meeting held between July 30 and August 1, 1959.[71] We know that of twenty full Politburo members and six alternates at least three were not present at Lushan during those days: Ch'en Yün, who was on vacation in Talien; Teng Hsiao-p'ing, who had left the conference because of his 'ailing legs'; and Marshal Ch'en Yi. Of the remaining twenty-three, Mao could safely reckon on seven: himself, Marshal Lin Piao, Marshal Lo Jung-huan, K'e Ch'ing-shih, T'an Chen-lin and the Politburo alternates Ch'en Po-ta and K'ang Sheng. It seems that P'eng was fully supported by the Politburo members Chu Te and Lin Po-ch'ü, and the alternate Chang Wen-t'ien — making four including himself. This meant that the decision depended on the remaining twelve: the Politburo members Liu Shao-ch'i, Chou En-lai, P'eng Chen, Li Fu-ch'un, Tung Pi-wu, Li Hsien-nien, Marshal Ho Lung, Marshal Liu Po-ch'eng, Li Ching-ch'üan and the alternates Lu Ting-i, Po I-po and Ulanfu. In this third group one can single out three sub-groups: Chou En-lai and Tung Pi-wu, who are on record as having always joined the stronger side in any intra-élite conflict where they were involved; the two remaining military leaders, Liu Po-ch'eng and Ho Lung, of whom Ho had been P'eng's rival in the last years of the Civil War; and the eight representatives of the civilian Party machine and the economic planning establishment: Liu Shao-ch'i, P'eng Chen, Li ching-ch'üan, Li Fu-ch'un, Li Hsien-nien, Lu Ting-i, Po I-po, and Ulanfu. Thus it was this last of the sub-groups which held the key in and it may well be assumed that Teng Hsiao-p'ing, although absent during the crucial days, communicated his views to this sub-group and went along with their position. Two major interests were represented in the sub-group around Liu Shao-ch'i and the absent Teng Hsiao-p'ing. First, they wanted, by whatever means, to preserve the outward unity of the Party , and avoid the split which Mao had threatened to create; and secondly, they wanted to make further revisions to the Three Red Banner policies.

In the event the Eighth Plenum, on August 16, 1959, passed two resolutions. One of them, published only in 1967, condemned the 'anti-Party clique headed by P'eng Te-huai' and called for P'eng's removal from his position as Minister of National Defence and First Vice-Chairman of the CCP/CC's Military Commission, while preserving his membership in the CCP/CC and the Politburo.[72] The other resolution, which was soon to be published, concerned the 'development of the campaign to increase and practice economy'.[73] It again paid lip-service to the Three Red Banners, but in fact confined the authority of the rural communes to administrative and planning duties, while the centre of gravity of social policy for the countryside now shifted to the production brigades (i.e. to the level of the former APCs), which were entrusted with the ownership of land and became the 'basic accounting unit' (*Chi-pen he-suan tan-wei*).

The substance of these two resolutions, I would suggest, reveals the nature of the compromise which Liu Shao-ch'i, Chou En-lai and — with his agreement from a distance — Teng Hsiao-p'ing concluded with Mao and his supporters sometime around the end of July and beginning of August 1959. The first point of significance is that Mao's attacks on P'eng were accepted. P'eng was to be removed from his positions and forced to undertake self-criticism at the forthcoming Eighth Plenum. However, he was not to be expelled from the Party, as Kao Kang and Jao Shu-shih had been in 1955. He was even to remain officially a member of the Politburo, although he was to be excluded from its meetings, at least for a considerable time. Finally, Mao accepted the revisions of the Three Red Banners policies proposed by the civilian leaders in the Party machine leaders and the economists. If these suggestions are correct, then P'eng's isolation when the Eighth Plenum convened was almost total. Liu, Chou and probably Teng too had dropped him like a hot brick in order to safeguard Party unity, and to secure Mao's consent to their policy of further revisions in the Great Leap and in the structure of the communes.

But what of the reactions of P'eng's loyalty group within the PLA? As we soon shall see, some of his old associates from the P'ingchiang uprising in 1928, and some generals with whom he had established close contacts during his time as Commander-in-Chief of the PVA in Korea, continued to support him and thereby showed considerable courage. However, the majority of the leaders of his former First FA did nothing to aid their one-time Commander-in-Chief. This should be explained by

the fact that most of them, as we have seen already,[74] had served under
Marshal Ho Lung for much longer than they had under P'eng. So it can
be concluded that Ho's decision to go along with the Mao-Liu-Chou
compromise deprived P'eng of whatever larger support base he might
otherwise have mobilised within the PLA.

The Eighth Plenum was opened on August 2, 1959, with a short
speech by Mao in which he reiterated that the Party should now defend
itself against 'rightist opportunism', attacking Chang Wen-t'ien by
name, but P'eng only by implication.[75] Throughout the course of the
meeting, only ten CCP/CC members or alternates spoke out in defence
of P'eng. These were, according to Red Guard sources published during
the Cultural Revolution, Marshal Chu Te and the old and infirm Lin
Po-ch'ü; and, according to a report submitted by Huang K'e-ch'eng in
1978, Huang himself, Chang Wen-t'ien, Chou Hsiao-chou, General
Hung Hsüeh-chih (Director of the General Rear Services Department
of the PLA), General Hsiao K'e (Vice-Minister of National Defence),
General Teng Hua (Commander-in-Chief, Shenyang Military Area),
General Chou Huan (Political Commissar, Shenyang Military Area),
and T'eng Tai-yüan (Minister of Railways).[76] Huang K'e-ch'eng also
reports that during the first few days of the Eighth Plenum P'eng did
not say a single word and gave no acknowledgement whatever of having
committed any mistake. Then, however, 'Liu Shao-ch'i, Premier Chou,
and Chu Te exhorted him to consider *protecting the authority of Chairman
Mao, and protecting the unity of the Party.* Thus, commander P'eng was
forced to present a public self-examination at the meeting.'[77] In this
'self-examination' P'eng admitted having committed 'severe mistakes',
not only with his 'rightist viewpoint' at the Lushan conference, but also
during large parts of his career. He also pleaded guilty to having 'implemented the [Li] Li-san line' in 1930 and the 'Wang Ming Line' in
1937–8. Moreover, he openly implicated Huang K'e-ch'eng and Chang
Wen-t'ien in his 'mistakes'.[78]

While his self-examination could be explained by the pressure
brought on him by Liu, Chou and Chu Te, the implication of others
shows the otherwise straightforward, if strategically weak, military man
in an unfavourable light. Indeed, P'eng apologised to Huang when the
latter visited him in the prison hospital in August 1974.[79] At the end of
the Eighth Plenum, the Marshal said privately to Chou En-lai: 'For the
first time in my life, I have spoken out against my very heart!'[80] On
August 16 P'eng, now almost totally isolated among the ruling élite
of the PRC, returned to his work in the Ministry of Defence

in Peking. On September 9 he once again humilitated himself with a
personal letter to Mao:

I have failed the Party, failed the people, and also failed you. In the future, I
must . . . ensure that I should never again do things to endanger the Party and
the people. For this, I beg to request the Party centre to consider . . . to permit
me to carry out studies or to leave Peking for the people's communes, so that I
may study and participate in some labour at the same time, so that, in the
collective living of the working people, I may steel myself and reform my
thoughts.[81]

His request to leave for the villages was not granted. He remained
officially at his post for eight more days, during which Marshal Ch'en
Yi, the Minister of Foreign Affairs, was the only member of the CCP
leadership who visited him.[82] Then on September 17 P'eng was removed
from his post as Minister of National Defence and replaced by his
long-time adversary and now Mao's trusted lieutenant, Marshal Lin
Piao. Along with P'eng, Huang K'e-ch'eng was dismissed as Chief-of-
the General Staff, with General Lo Jui-ch'ing, the former Minister of
Public Security, being appointed as his successor.[83] Also dismissed or
criticised were the following:

Chang Wen-t'ien, Vice-Minister or Foreign Affairs and alternate
member of the Politburo;

Hsi Chung-hsün, Vice-Premier, Secretary General of the State Council,
and member of the CCP/CC (in 1960);

General T'an Cheng, Director of the PLA's GPD and member of the
CCP/CC (in 1960 or 1961);

General Hsiao K'e, Vice-Minister of National Defence and member of
the CCP/CC (demoted to a less important position);

General Teng Hua, Commander-in-Chief of the Shenyang Military Area
and member of the CCP/CC;

Chou Hsiao-chou, First Party Secretary of the CCP's Hunan Provincial
Party Committee and alternate member of the CCP/CC;

General Hung Hsüeh-chih, Director of the PLA's GRSD and alternate
member of the CCP/CC;

General Li Ta, Vice-Minister of National Defence (only in that position);

Lieut.-General Nieh He-t'ing, Vice-Commander of the PLA armoured
troops;

Lieut.-General Han Chen-chi, Military Attaché to the Soviet
Union;

Lieut.-General Wan Yi, Director of Staff Operations, PLA;
Lieut.-General Ch'en Cheng-hsiang.[84]

P'eng, Chang, Hsi, Huang and Chou were, until further notice, forbidden to attend meetings of the CCP/CC or the Politburo, but they continued to receive the documents circulated among the members of these bodies. For P'eng himself there quickly followed significant changes in personal circumstances. By late September 1959 he was moved from the residential area of the major Party Leaders, the Chungnanhai in Peking, to an old run-down estate in the outskirts of the capital, called the Wu-chia hua-yüan (Wu Family's Garden). Of his whole staff only his bodyguard and personal secretary were allowed to stay with him. Before he quit his old premises, he handed over his Marshal's uniform, his fur coat and his decorations to the Ministry of Defence.[85] After more than forty-three years, his military career had come to an abrupt end.

P'eng's removal brought about major changes in the work and style of the PLA.[86] Immediately after the new Minister of Defence, Marshal Lin Piao, had taken office, a campaign for the glorification of Mao and for widespread circulation of his writings — now placed on an equal footing with the Marxist-Leninist classics — began within the armed forces.[87] This campaign aimed not only to restore the Chairman's prestige, which had suffered through the failure of the Three Red Banners policy, but also to reinforce political work among the military and to enhance the role of political commissars. After only twelve days in office, Lin Piao formulated the new concept for the PLA in a *JMJP* article. The army was to be placed under the command of the Party; the individual should submit to 'absolute leadership by the CCP' because the task of the PLA was to 'serve politics'. Hence the soldiers were exhorted 'Never forget politics' and 'Put politics in command.'[88] Between early 1960 and 1964, a number of conferences on political work in the army set the guidelines for the drive for a thorough indoctrination with the 'Thought of Mao Tse-tung' and the strategic principles of Mao's idea of 'people's war'. Political education in the PLA should be determined by the 'living study and living use of Mao Tse-tung's thought'. The style of activity now prescribed for the PLA was called the 'Three-Eight style' (*San-pa tso-feng*), stressing 'three sentences and eight ideograms'. The 'three sentences' called for correct political orientation, hard work and the simple life, and flexibility in strategy and tactics. The 'eight ideograms' represented the Chinese terms for unity, sincerity, energy and vitality, all interpreted as a return to the guerrilla ethics of the early 1930s and mid-1940s.

Yet despite these changes in style, doctrine and ethics which Lin Piao tried to implement after P'eng's removal, it would be wrong to suggest that P'eng's defeat at the Lushan conference was even partly due to his military convictions. It was, rather, part of a major intra-élite conflict which had begun to develop from 1958 onwards. We therefore have to ask how we can gain a clearer understanding of such intra-élite conflicts in the PRC from the confrontation at Lushan and its outcome. At the Lushan conference, as we have seen, there was no clear-cut confrontation between two structured factions with obvious alternative platforms; rather two loosely-knit groups attacked and counter-attacked, with a third group — the largest one! — holding the balance and working for a compromise solution. The basis for this solution, which meant the removal of P'eng without his being expelled from the Party and with some adaptation of the revisions to the Three Red Banners policy which he had advocated, was a consensus on procedures which still operated. The group around Liu Shao-ch'i and Chou En-lai wanted, by whatever means, to preserve this consensus on procedures, which meant the agreement of all participants that decisions should be made within the formal organs of the Party. Mao won his cause by threatening to break this consensus, and P'eng, egged on by Liu, Chou and Chu Te, humiliated himself in order to save it.

In a number of systematic presentations since 1971, I have suggested that during intra-élite conflicts in the PRC factors of primary group formation (structural or functional groups) and, since the Cultural Revolution, also of proto-secondary group formation (experience groups) have not, as a rule, acted independently. They have acted rather, as elements of both programme- and power-oriented alliances, formed in a process of secondary group formation.[89] Two types of such secondary group formation should be clearly distinguished. First, there are latent and short-term *opinion groups,* which are formed in clearly defined conflicts and based on individual decisions reached in the course of such conflicts; thus they are concerned only with the immediate issue at stake. And secondly there are intermediate-range to long-term *factions,* i.e. coherent circles based on alternative platforms, which claim exclusive political power and overall control.

The difference in character between these two types of intra-élite secondary group formation can be further explained by introducing the term 'coalition': 'opinion groups' are issue-based coalitions limited, by their very nature, to short-term co-operation, whereas 'factions' are programme-based coalitions which, by their very nature, are not limited in time. These types of group formation appear to be linked to different stages of intra-élite conflict, of which, so far, two can be distinguished: first, a stage of differentiation; and secondly, a stage of conflict resolution. During the stage of differentiation, intra-Party group formation is dominated by opinion groups, occasionally (though not in 1958–9) even by the independent actions of functional groups. In this stage the intra-élite consensus on issues evaporates, while the consensus on procedures is maintained, at least to begin with. *Pre-critical* confrontations, which result either in removals or in short-term compromise on policies (or, as at the Lushan conference, in both), appear either as a climax in the stage of differentiation, or as a point of intersection with the second stage of the conflict. This second stage, conflict resolution, starts with the condensation of opinion groups into factions, and the factional strife then results in the breakdown of the consensus on procedures. Thus a critical confrontation becomes unavoidable, which brings about the elimination of the defeated faction's leadership — either by expulsion from the Party or even by physical liquidation.

All the available evidence suggests that the events at the Lushan conference were a quite typical case of pre-critical confrontation. After the Eighth Plenum the intra-élite conflict continued, and from the winter of 1961–2, because the previously latent opinion groups began to condense into factions, it escalated gradually into the stage of conflict resolution. This process was definitely concluded by the summer of 1965, and thereafter the conflict developed into the critical confrontations which took place in the cataclysms of the Cultural Revolution. For P'eng this critical confrontation was to spell agony of a degree which put the isolation and the humiliations at Lushan into the shade.

NOTES

1. For this chapter consult the succinct and detailed account of Roderick MacFarquhar in *The Origins of the Cultural Revolution 2: The Great Leap Forward, 1958–1960* (Oxford University Press, 1983) (hereafter *Origins 2*). Cf., among others, Cheng Chu-yüan, *The People's Communes* (Hong Kong: URI, 1959), *passim*; Schurmann, *op. cit.*, pp. 464–500; Tang/Maloney, *op. cit.*, pp. 374–83; and Domes, *Socialism, op. cit.*, pp. 19–45.
2. *JMJP*, Sept. 29, 1958; also, quoting Mao Tse-tung: Liu Shao-ch'i in URI (ed.), *Collected Works of Liu Shao-ch'i, 1958–1967* (Hong Kong: URI, 1968), p. 10; and P'eng Te-huai in URI, *Peng, op. cit.*, p. 400.

3. *JMJP,* August 18, 1958.

4. Ch'en, Po-ta, 'Under the banner of Comrade Mao Tse-tung', *HC,* no. 4/1958, p. 8.

5. *JMJP,* Sept. 10, 1958.

6. *JMJP,* Sept. 30, 1958.

7. *JMJP,* Nov. 15, 1958. Cf. Schurmann, *op. cit.,* p. 493.

8. 'Salute to the high tide of the establishment of people's communes!, *JMJP,* editorial, Aug. 29, 1958; also in *HC,* no. 7/1958, pp. 13–15.

9. *Nung-ts'un kung-tso t'ung-hsün (Rural Work Bulletin),* Peking, no. 11/1958; *Ching-chi yen-chiu (Economic Studies),* Peking, no. 12/1958; and *JMJP,* Aug. 30 and Oct. 7, 1958.

10. *JMJP,* Sept. 30, 1958; and *Chung-kuo ch'ing-nien pao* (China Youth Daily), Peking (hereafter *CKCNP*), Sept. 27, 1958. Cf. Domes, *Socialism, op. cit.,* p. 32 f.

11. Reports on the chaotic situation in a number of communes were published, e.g. in *JMJP,* Oct. 3 and 29, and Nov. 11, 1958; *Kuang-ming jih-pao (The Light Daily),* Peking (hereafter *KMJP,*), Oct. 14, 1958; and *Honan jih-pao* (Honan Daily), Chengchow, Dec. 2, 1958.

12. Reports on such resistance are given by Cheng, *op. cit.,* pp. 124–9.

13. Among others *Hupei jih-pao,* Wuhan, Jan. 11, 13 and 24, 1959; *Ssuch'uan jih-pao,* Chengtu, April 3, 1960; *Hsin Hunan jih-pao,* Changsha, Nov. 19, 1959; *Ch'inghai jih-pai,* Hsining, Dec. 4, 1959; and *Nei-meng-ku jih-pao,* Huhehot, April 25, 1960.

14. When the research for this study was still under way, a very detailed narrative of the antecedents and the development of P'eng Te-huai's conflict with Mao in 1958–9 was published. The following account draws heavily on it, wherever the present author has reasons to agree. It is MacFarquhar, *Origins 2, op. cit.,* pp. 187–251.

15. Cf. *ibid.,* pp. 63–5.

16. Shanghai People's Publishing House (ed.), *Jen-min-te hao tsung-li* (The good premier of the people), vol. I (Shanghai: People's Publishing House, 1977), p. 197.

17. MacFarquhar, *Origins 2, op. cit.,* pp. 100–2.

18. Ssuma Lu, *op. cit.,* pp. 135 and 136.

19. Ching/Ting, *op. cit.,* p. 69.

20. *ibid.,* pp. 69 ff.

21. URI, *Peng,* pp. 120 and 446.

22. *PTHTS,* p. 265. Cf. MacFarquhar, *Origins 2, op. cit.,* pp. 196–2.

23. *JMJP,* Dec. 18 and 29, 1958. Cf. *CNA,* no. 258, Jan. 8, 1959.

24. *JMJP,* Dec. 18, 1958.

25. *JMJP,* Jan. 1, 1959. After 1977 this figure was revised to 200 million tons.

26. *NCNA,* Peking, March 28, 1959. Cf. *CNA,* no. 270, April 3, 1959, and no. 282, June 26, 1959; George N. Patterson, 'China and Tibet: Background to the Revolt', *CQ,* no. 1, Jan.–March 1960, pp. 87–102; *idem,* 'The Situation in Tibet'; *ibid.,* no. 6, April–June, 1961, pp. 81–6; and Tang/Maloney, *op. cit.,* p. 289 f.

27. Ching/Ting, *op. cit.,* p. 72 f.; and *CKCN* reporters, 'The great General P'eng returns to his native place'; in *Hsin-hua yüeh-pao wen-chai-pan,* no. 4/1979, pp. 144–6.

28. Ching/Ting, *op. cit.,* p. 74. Cf. MacFarquhar, *Origins 2, op. cit.,* pp. 197–200.

29. URI, *Peng,* pp. 120, 203 f., 446 and 479.

30. *Kung-jen p'ing-lun* (Workers' Review), Canton, no. 5, June 1968.

31. *Wen-ke feng-yün* (Storm clouds of the Cultural Revolution), Peking, no. 4/1967 (no date).

32. Mao Tse-tung, speech at the Lushan Conference (July 23, 1959); in *Mao Tse-tung t'ung-chih shih tang-tai tsui wei-ta-te Ma-k'e-ssu-Lieh-ning-chu-yi-che* (Comrade Mao Tse-tung is the greatest Marxist-Leninist of the present) (no place, presumably Canton: no publisher, presumably a volume distributed internally within the CCP, Aug. 1969), pp. 294–305 (hereafter Mao, *Lushan I*), here: p. 301. The same speech in an abridged and slightly different version can be found in URI, *Peng*, pp. 15–26 and 405–12 (here pp. 23 f. and 410).

33. *CNA*, no. 761, June 20, 1969.

34. *JMJP*, Aug. 28 and 29, 1959. Cf. MacFarquhar, *Origins 2, op. cit.*, pp. 146–55.

35. *JMJP*, April 8, 1959. Cf. MacFarquhar, *ibid.*, pp. 172–80.

36. Ssuma Lu, *op. cit.*, p. 137.

37. URI, *Peng*, pp. 387–9.

38. Ssuma Lu, *ibid.*

39. David A. Charles, 'The Dismissal of Marshal P'eng Teh-huai', *CQ*, no. 8, Oct.–Dec. 1961, pp. 63–76. A contrary argument is presented by J.D. Simmonds, 'P'eng Teh-huai: A Chronological Re-Examination', *CQ*, no. 37, Jan.–Mar. 1969, pp. 120–38.

40. MacFarquhar, *Origins 2, op. cit.*, p. 228.

41. URI, *Peng*, p. XII.

42. MacFarquhar, *ibid.*

43. For the Lushan Conference, cf. among others *ibid.*, pp. 200–25; Charles, *loc. cit.*; Simmonds, *loc. cit.*; Domes, *Socialism, op. cit.*, pp. 42–5; Frederick C. Teiwes, *Politics and Purges in China* (White Plains, NY: M.E. Sharpe, 1979), chapter 9; Ellis Joffe, *Between Two Plenums: China's Intra-leadership Conflict 1959–1962* (Ann Arbor, Mich.: Center for Chinese Studies, University of Michigan, 1975), pp. 8–22; Byung-Joon Ahn, *Chinese Politics and the Cultural Revolution: Dynamics of Policy Processes* (Seattle: University of Washington Press, 1976), pp. 38–42; Peter R. Moody, *The Politics of the Eighth Central Committee of the Communist Party of China* (Hamden, Conn.: Shoe String Press, 1973), pp. 139–146; Franz Michael, *Mao and the Perpetual Revolution* (New York: Barron's/Woodbury, 1977), p. 148 f.; and Thornton, *op. cit.*, pp. 253–5.

44. *PTHTS*, p. 266 f.; and Ching/Ting, *op. cit.*, p. 75.

45. Quoted by MacFarquhar, *Origins 2, op. cit.*, p. 191.

46. Huang K'e-ch'eng, 'Please, give Comrade P'eng Te-huai his reputation back!', Letter to the Organisation Department of the CCP/CC, Nov. 29, 1978 (Internal CCP document, copy in the author's possession) (hereafter Huang, *Letter*), p. 4.

47. Excerpts from P'eng Te-huai's Talks at the Meetings of the Northwest Group of the Lushan Meeting (July 3–10, 1959); in URI, *Peng*, pp. 1–5 and 393–5 (here pp. 1 and 393).

48. *ibid.*

49. *ibid.*, p. 3 and 394.

50. *ibid.*

51. *ibid.*, p. 4 and 395.

52. MacFarquhar, *Origins 2, op. cit.*, pp. 204–6.

53. P'eng Te-huai, 'Letter of Opinion', July 14, 1959, in URI, *Peng*, pp. 7–13 and 397–401 (hereafter P'eng, *Letter*).

54. *PTHTS*, p. 276.
55. P'eng, *Letter,* p. 7 and 397.
56. *CNA*, no. 274, May 1, 1959.
57. P'eng, *Letter,* p. 8 and 397.
58. *ibid.*, p. 9 and 398. Author's emphasis.
59. *ibid.*, p. 10 and 399.
60. *ibid.*, pp. 10–12 and 399 f. Author's emphasis.
61. Huang, *Letter,* p. 5. Cf. MacFarquhar, *Origins 2, op. cit.*, p. 217 f.
62. Huang, *Letter, ibid.*
63. In an earlier treatment of the Lushan conference, the present author has suggested that two votes were taken, probably one in favour of P'eng's criticism, and one as a vote of confidence in Mao (Domes, *Politics, op. cit.*, p. 112). Roderick MacFarquhar (*Origins 2, op. cit.*, note 163 on p. 404) doubts this statement because 'there is little evidence that the CCP's leading bodies actually take decisions in that way'. This may be correct, but I would still suggest that — most probably with a vote among the members of the Politburo who were present — P'eng's letter was approved, and that — either by vote or by a presentation of opinions — Mao was ensured of the confidence of a majority among the conference's participants.
64. Mao, *Lushan I, passim*.
65. *ibid.*, p. 295 f.
66. *ibid.*, p. 296.
67. *ibid.*, pp. 298 ff.
68. *ibid.*, p. 300 (author's emphasis).
69. Huang, *Letter,* p. 5.
70. *ibid.*
71. *ibid.*
72. This was only published in 1967: *JMJP,* Aug. 16, 1967. Its text can also be found in URI, *Peng,* pp. 39–44 and 423–7.
73. *JMJP,* Aug. 26, 1959. Cf. Domes, *Socialism, op. cit.*, p. 44.
74. See above, p.
75. Mao Tse-tung, 'Speech at the Eighth Plenum of the Eighth CCP/CC', Aug. 2, 1959; in URI, *Peng,* pp. 27–30 and 413–15 (hereafter Mao, *Lushan II*).
76. Huang, *Letter,* 1–5.
77. *ibid.* (author's emphasis).
78. URI, *Peng,* pp. 31–38 and 417–21.
79. Huang, *Letter,* p. 1.
80. *ibid.*, p. 5.
81. URI, *Peng,* pp. 45 f. and 429.
82. Ching/Ting, *op. cit.*, p. 67 f.
83. *JMJP,* Sept. 18, 1959.
84. Huang, *op. cit.*, p. 443 f.
85. Ching/Ting, *op. cit.*, p. 81 f.
86. For the changes in military style and doctrines under Lin Piao, cf. Samuel B. Griffith II, *The Chinese People's Liberation Army* (New York: McGraw-Hill, 1967), pp. 214–64 and 279–96; John Gittings, *The Role of the Chinese Army* (Oxford University Press, 1967), pp. 225–62; Ellis Joffe, *Party and Army: Professionalism and Political Control in the Chinese Officer Corps* (Cambridge, Mass.: East Asian Research Center, Harvard University, 1965), pp. 114–46; Whitson/Huang, *op.*

cit., pp. 447 f. and 526–30; and Domes, *Politics, op. cit.*, pp. 130–134.

87. Cf. James T. Myers, 'The Fall of Chairman Mao', *Current Scene*, Hong Kong (hereafter *CS*), vol. VI, no. 10, June 15, 1968.

88. *JMJP*, Sept. 29, 1959.

89. The following proposals have been gradually developed by the present author since 1970. A first version was published in the German edition of Domes, *Politics, op. cit.*, (English edn, p. 236) in 1971. The most recent published version, which is followed here, can be found in Jürgen Domes, 'Intra-Elite Group Formation and Conflict in the PRC', in David S.G. Goodman, (ed.), *Groups and Politics in the People's Republic of China* (Cardiff: University College Press, 1984), pp. 26–39 (here pp. 28–31 and 35).

5

ISOLATION, PARTIAL REHABILITATION AND PERSECUTION, 1959–1974

The historical framework

The revisions of the organisational structures in the rural communes enacted at the Lushan conference did not alleviate the economic crisis into which Mao's mobilisatory policy of the Three Red Banners had thrown the country.[1] On the contrary: as P'eng Te-huai had predicted at Lushan, this crisis began to assume threatening proportions in the autumn of 1959, and became further aggravated in 1960. The result was a veritable famine in most regions of China — the most severe one, in fact, which the country experienced in the twentieth century. During 1959–61, which the Chinese still call the 'three bitter years', between 16.4 and 29.5 million people died of starvation,[2] and in 1961–2 the famine had the further result of a severe recession in industrial production. This crisis caused most of the leaders in the civilian Party machine, led by Liu Shao-ch'i and Teng Hsiao-p'ing, to intensify their opposition to Mao's prescriptions. By early 1962 their suggestions had condensed into a comprehensive platform calling for ownership of arable land, lifestock, machine tools and seedgrains to be transferred from the production brigades to the production teams, for peasants to have more leeway in deciding whether to work for their families' benefit as a sideline, for the distribution of private plots to the peasants, and for the opening of free markets in the villages. They managed to introduce a new concept of development, in many ways diametrically opposed to that of Mao, and this was implemented under the name of the 'policy of readjustment' between 1961/2 and 1965. As the result, the economic situation was stabilised and underwent marked improvements after 1963.

At the 10th plenum of the Eighth CCP/CC, which convened in Peking in September 1962, all changes in structure of the communes which had been made up till then were written into a 'Revised Draft of Working Regulations for the Rural People's Communes'; this provided for an organisation of agricultural production which had little more in common with the original Maoist model of 1958 than the name.[3] It was

107

to be one of the last compromises to be achieved in the unfolding intra-élite conflict within the ranks of the CCP leadership. With the 1962 compromise, the consensus on procedures was saved for the time being, but the consensus on issues could not be retrieved. From now on, during the three years between the autumn of 1962 and the late summer of 1965, the latent opinion groups within the élite condensed into factions with alternative platforms. In terms of policies, the conflict was basically over whether the PRC should in future follow Mao's concept of development through mass mobilisation and enthusiastic austerity, or the 'readjustment' concept which stressed traditional economic growth criteria, material incentives and a widening of the limits to individual initiatives. Mao's first major attempt to stage a return to the developmental concept of 1958 threw the country into the devastating experience of the 'Great Proletarian Cultural Revolution'.[4] The Party Leader's offensive was staged after he had realised that the policy-making bodies of the CCP were no longer willing to follow his suggestions.

In October 1965 Mao went to Hangchow and Shanghai, and for about seven months, competing leadership circles around him in Hangchow and around Liu Shao-ch'i in Peking issued conflicting orders. Mao and his supporters enlisted the help of the majority of PLA leaders, and as the result of a show of military force in the capital, P'eng Chen was forced to resign. Mao returned to Peking and managed, on May 16, 1966, to win a Standing Committee decision which defined the debate with the intellectual critics of 1961/2 as an 'antagonistic contradiction'. This meant that physical coercion could now be employed against them. From late May 1966 the conflict took a further bound forward. The Maoist faction of the Cultural Revolutionary Left, led by Mao, Lin Piao, Ch'en Po-ta and the Party Leader's wife Chiang Ch'ing, with the support of sections of the PLA, now started to mobilise university and secondary school students into the *ad hoc* youth organisations of the 'Red Guards' (*Hung-wei-ping*). At first these new shock forces of the Maoist offensive concentrated on criticism and the application of physical violence against opponents of Mao among the teachers and university professors. Already by mid-May, all secondary schools and universities had been closed, the schools for about eighteen months, one-third of the universities for more than four years, and the other two-thirds for between seven and eleven years. Under pressure from the Red Guards, and again with the help of shows of military force, the Maoists, in early August, convened the 11th plenum of the Eighth

CCP/CC, which formally expelled P'eng Te-huai and P'eng Chen from the Politburo, demoted Liu Shao-ch'i from the Standing Committee to simple Politburo membership, and decided to elevate the Great Proletarian Cultural Revolution to the status of the Party's 'general line'. On August 18, at a mass rally of about one million Red Guards in Peking, Mao and Lin Piao officially legitimised the activities of the new youth organisations, which now considerably broadened their devastating activities. The actions of this Leftist vanguard soon aroused resistance, but by late December 1966, in spite of mounting opposition, the Cultural Revolutionary Left had finally gained the upper hand in the Party Centre. On Mao's birthday, December 26, the leaders of the left decided to initiate 'a new high tide of the Cultural Revolution in industry and mining'. The Red Guards were now joined by workers' organisations, the 'Revolutionary Rebel Factions', which gathered together 'temporary' workers, apprentices and some workers from the lower end of the pay scale. During January 1967 the Red Guards and Revolutionary Rebel Factions, staged an all-out attack on the civilian Party leaders in most provincial capitals. This drove the country close to civil war; the structures of the Party and state administrative machines broke down, while popular resistance, which many anti-Maoist cadres had begun, largely defeated the Leftists' drive to seize power. Yet this resistance soon became uncontrolled, and strikes, factory closures and attacks on railways and harbours crippled the economy.

The situation had become so dangerous that Mao himself, had to call upon the PLA to intervene in the domestic crisis.[5] The reaction of the regional military commanders to this call, however, was ambivalent. Only in six of China's twenty-nine provinces did they support the Cultural Revolutionary Left; in some others they turned against Maoist organisations, but in most cases they remained neutral. Yet almost everywhere the generals forced the Party leaders out of office and took over control of the administration and the economy themselves, establishing new local and regional power organs under direct military leadership, which soon came to be known as 'revolutionary committees'. However the leaders of the Cultural Revolutionary Left tried, in a second offensive, to overthrow the regional military power-holders. But the military, mainly using the instrument of its own newly-founded mass organisations, offered staunch resistance, and the confrontations often escalated into violence. The culmination, on July 20, 1967, was an abortive military *coup* in Wuhan; and although it was possible to suppress this local *coup*, this was the turning-point of the Cultural

Revolution. Mao and Lin Piao saw themselves forced into a compromise with the regional military leaders, who agreed to establish new power-organs ('revolutionary committees') in every province, provided that these bodies remained under PLA control. In return for this concession to Cultural-Revolutionary terminology, the generals received permission from the centre to proceed with a drive to discipline the Maoist organisations. In the late summer of 1968 the last resistance by the Red Guards and 'Revolutionary Rebels', — now deserted by their idol Mao Tse-tung — finally collapsed. The Cultural Revolution in fact ended with the Ninth CCP Party Congress in April 1969, although it was only officially proclaimed to be 'successfully completed' at the Eleventh Party Congress in August 1977. Lin Piao became the only Vice-Chairman of the CCP/CC, and in the new Party statute he was mentioned by name as 'Chairman Mao's close comrade-in-arms *and successor*'. Yet exactly half of the 170 members of the new Ninth CCP/CC were military men, and so were twelve out of the twenty-one members of the new Polit-buro: the PLA had become the decisive political factor in the PRC.

Grave damage was done to the country by the crisis of the Cultural Revolution. At least three million people were killed, mostly in the cities and towns.[6] In terms of education and scientific development, the PRC — as Teng Hsiao-p'ing stated in 1977 — had been 'thrown back by at least twenty years', and 'a whole generation of youth had become intellectual cripples'.[7] Yet the countryside was only marginally affected by the fights and convulsions of the Cultural Revolution. There from early 1967 onwards, the crisis had the diametrically opposite result to that intended by Mao and his supporters. Wherever the control structures broke down, the peasants returned to individual production and to the selling of their products on free village markets.[8] It was only after the reconstruction of the Party machine began with strong military assistance in the course of 1969 that CCP control over the villages was gradually re-established.

In the context of the drive to reassert Party leadership in the country-side, Lin Piao and most leaders of the central PLA machine made a second attempt to implement the Maoist developmental concept of 1958 and the original structures of the rural people's communes, albeit not this time through mass mobilisation but through an effort to impose strict military discipline on all sectors of society. This attempt promoted the PRC's next grave domestic political crisis, that concerning Lin Piao in 1970–1.[9] In this conflict the coalition which had triumphed in the Cultural Revolution split up, and by the spring of 1971 Lin Piao and his followers in the central PLA organs were almost entirely isolated. In September Mao's 'closest comrade-in-arms and successor' lost his position — and his life — in a palace *coup* in Peking.

After the fall of Lin Piao, Chou En-lai engineered a new line in developmental, cultural and personnel policy, which tried to combine an all-out return to the concept of 'readjustment' with the gradual rehabilitation of those cadres and generals who had been purged and persecuted during the Cultural Revolution. The wave of rehabilitations reached its apex on April 12, 1973, when Teng Hsiao-p'ing re-appeared in his position as Vice-Premier of the State Council.[10] When Chou En-lai went into hospital with an incurable cancer on May 7, 1974, Teng took over the responsibilities of the State Council leadership. However, this, together with an escalating drive to combine a return to pre-Cultural-Revolutionary policies with an all-out rehabilitation of pre-Cultural Revolutionary leadership personnel, provoked opposition from the Cultural Revolutionary Left and Leftist cadres in the civilian Party machine as well as from the security establishment and groups which, late in 1975, united into a faction that one may call the United Left. After Chou's death on January 8, 1976, this faction managed to prevent Teng from taking over as Prime Minister and to engineer his second purge on April 7, 1976. For some time it seemed as if the ideas and platforms promoted by Mao and the other leaders of the Cultural Revolutionary Left would prevail. But from late March, massive manifestations of popular opposition to Mao and his policies shook the country. As if this were not enough, a third major crisis, that of the succession to Mao Tse-tung, started to unfold in 1976. In the early morning of September 9, 1976, the Chairman died, and less than four weeks later, on October 6, in a military *coup* in Peking, a combination of veteran civilian cadres and the leadership of the PLA overthrew and arrested Chiang Ch'ing and three other members of the core of the Cultural Revolutionary Left, which thereby ceased to be a major force in PRC politics. The country entered a new political era — one dominated not by the concepts of Mao but increasingly by the ideas which P'eng Te-huai had held against the Party Leader at the Lushan conference.

Living in disgrace — and a limited comeback

In trying to reconstruct the course of P'eng's life after his dismissal as Minister of National Defence, we have the difficulty that, at least for the period up till late 1966, we have to rely entirely on sources published in the PRC since early 1979, i.e. at a time when the CCP élite had already decided to re-create the dead Marshal's image as that of a hero. Nevertheless, we would suggest that these sources,[11] apart from the fact that their evaluation of his character is positive, do present a fairly reliable account of his activities and those occurring around him.

After he had left the ministry and moved to the *Wu-chia hua-yüan*, life for P'eng became somewhat lonely, with only his personal secretary and his bodyguard still with him. Under surveillance by a group of eight or ten soldiers from the Central Guard Division of the PLA,[12] he had difficulty in making contact with his neighbours — some peasant families — until he threatened to complain to Mao Tse-tung. Only then did the guards allow the peasants to visit him, but he was still closely followed and observed whenever he went out.[13] His wife P'u An-hsiu had to stay in Peking to attend to her position as a Party secretary at the Normal University, and she was thus able to join him in his new house on the outskirts of the city only on her free days. However, he did not encourage visitors, apparently because he thought that this could compromise their position with the authorities; he mentioned this to the Politburo's physician, Dr Fu Lien-chang, who once came to see him.[14] Occasionally his niece P'eng Mei-k'uei stayed with him, and it seems that the two developed a close and trusting relationship.[15]

Around the delapidated Wu-chia hua-yüan was a little park close to the Summer Palace, which seems to have been in a very neglected condition when he moved in, with only a few dead trees, and overgrown with weeds. P'eng immediately set to work on it — something his peasant youth had trained him to do. He removed the weeds, dug a pond and started to raise fish. When the spring of 1960 came, he planted some apple-trees and vines and began growing cabbage, beans and egg-plant.[16] Thus he spent much of his time working in the garden, and this gave him the opportunity of closer contacts with his peasant neighbours and their children, all of whom were said to have been quite fond of him.[17] At other times he read, and began to study Marxist theory, economics and agriculture. At his request, the Director of the Higher Party School, Yang Hsien-chen, regularly sent two teachers to help P'eng with his studies.[18] Thus, although he was in deep disgrace with Mao and his close associates, P'eng was clearly not to be considered as totally purged, even during the first two years after his dismissal. He was still officially a member of the Politburo and a Vice-Premier of the State Council, and while he could not attend meetings, he still received and read attentively all documents distributed among the members of these bodies.[19] The Party Centre even appointed Yang Shang-k'un, an alternate member of the Secretariat and Director of the CCP/CC General Office, who had worked with P'eng as a political commissar for some time in the early 1940s, to keep in regular contact with him.[20]

Once only during the whole period from September 1959 to August 1967 did P'eng's name appear in the official media, thus indicating that he had not been entirely excluded from the élite: he was mentioned as a member of the funeral committee for the deceased Politburo member Lin Po-ch'ü in May 1960.[21] He also seemed to get over the shock of the Lushan conference quite quickly, and in spite of having surrendered to Mao and made a confession at the 8th plenum of the Eighth CCP/CC, he resumed his scathing criticism of Mao's mobilisatory policies. Already on October 10, 1959, he wrote some notes on the clashes that had taken place in July and August. He reiterated that when the communes were established 'there was an unchecked flight of peasant population from the land, which created a period of social chaos'. The steel campaign during the Great Leap Forward, according to these notes of P'eng's, 'was actually one big widespread destruction. A destruction which damages the people's vigour and vitality can be made good only over a period of years, if not decades. . . .'[22] As the economic conditions in the country deteriorated and the great famine of 1960–1 — largely a man-made one — increased in severity, his criticism, made in conversations with relatives and friends, became ever more pointed. In late 1960 he said to his niece:

'Do not forget: I am still a member of the CCP/CC, I can still look at [internally circulated] documents. The peasants are very badly off. Szechuan used to be like heaven, but now, alas, the peasants there have nothing to eat. In the —— region, several tens of thousands of people have already starved to death! . . . I have experienced hunger, I know the taste of it, and it frightens me! We have fought decades of war, and the people, poorly clothed and poorly fed, have spilt their blood and sweat to help us, so that the CCP could win over the country and seize power. How can we let them suffer again — this time from hunger?'[23]

The worsening economic crisis, on the other hand, contributed indirectly to an improvement in P'eng's standing with a considerable part of the ruling élite. As the famine spread and the industrial recession began to bite, Liu Shao-ch'i, Teng Hsiao-p'ing and other Party leaders, who had agreed to P'eng's dismissal at Lushan, came increasingly to realise that his criticism of the Three Red Banners policy had been correct. They made some first cautious attempts to enlist his support in their drive towards further revisions of Mao's concept of 1958, and it was most probably due to Liu's and Teng's influence that, around late November or early December 1961, for the first time since September 1959, P'eng was allowed to leave the capital for an inspection tour of his home province, Hunan, which brought him again to his native village. He stayed in Hunan for some six weeks, visiting four communes, nine production brigades and one coal mine,[24] and found the situation there even worse than it had been in late 1958. In his home village and all over the province there was malnutrition, and in many places severe famine. The mess-halls had broken down, and because the people were frustrated and angry, they naturally turned to P'eng, whose stand at Lushan had gradually become known even in the villages, to express their complaints. He decided once again to write a report to the Party Centre demanding rapid relief for the countryside through sweeping reforms in the commune system. Even before he wrote this report, his message was taken up by Liu Shao-ch'i, who now set out to attempt a full rehabilitation of P'eng. At a 'Central Work Conference' of the CCP/CC in Peking on January 26 and 27, 1962, at which more than 7,000 leading Party cadres were present, Liu repeated most of the criticisms P'eng had voiced at the Lushan meeting, and he openly called for a 'reversal of the verdict against the so-called "rightist deviationists" '.[25] A few weeks later Ch'en Yün, who had not been seen in public for almost two years, reappeared, and was entrusted with the responsibility of readjusting the state budget.

Liu and Teng soon tried to enlist P'eng Te-huai's support in their drive to even more thoroughgoing revisions in the commune structure. In April or May 1962 they encouraged him to present a memorandum to the Party Centre, in which he should discuss the whole history of his career, ask for a reversal of the Lushan conference's decision to censure him, report on his findings in Hunan during the winter of 1961/2, and suggest further changes in the CCP's rural societal policies.[26] Accordingly, on June 16, 1962, he presented to the CCP/CC Secretariat a document for the hands of Mao Tse-tung and the Politburo, which has since become known as the 'Letter of 80,000 Words'.[27] Unfortunately this document, to which almost every article attacking or praising P'eng since 1967 has referred, remains unpublished, even in excerpts, either inside or outside the PRC. Yet we can infer that he presented here a full account of his life, admitted a number of his supposed 'mistakes', but defended himself against most of the allegations in the resolution of the 8th plenum at Lushan which had censured him. He apparently even went beyond his Lushan 'Letter of Opinion' in his criticism of the 'Great Leap' and the communes, and probably suggested that the large rural collectives be abolished altogether. It is also probable that he asked to be allowed to participate in policy-making bodies again, preferably in a leading position in the economic planning and administrative establishment. Yet although no part of the text has ever been revealed to the public eye, one phrase of P'eng's has been quoted again and again, and soon became of great symbolic importance: 'I want to be Hai Jui! [*Wo yao tang Hai Jui!*]'.

What meaning are we to attribute to this phrase? Hai Jui (1515–87) was an honest and efficient *hsien* magistrate in the period of the late Ming dynasty. When imperial officials exploited and oppressed the peasantry in his *hsien* and elsewhere in China, he went to the capital, requested to see the emperor and, when he was received in audience, criticised him for tolerating the abuses by the imperial bureaucracy. Thus Hai Jui carried the complaints of the people right to the throne itself. The emperor, however, was infuriated by the Hai Jui's harsh criticism and dismissed him. The meaning of P'eng's statement was clear: he compared Mao to the emperor, the mobilisation cadres of the Three Red Banners drive to the corrupt and oppressive bureaucracy, and himself to Hai Jui, the valiant and honest official who 'spoke up for the people'. His remark was particularly sensitive because the drama 'Hai Jui's Dismissal' (*Hai Jui pa kuan*) by Wu Han, the close associate of P'eng Chen, had been staged in Peking in February 1961, and this event had already been interpreted as an attempt to vindicate P'eng Te-huai's attack on Mao at Lushan.[28]

The drive by Liu and Teng to effect a full rehabilitation of P'eng and other 'rightist deviationists' in 1962 did not succeed. The Marshal was again not allowed to participate in the 10th plenum of the Eighth CCP/CC, which convened in Peking in September 1962, and this conference failed to reverse the 1959 verdict on P'eng. Nevertheless, although he continued to live in involuntary retirement, his isolation from other Party leaders, which had been almost total in 1959–60, gradually ceased. He continued working in his garden at Wu-chia hua-yüan and reading books throughout the three years from September 1962 to September 1965, but he started to make tours of the capital, and thus his contacts with the ordinary people increased. Even more important was the fact that from the summer of 1964 a number of his Politburo colleagues started to visit regularly and openly, and discuss politics with him, most of all his former PLA colleagues Chu Te, Ch'en Yi, Liu Po-ch'eng and also Ho Lung. Lin Piao, however, never came.[29] Then in September 1965 Mao Tse-tung seems finally to have bowed to the increasing pressure from other members of the ruling élite to agree to a partial rehabilitation of P'eng. In early September P'eng Chen received P'eng Te-huai in the 'Great Hall of the People', the seat of the NPC, and conveyed to the Marshal a suggestion of Mao that he should go to Southwest China and there assume responsibility for what was then called the 'Third Line of Construction', i.e. the development of new industries.[30] P'eng, however, did not immediately accept this offer. A few days later Mao himself phoned (a telephone had only just been installed at Wu-chia hua-yüan) inviting him to come to the Chairman's residence.

On September 23, 1965, the two adversaries of the Lushan confrontation met for the first time in six years. It was also the last meeting.[31] Liu Shao-ch'i, Teng Hsiao-p'ing and P'eng Chen also joined the two of them somewhat later. The Chairman tried to crack a joke as he received P'eng: 'You are some kind of fellow. At quiet times, you never come. You do not even write letters, and when you write, you write 80,000 words.' He then referred to 'many decades of common work', and to the fact that the two had 'parted ways at Lushan': 'Now we are both in our sixties or seventies, we must think about the next generation, and we must make a greater effort.' This effort was defined by Mao as P'eng's 'going to the Southwest to do work in the third line of construction'.[32] P'eng, however, still hesitated, and blamed the Party Leader for having 'put so much abuse on my neck'. Yet in the course of the conversation, Mao — probably grudgingly — was ready to admit: 'The Lushan conference is already past history. From the perspective of today, the truth may have been on your side! [. . .] Now, let us go forward together again.'[33] This seems to have placated P'eng, and a few weeks later he abandoned his resistance to the new appointment in the Southwest, and accepted the position as 'Deputy Commander of the Great Third Line of Construction in South-west China', which in fact meant that he was to be in charge of industrial construction (particularly in arms and military logistics) for the provinces of Szechuan, Kweichow, Yunnan and Tibet. So that he would have a post in the official Party structure, in which the 'Third Line' was not included, he was also appointed Third Secretary of the Control Commission of the CCP's

Southwestern Bureau. These positions were in no way comparable with P'eng's former rank, but it meant that his retirement had ended, and he had been able to stage at least a limited comeback.

On November 28, 1965, the Marshal left Peking by train for Chengtu, the capital of Szechuan province, where he took up residence in a well-built house with garden (no. 7, Yung-hsing Alley).[34] He was of course without P'u An-hsiu, who continued her work in Peking, but with a much larger entourage than at Wu-chia hua-yüan. However for the next eight months, till July 1966, P'eng hardly occupied his new home at all. His main work now consisted of inspection tours of industrial establishments, construction sites and mines, and he visited more than twenty cities and counties and fifteen factories and mines[35] in the course of preparing plans for the expansion of industry in the region. One of his last trips, in the summer of 1966, took him into the province of Kweichow, where he again investigated the situation in the villages, making caustic comments on the poverty of the peasants but also occasionally talking nostaligically of the Long March.[36] Then from early August 1966 he mainly laid low at Chengtu, while in the capital the forces of the Cultural Revolution under the leadership of Mao, Lin Piao and Chiang Ch'ing had started their attack on all their former critics and opponents among the élite. In Chengtu the vanguards of Maoism, the Red Guards, had already started to roam the streets, set on the violent persecution of their perceived enemies. At first P'eng obviously did not realise the danger he was in, and when his bodyguard warned him not to walk in the streets in order to avoid attacks, he would still insist that 'a CCP member does not have to be afraid of the masses'.[37] That was another of his occasional miscalculations. Soon the Cultural Revolution reached him too, and his long final ordeal began. His partial rehabilitation had lasted less than thirteen months.

Years of persecution

On May 16, 1966, Mao Tse-tung had succeeded in rallying enough support at a meeting of the CCP Politburo's Standing Committee to launch his attack against his opponents, which became known as the Great Proletarian Cultural Revolution. As the leading organ for this drive, a 'CCP/CC Cultural Revolution Group' (CRG) was formed at the same time, with Ch'en Po-ta as Chairman, Chiang Ch'ing as First Vice-Chairman, and the major figure of the secret police establishment since the late 1930s, K'ang Sheng, as 'adviser'.[38] For the time being the CRG had to co-ordinate the criticism of those scholars, artists and political leaders, ever larger numbers of whom were now about to be purged, and to oversee the activities of the Red Guards. It was still supposed to work through the Party's Secretariat, but since the last days of 1966 or January 1967 the CRG, for all practical purposes, had taken the place of the Secretariat, which by then was officially disbanded after ceasing to function in late November 1966.

The CRG became instrumental in the arrest of P'eng Te-huai, an event which indicated that a new stage in the Cultural Revolution had been reached.[39] Already on June 16, 1966, two younger CCP theoreticians and members of the CRG, Kuan Feng and Ch'i Pen-yü, both close associates of Chiang Ch'ing wrote a letter to Ch'en Po-ta, Chiang Ch'ing and K'ang Sheng, from which the following is an extract:

We already expressed our concern about P'eng Te-huai's appointment as Vice-Commander of the Third Line when you last came to Shanghai. Now we understand that P'eng Te-huai, in the Third Line, started incorrect activities . . . Hence, we again suggest that the Centre should dismiss him from his position as Third Line Vice-Commander. [. . .] P'eng Te-huai . . . is a black banner of revisionism . . ., who always pursues anti-Party, anti-socialist criminal activities![40]

After receiving this letter, Ch'en passed it on to the Secretariat, then still headed by Teng Hsiao-p'ing. But the Secretariat ignored it and took no action. After some time Ch'i Pen-yü sent another copy of the letter to Chiang Ch'ing, reminding her that the Secretariat had remained inactive on this case. When she received this message Mao's wife phoned Ch'i, who was then in Shanghai, and told him that the Secretariat refused to act against P'eng. She told Ch'i: 'Let us wait until the revolutionary little generals [meaning the Red Guards] take action!'[41] Chiang Ch'ing and Ch'i Pen-yü had to wait until mid-December 1966 before they could make progress in their drive to purge P'eng again, this time more thoroughly than in 1959. Then, in a break during a reception for cadres of Red Guard units from PLA organisations, Ch'i brought representatives of the Maoist vanguard forces from the Peking Aeronautical School to meet Chiang Ch'ing. During the conversation the Red Guards suggested that Yeh Chien-ying should now be attacked, to which the wife of the Party Leader said: 'Now, you cannot deal with Yeh Chien-ying. "Hai Jui" [P'eng Te-huai] has not yet been struggled.' A Red Guard representative replied: 'We don't know where he is now.' To which Chiang Ch'ing said 'In Chengtu. Send out people to find him!'[42] Following this order of Chiang Ch'ing, two Red Guard organisations — the Red Flag of the Peking Aeronautical School (*Pei-hang hung-ch'i*) and the Peking Institute of Geology's The-East-is-Red (*Ti-yüan tung-fang-hung*), both of which had particularly close links to Mao and his wife — were entrusted with the task of arresting P'eng and bringing him to Peking to be 'struggled against'. Both organisations had their own 'liaison stations' in Chengtu which they contacted by phone. Han Ai-ch'ing, a leader of the *Pei-hang hung-ch'i*, told his comrades in the provincial capital of Szechuan: 'Find P'eng Te-huai, seize him and bring him to Peking so that he can be struggled against until he stinks. Yes! This is an order of comrade Ch'i Pen-yü from the CRG. This is of utter importance . . . put off everything else!'[43]

Similar orders were given by the Red Guard leader Chu Ch'eng-chao from the *Ti-yüan tung-fang-hung*. But the Chengtu 'liaison stations' were not keen to carry out orders from Peking. On December 18 Red Guards from these units visited P'eng in his home, and merely told him that his old subordinate Ho Ch'ang-kung had been arrested, and on December 22 they returned to say that Liu Shao-ch'i and Teng Hsiao-p'ing would soon be 'overthrown', probably to frighten the Marshal. No other action was taken until December 24.[44] On that day the 'liaison stations' in Chengtu cabled to their organisations in the capital to find out what they should do. They received no reply, nor could they get through by telephone. However, at this moment the leader of the *Ti-yüan tung-fang-hung* unit in Chungching, Wang Ta-pin, arrived in Chengtu by train with some of his Red Guards. Wang immediately went into action, and told his Chengtu comrades they were 'rightists' and 'traitors' because they had not yet seized P'eng.[45] The geology students discussed how they could arrest 'Hai Jui'; but meanwhile the Chengtu group of the *Pei-hang hung-ch'i* were quicker off the mark. In the early morning of December 25 they arrived at P'eng's home, seized him and took him to a detention cell near the Chengtu railway station. When the geology students arrived and found P'eng gone, they had to be content with 'searching' the house, destroying pictures and tearing up books. When P'eng's bodyguard came to look for him at 4 a.m., the Marshal had already been abducted.[46]

It appears that at this moment Chou En-lai in Peking made a last effort to save P'eng from Red Guard violence, and to put him under PLA surveillance. On the morning of December 25 the Prime Minister's office cabled the two Red Guard organisations, ordering them to accompany P'eng to the capital, but to do so along with men of the Chengtu Military Area Command. They were not to bring him by plane (because at that moment Peking airport was under Red Guard Control) but were to hand him over to a unit of the PLA Peking Garrison Command when they arrived at the Peking railway station.[47] At the Chengtu railway station, however, the *Pei-hang hung-ch'i* group, which actually had the custody of P'eng, met the geology students and a number of soldiers. All of them entered a special wagon bound for the capital on December 27. Wang Ta-pin, anxious not to let P'eng be turned over from the Red Guards to the PLA, joined them. The group arrived in Peking on December 29. When they arrived the Red Guards, led by Wang who claimed to be acting on behalf of the CRG, were able to forestall the Peking Garrison unit which was waiting to take charge of P'eng. And so he was led away, with his hands and feet in chains, by the 'revolutionary little generals'.[48]

From this moment on, information on P'eng Te-huai's fate is scanty. We only know that in January 1967 he was taken to a 'struggle meeting' of several thousand Red Guards, again in chains and wearing a white paper hat and with a wooden board around his neck inscribed with his 'crimes'.[49] In April he was handed over to the PLA, and put up in a military prison in the outskirts of Peking.[50] This seems to have brought a slight respite in his situation; in April or May his niece, P'eng Mei-k'uei, was allowed to send some clothes and other necessities into the prison, which he acknowledged having received with a short written note.[51] This improvement, however, did not last long. In July the PLA formed an 'investigation group' under the personal orders of Mao and Lin Piao, which was supposed to prepare P'eng for a large military 'struggle meeting' against him. In order to stabilise their hold over the central military organs, the leaders of the Maoist faction had decided to make P'eng the major target of the purge campaign within the PLA. The aim was to force him to admit publicly that he was a 'great warlord', a 'great ambitionist' and a 'great conspirator', who had 'crept into the Party and the army'. Yet P'eng refused to confess or to 'surrender to the masses'. He was then placed in an unlit cell, and for several days not allowed to rise, to drink water, to go to the toilet or to turn in his sleep. Then 'interrogations' began. He was beaten several times, so that he fell to the ground. His ribs were broken and he suffered pain in his lungs. The 'interrogations' mostly lasted for more than ten hours, with the interrogators changing every two hours in the 'conveyor belt' style used by the Soviet political police under Stalin in the

1930s. Altogether P'eng underwent more than 130 such 'inter-rogations'.[52]

In late July, in the critical days after the mutiny of General Ch'en Tsai-tao in Wuhan, the CCP leaders decided that P'eng should now be publicly criticised by name. On July 31, the eve of the PRC's Army Day, *JMJP* reprinted the editorial of the PLA paper, the *CFCP*, of the same day in which P'eng was called 'the representative of the greatest capitalist–roader in power [Liu Shao-ch'i] in the army'. The editorial said:

P'eng Te-huai stubbornly promoted the capitalist military line. This great ambitionist and great conspirator has always opposed Chairman Mao, he has always opposed the correct military line represented by Chairman Mao. [. . .] He conspired with foreign countries! Singing the same tune as the imperialists, revisionists and counter-revolutionaries, he waged a wild attack against the Party.

Then, on August 16, 1967, the resolution of the Lushan plenum which censured P'eng was published for the first time inside the PRC, accompanied by an even more outspoken editorial in *JMJP*:

P'eng Te-huai was never a Marxist, he has the psychology of a speculator. He is a totally capitalist great warlord, great ambitionist and great conspirator who has crept into the Party and into the army. [. . .] We have to struggle him until he falls, until he breaks down, until he stinks.

This editorial sounded the clarion call for a nationwide campaign of vilification of P'eng, lasting several months till late 1967. In the context of this campaign, another 'struggle meeting' was held at the end of August in the stadium in Peking, attended by about 40,000 PLA soldiers. He was taken to this meeting in chains and had to listen to recriminations, on his knees, for several hours. At the end of the meeting, Lin Piao personally appeared and said to the crowd, as well as to his still kneeling predecessor:

'P'eng Te-huai has always ganged up with this man or that man, he has committed this mistake, then that mistake, all because of his ambition. This rightist opportunist must be thoroughly exposed, he must be struggled against to the end, until he stinks. Nothing else is good enough. This is advantageous for you and for the Party, only in this way can we achieve reform, otherwise this is impossible. At the Lushan conference, this problem was exposed. The

solution of this problem was a great victory, we destroyed a great danger for
the Party. The Chairman has said many times that only P'eng Te-huai and ——
[possibly Ho Lung or Chu Te] can split the Party. [. . .] Now, we fully wage
the struggle, we protect the general line. We educate the whole Party, we
strengthen the Party Centre led by Chairman Mao. This is in the interest of the
whole Party, the whole army, and the whole people of the whole country. We
must expose, we must fight to the end. If you [meaning P'eng] reform yourself,
all right, if not, it is all right too. But of course we hope you reform yourself'.[53]

We do not know whether P'eng made a 'self-criticism' or a 'confession'
at the Peking 'struggle meeting', and we still know very little of what
befell him during the next seven years.

What we do know is that P'eng stayed in prison till the spring of
1973, and was then moved for a few months to a prison hospital; then he
was sent back again to prison sometime during the second half of 1973.
In late 1969, the PLA central leadership formed a 'special investigation
group' (*Chuan-an hsiao-tsu*) to reach a final verdict on his case. For this
group he had to write, over and over again, an account of his whole
life — in which he still did not fully confess his alleged 'crimes'. This
new ordeal, accompanied by new tortures and 'interrogations', lasted
throughout most of 1970.[54] Then it seems that a special military tribunal
— whether in his presence or not we do not know — condemned him
to life imprisonment, a sentence immediately approved by the then Chief
of the General Staff, Huang Yung-sheng.[55]

Some improvements in the conditions of his life in prison were made
after Lin Piao and Huang Yung-sheng were overthrown on September
12/13, 1971. But P'eng now had to contend with worsening health.
The torture to which he was subjected in 1967 and again in 1970 may
not have broken his mind, but it did break his body. From late 1972
he was seriously ill. The sources now available to us do not specify the
nature of his illness, but his symptoms have been partly recorded, and
these suggest tuberculosis or a thrombosis, or a combination of both.
On April 10, 1973, he was transferred from the military prison to a
prison hospital, and on April 23 his niece P'eng Mei-k'uei was informed
by a PLA soldier that she could visit him two days later. She found him
very weak, lying on a wooden bed in an almost empty room which had
its windows sealed with paper. But his spirit was clearly unbroken. At
the behest of his guards, she tried to convince him that he should agree to
undergo a surgical operation, and after some resistance he finally gave in.
It seems that he was then operated upon, but we do not know the nature
of the operation, or its result.[56]

On July 11, 1973, he wrote his last letter, a note to his niece:

Mei-k'uei,

I thank you for your help after my arrest. Since 1967, you have sent me articles of daily use and books. I do not know how much they have cost you. The other day I received 800 Yüan from a responsible person of the prison administration. I want to give this money to you as compensation. I do not want to cause difficulties for you, and you should not think about me, so that you may be able to concentrate on your work. With this letter, I send you a blue cotton winter-suit, the leather overcoat of the PVA, and two pieces of cotton, meant as a compensation for the clothes which you bought for me in the 1960s. You may sew yourself cotton trousers.

P'eng Te-huai
July 11, 1973[57]

This suggests that by the summer of 1973 some of the goods which had been seized in his house at Chengtu had been returned to him. But he was never released from prison, and after his death the only items which he left behind were a pair of patched undershorts, a patched pair of trousers, a patched jacket, a blanket, an aluminium spoon and a wrist-watch.[58] It seems that the conditions in which he was kept became worse between August and November 1974. In mid-August his old associate and follower Huang K'e-ch'eng, himself not yet officially rehabilitated though released from prison, was allowed to visit P'eng in the prison hospital. Huang found him extremely weak and a shadow of his former self, but with a very clear mind. He apologised for having implicated Huang in his 'self-criticism' at the Lushan plenum, and then added:

'Besides apologising to the comrades who have suffered because of my implicating them, I feel no guilt. I have given my whole self to the Party, and I firmly believe in the cause of communism. My only wish is that, before I die, the oganisation gives me a fair final decision [on my case]. I have written to Chairman Mao asking for this, but I have received no answer so far'.[59]

It may well be that the Chairman, who in late 1974 still had considerable influence on the decision-making process within the élite, was resentful of P'eng's insistence on a new hearing of his case. There is some scattered information that when P'eng's sickness again became worse in September 1974, he received no substantial medical aid, presumably due to direct orders from Mao.[60]

The old soldier died on November 29, 1974, at 3.35 p.m. A few hours later his niece was allowed to see his body in the prison hospital for twenty minutes; the guards then whisked her away.[61] After his body had been cremated, the ashes were sent to Chengtu — so even in death P'eng Te-huai remained a non-person for the ruling élite. The casket containing his ashes was marked with a slip of paper which read: 'No. 327 — Wang Ch'uan, 32 years, from Chengtu'.[62]

Epilogue: The posthumous rehabilitation in December 1978

In late 1974 the CCP leadership was obviously interested in concealing the fate of P'eng Te-huai. His niece was given a strict warning not to pass on any information about his death, and she seems to have heeded this advice so as to protect herself. Only in the spring of 1976 did P'eng's former driver and his bodyguard learn of the death of their old master.[63] His widow P'u An-hsiu, who had not joined him in Chengtu in 1965 but stayed behind in Peking because of her job as a Party secretary at the Normal University, was arrested by Red Guards around New Year 1967, and at some time during the ensuing months — the exact date is impossible to ascertain from the available sources — she was tried at a Red Guard 'mass trial' by a kangaroo court of the kind which is so common in the PRC.[64] She was then taken to a 'labour reform camp' and remained there until early in 1975, when she was released and sent to work as a peasant in a Northern Chinese village. Only when she was allowed to return to Peking in early 1978 did she learn of her husband's fate.[65] In December 1978 Party cadres and peasants in Shensi still believed the former military and administrative head of Northwest China to be alive.[66]

However by that time a new evaluation of P'eng was in the making. After the overthrow of the core leadership group of the Cultural Revolutionary Left in the military *coup* of October 6, 1976, the new Party Leader, Hua Kuo-feng, was forced by regional military commanders and veteran cadres to agree to the second rehabilitation of Teng Hsiao-p'ing; this was officially announced to the public in July 1977. After stabilising and broadening his political base within the ranks of the ruling élite, Teng, in May 1978, launched a political offensive with the aim of enacting thoroughgoing revisions of the policies of late Maoism which Hua and his close associates were still partly sustaining; removing Hua from his position as Party Leader; and reevaluating both the ideological concepts and the person of Mao Tse-tung.[67] In order to push this offensive forward, Teng and his supporters, in late October 1978, tolerated and to some extent even promoted an incipient popular movement in Peking and other cities which called for a widening of the parameters of cultural and even political competition — the manifestation of opposition and dissent soon to be called the 'Democracy and Human Rights Movement'. It was in the context of this movement that in the second half of November 1978 a full rehabilitation of P'eng, which till then had been resisted by a number of members of the ruling élite and particularly by Hua Kuo-feng,[68] was increasingly demanded on wall-posters in the capital.

By this time a number of generals and civilian cadres who had been censured or at least demoted or criticised with P'eng in 1959[69] had already been rehabilitated. The first to re-appear was General Hsiao K'e in March 1972, only six months after the death of Lin Piao; he was followed by General Li Ta in November 1972, General Teng Hua in September 1974 and General T'an Cheng in January 1975. Others had to wait to be rehabilitated until Mao's death and Teng Hsiao-p'ing's triumphant return to the political scene. Only then followed the rehabilitation of Huang K'e-ch'eng in August 1977, Hung Hsüeh-chih and Wan Yi in October 1977, Hsi Chung-hsün in February 1978 and finally Ch'en Cheng-hsiang in March 1978, about the time that P'u An-hsiu received permission to return to Peking. However, four former associates of P'eng did not reappear: Chang Wen-t'ien died in disgrace, Chou Hsiao-chou was killed during the Cultural Revolution,[70] and the two generals Nieh He-t'ing and Han Chen-chi disappeared in 1968–9.

Pressure from the public in Peking for a reversal of the decisions on P'eng Te-huai made at the Lushan plenum in August 1959 and by the PLA leadership in 1970 had obviously encouraged Huang K'e-ch'eng, the late Marshal's most loyal follower, to ask the Party Centre formally for P'eng's rehabilitation. On November 29, 1978, Huang addressed a letter to the Organisation Department of the CCP/CC, which began:

Today is the fourth anniversary of Comrade P'eng Te-huai's passing away. I cannot help being very sad. I mourn my old commander, my outstanding teacher and good friend, the loyal soldier of the Chinese people, Comrade P'eng Te-huai! After the overthrow of the 'Gang of Four' [Chiang Ch'ing and her chief associates] the whole Party, the whole army and the whole people, under the brilliant leadership of the Party Centre with Comrade Hua Kuo-feng as its head, are fuming with wrath because of the injustice done to Comrade P'eng Te-huai. One after the other, a number of people have asked for his acquittal.[71]

Huang went on to describe his last meeting with P'eng, and to discuss in detail the events of the Lushan conference, arguing that P'eng had been correct in his stand at that time. Huang's letter ended with the sentences that follow, parts of which have since become standard verbiage in many official CCP evaluations of the former Minister of National Defence:

The whole life of Commander P'eng was a life of revolution, was a life of loyalty to the Party and the people. He was open and straightforward, incorruptible and impeccable, strict towards himself. He always cared about the miseries of the masses. Never concerned about his own advantage, he fought all his life for the cause of communism. . . .

Today both right and wrong have come to the fore as clearly as stones washed by the water. I hope that the Organisation Department will catch this proper moment to arrive at a just decision on his case, so that his soul may be comforted. Give back to Comrade P'eng Te-huai his innocence![72]

Huang's move was rewarded with success. At the 'Central Work Conference' which had convened in Peking in mid-November to make the decisions which would be ratified by the impending 3rd plenum of the Eleventh CCP/CC, Teng Hsiao-p'ing announced for the first time that P'eng was in fact dead and elaborated the circumstances of his death. The information was circulated to Party cadres all over the country in a CCP/CC document on December 7, 1978.[73]

When the 3rd Plenum met on December 18–22, the reversal of the verdicts on P'eng Te-huai had already been decided upon. To ratify this decision the communiqué of the plenum, passed on December 22, contained the following sentence:

The plenary session examined *and corrected the erroneous conclusions* which had been adopted on P'eng Te-huai, T'ao Chu, Po I-po, Yang Shang-k'un and other comrades, and it affirmed their contributions to the Party and the people.[74]

The same day, the CCP/CC plenum elected P'eng's widow, P'u An-hsiu, as one among 100 members of the Party's newly-established 'Central Disciplinary Investigation Commission'.

Yet while Po I-po, Yang Shang-k'un 'and other comrades' were still alive to enjoy their reception back into the ruling élite, T'ao Chu (former First Secretary of the CCP's Central-South Regional Bureau, who had become a Politburo member in August 1966 but was arrested in early 1967 and killed in prison in November 1969) and P'eng Te-huai were not. For them the obsequies, delayed by nine and four years respectively, were staged on the afternoon of December 24, 1978.[75] In the Great Hall of the People in Peking there assembled more than 2,000 people. Among them were almost all the Politburo members, including Hua Kuo-feng, who had already been in charge of the Ministry of Public Security at the time of P'eng's death in November 1974; Marshal Yeh Chien-ying, who had been acting as Minister of National Defence and Vice-Chairman 'entrusted with the daily work' of the CCP/CC Military Commission in November 1974; Teng Hsiao-p'ing, who had acted as temporary leader of the state administrative machine, standing in for the ailing Premier Chou En-lai (then in hospital); and General Wang Tung-hsing, who had commanded the 'Central Guard Division', 'PLA unit no. 8341', which had been in charge of P'eng's prison.

Teng Hsiao-p'ing, who had probably been a major promoter of P'eng's posthumous rehabilitation, gave the funeral oration, of which the most important extracts are given below:

'Comrades!
'With a heart full of sadness, we are now holding the obsequies for Comrade P'eng Te-huai.

'Comrade P'eng Te-huai was an excellent member of our Party, a proletarian revolutionary of the old generation. He was the most important leader of the P'ingchiang uprising, the founder of the Red Third Army. He was an outstanding leader of our Party, our country, and our armed forces, who held many important positions in the Party, the government, and the army. Under the persecution of Lin Piao [*sic*] and the 'Gang of Four' he passed away in Peking on November 29, 1974, at the age of 76. Today, in the spirit of seeking the truth from the facts, the Party Centre under the leadership of Comrade Hua Kuo-feng, sincerely emulating the Party's policy, pronounces for Comrade P'eng Te-huai a total and just evaluation: his honour is herewith restored.

'During the revolutionary struggle of the recent half-century, Comrade P'eng Te-huai, under the leadership of the great teacher, Comrade Mao Tse-tung, has fought all through the country. Experiencing difficulties and dangers, he has made outstanding contributions to the victory of China's revolutionary war, to the strengthening of the people's armed forces, as well as to the protection and construction of our socialist fatherland. His whole life was a life of revolution, was a life of loyalty to the Party and the people. His unfortunate death is a very great loss for our Party and our army. . . .

'Comrade P'eng Te-huai had warm love for the Party and warm love for the people, he was loyal to the great cause of the proletarian revolution. He was courageous in battle, open and straightforward, incorruptible and impeccable, and strict towards himself. He cared about the masses, and was never concerned about his own advantage. He was never afraid of difficulties, neither of carrying heavy loads. In his revolutionary work, he was diligent, honest, and he had an utmost sense of responsibility.

'Comrade P'eng Te-huai was a military man and politician, well known in the country as well as internationally. He will always be remembered and loved by the Party members and the broad masses . . . Comrade P'eng Te-huai will always be in our minds!'[76]

Starting from January 1979, the country was swept by a veritable avalanche of memoirs, stories and articles in praise of P'eng. Finally — or should one say 'for the time being'? — he had become a hero again.

In the resolution passed by the 6th Plenum of the Eleventh CCP/CC in June 1981,[77] which gave the official evaluation by the current CCP élite on the history of the PRC since 1949, the man who had opposed Mao at Lushan was fully vindicated. Mao Tse-tung, so this major decision informed the public,

. . . .erred in initiating criticism of Comrade P'eng Te-huai, and then in launching a Party-wide struggle against 'rightist opportunism'. The resolution [of the Lushan plenum] concerning the so-called anti-Party group of P'eng Te-huai, Huang K'e-ch'eng, Chang Wen-t'ien, and Chou Hsiao-chou was entirely wrong. Politically this struggle gravely undermined intra-Party democracy from the central level down to the grassroots, it cut short the process of the rectification of 'Left' errors, thus prolonging their influence.

More than two years later the Intermediate Court of Justice at Wuhan announced a verdict which should serve as a final note to our account of P'eng Te-huai's life and death. Wang Ta-pin, the former Red Guard leader who had been involved in P'eng's arrest on December 25, 1966, was sentenced to nine years in prison for 'the persecution and torture of Comrade P'eng Te-huai'.[78] CCP policies had indeed gone through a complete about-turn.

NOTES

1. For the present author's discussion of rural developments and policies between 1959 and 1962, cf. Domes, *Socialism, op. cit.*, pp. 45–54. Data taken from Kraus, *op. cit.*, table A. 7 on p. 335.

2. These figures are given by Roderick MacFarquhar (*Origins 2, op. cit.*, p. 330), who relies on estimates provided to him by John Aird, probably in 1981 or 1982. The unwillingness of many Western observers of PRC politics to accept the facts of the 1959–61 famine on is one of the dark spots on the reputation of our discipline. When the present author suggested, on the basis of contemporary Taiwan sources, a figure of about 10.5 million people who had died of starvation during the famine in a study published in German in 1964 (Jürgen Domes, *Von der Volkskommune zur Krise in China* [China from the commune to crisis], Duisdorf: Studiengesellschaft für Zeitprobleme, 1964, p. 51), this was doubted by many German China scholars, most notably by Wolfgang Franke. When he assumed a figure of 'at least ten million' in 1971 (Domes, *Politics, op. cit.*, p. 115), this was called an 'exaggeration' by a number of reviewers. Even in 1975, Mark Selden, while admitting that there had been 'starvation in some areas' in 1960 and 1961, argued that 'the damage of hunger' had been 'minimized' (Selden in Victor Nee/James Peck (eds), *China's Uninterrupted Revolution: From 1840 to the Present*, (New York: Random House, 2nd edn, 1975, p. 96). In 1976, Ivan and Miriam London presented the first comprehensive account of the 1959–61 famine in the Anglo-Saxon countries ('The other China: Hunger' in *Worldview*, New York, vol. 19, no. 5, May 1976, pp. 4–11; and no. 6, June 1976, pp. 43–8). Finally, in the spring of 1981, an official PRC source (*Ching-chi kuan-li* [Economic Management], Peking, no. 2, March 1981, p. 3) gave a figure of 'more than 20 million' for those who had starved to death.

3. Revised draft of working regulations for rural people's communes, Sept. 29, 1962. English translation in Domes, *Socialism, op. cit.*, pp. 128–58.

4. For the Cultural Revolution, cf. among others Ahn, *op. cit.*, Parris Chang, *op. cit.*; Michael, *op. cit.*, pp. 147–82; Thornton, *op. cit.*, pp. 278–38; and Domes, *Politics, op. cit.*, pp. 151–222.

5. *Tung-fang-hung* (*The East is Red*), Peking, Jan. 28, 1967.

6. This estimated figure was given to the present author individually by eleven scholars from the PRC in the United States between March and July 1981, and by three leading CCP cadres in Peking in September 1980.

7. In an interview with Han Su-yin, published in German in *Der Spiegel*, Hamburg, Nov. 28, 1977, p. 198.

8. This description summarises data from 67 interviews with refugees which the present author conducted in Hong Kong between 1969 and 1977. Of these interviews 41 dealt entirely, the remaining 26 mainly, with developments in the Chinese countryside during the Cultural Revolution. Cf. William L. Parish/Martin King Whyte, *Village and Family in Contemporary China* (Chicago University Press, 1978) pp. 78 f., 261–3, 280 f. and 289 f.

9. For the present author's account of the Lin Piao crisis, cf. Jürgen Domes, *China after the Cultural Revolution: Politics Between Two Party Congresses* (London: C. Hurst & Co., 1976), pp. 77–137.

10. *NCNA*, Peking, April 12, 1973.

11. For the period until late 1966, the most important sources are Ching/Ting, *op. cit.*, pp. 81–156; *PCC, op. cit.*, pp. 71 f., 140–7, 160–75, and 176–89; 'Jung Jung', 'After P'eng Te-huai's Dismissal'; in *Cheng-ming* (Debate), Hong Kong (hereafter *CM*), no. 57, July 1982, pp. 66–77; and 'Jung Jung', 'P'eng Te-huai at the third line'; *ibid.*, no. 58, Aug. 1982, pp. 77–9 (hereafter Jung II, *loc. cit.*).

12. Jung, *loc. cit.*, p. 67.
13. *ibid.*
14. *JMJP*, March 6, 1981.
15. *PCC*, pp. 140 ff., and Jung, *loc. cit.*, pp. 66 ff.
16. *ibid.*, p. 66 f.
17. Ching/Ting, *op. cit.*, pp. 90–2 and 96–9.
18. *ibid.*, p. 107.
19. *ibid.*, p. 109.
20. *PCC*, p. 71.
21. *NCNA*, Peking, May 29, 1960.
22. *Chin-tai-shih yen-chiu* (Studies of Modern History), Peking, no. 4/1980, p. 3–5. Cf. MacFarquhar, *Origins 2, op. cit.*, p. 239 f.
23. Jung, *loc. cit.*, p. 68 f.
24. *ibid.*, p. 69 f.; and Ching/Ting, *op. cit.*, pp. 102–4.
25. A reconstruction of the speech of Liu Shao-ch'i was presented in German by Erik von Groeling, *Der Fraktionskampf in China* (Faction fighting in China) (Cologne: Bundesinstitut für Ostwissenschaftliche . . . Studien, 1970), pp. 31–4.
26. *Haik'ou tsao-fan pao (Haikow Rebel News)*, Oct. 19, 1967.
27. *CNP*, unpaginated; Jung, *loc. cit.*, p. 71; and Lung Chi-shih, 'The death of P'eng Te-huai', *CM*, no. 55, May 1982, pp. 60–4 (here p. 62 f.). The article of Lung Chi-shih seems to rely quite heavily on information from P'eng's niece P'eng Mei-k'uei and from his nephew P'eng Kang.
28. Cf. MacFarquhar, *Origins 2, op. cit.*, pp. 207–12.
29. Information provided to the present author by a cadre of the CCP/CC Secretariat in Peking in Sept. 1980.
30. Ching/Ting, *op. cit.*, p. 112.
31. *ibid.*, pp. 113–116; Jung, *loc. cit.*, p. 71; Jung II, *loc. cit.* p. 77; and *PTHTS*, appendix 2, p. 288 f.
32. Jung, *loc. cit.*, p. 71.
33. Jung II, loc. cit., p. 77.
34. Ching/Ting, *op. cit.*, p. 119 f.
35. Jung II, *loc. cit.*, p. 77.
36. Ching/TIng, *op. cit.*, pp. 132–6.
37. *ibid.*, p. 140.
38. Among others, *I-chiu-liu-chiu fei-ch'ing nien-pao/1969 Year-book on Chinese Communism* (Taipei: Intelligence Bureau, MND, 1969), chapter III, p. 3 f.
39. The major sources for P'eng Te-huai's arrest are: Wang Ying, 'The inside story of the arrest and struggle against P'eng Te-huai', *Tung-hsi-fang/East and West*, Hong Kong, no. 26, March 5, 1981, pp. 16–21 (hereafter Wang, *loc. cit.*); Lung, *loc. cit.*, p. 63 f.; Ching/Ting, *op. cit.*, pp. 151–160; and PCC, p. 142 f.
40. Wang, *loc. cit.*, p. 17.
41. *ibid.*
42. *ibid.*
43. *ibid.*
44. *ibid.*
45. *ibid.*, p. 18 f.
46. *ibid.*, p. 20, and Ching/Ting, *op. cit.*, p. 151 f.
47. Lung, *loc. cit.*, p. 63.

48. *ibid.*, p. 64.

49. Huang, *op. cit.*, p. 444.

50. *CNP*, unpaginated.

51. *PCC*, p. 143.

52. *CNP*, unpaginated, and Lung, *loc. cit.*, p. 64.

53. *Ta-p'i-p'an T'ung-hsün*, October 5, 1967. That Lin Piao gave this speech at the 'struggle meeting' against P'eng, was confirmed to the present author, together with details of that meeting by CCP cadres and scholars from the PRC in Peking in Sept. 1980, and in the United States in the spring of 1981.

54. *PTHTS*, publishing note, p. 2.

55. Lung, *loc. cit.*, p. 64. Huang Yung-sheng himself was put into prison for more than twelve years only a year later, in Sept. 1971.

56. *ibid.*; *CNP*, unpaginated; and *PCC*, p. 144 f.

57. *CNP*, picture no. 352.

58. *CNP*, picture no. 351.

59. Huang, *Letter*, p. 1.

60. This was reported to the present author by a leading cadre of the CCP in Peking in Sept. 1980.

61. Lung, *loc. cit.*, p. 64; and *CNP*, unpaginated.

62. *ibid.*, picture no. 353.

63. Ching/Ting, *op. cit.*, foreword, p. 2.

64. 'Trial of P'u An-hsiu (P'eng Te-huai's stinking wife)' in URI, *Peng, op. cit.*, pp. 123 f. and 447 f.

65. This information was provided to the present author by an American woman, a former teacher of P'u An-hsiu, who had given an account of her Cultural Revolution experiences to the teacher in a letter in November 1980.

66. 'Shih Che', 'Eminent commander, brilliant example: Remembering comrade P'eng Te-huai' in *HCPP*, vol. XVII (1979), p. 154 f.

67. For the present author's account of these developments, cf. Jürgen Domes, '1976–1982: Evolution of a New CCP Line?' *Issues and Studies*, Taipei, vol. XVIII, no. 7, July 1982, pp. 40–65.

68. Hua Kuo-feng's resistance to a rehabilitation of P'eng was officially revealed in a resolution of the CCP Politburo on Dec. 5, 1980. Text in *Chung-kung yen-chiu/Studies on Chinese Communism*, Taipei, vol. XVII, no. 4, April 1983, p. 82 f.

69. See above, p. .

70. *Hsin-hua yüeh-pao* (*New China Monthly*), Peking, no. 5/1979, p. 63 f. Cf. MacFarquhar, *Origins 2, op. cit.*, p. 236.

71. Huang, *Letter*, p. 1.

72. *ibid.*, p. 6.

73. 'Shih Che', *loc. cit.*, p. 155.

74. *JMJP*, Dec. 26, 1978 Author's.

75. *KMJP*, Dec. 26, 1978.

76. *ibid.* It should be remembered that Lin Piao had already died on about Sept. 13, 1971.

77. 'Resolution on several problems of Party history since the establishment of the PRC', adopted by the 6th plenum of the Eleventh CCP/CC on June 27, 1981, in *HC*, no. 13, July 1, 1981.

78. *Ch'ang-chiang jih-pao* Aug. 29, 1983.

6

PERSONALITY, PERSONAL IMAGES AND CCP POLITICS: THE CASE OF P'ENG TE-HUAI

P'eng Te-huai, the man: a tentative evaluation

We have reviewed the life of P'eng Te-huai from his birth in an impoverished (though originally middle-income) peasant family to his death in a military prison of the PRC during the late years of Mao Tse-tung's rule. It is now time to attempt a tentative evaluation of his character, personality and abilities, in so far as they can be judged from his life history.

We have seen that P'eng experienced considerable hardship and privation in his childhood and youth. In 1905 and 1906, when he was seven and eight years old, P'eng learned the bitterness of hunger, and from then until he was seventeen he did hard menial jobs and suffered the stresses and strains of living on an income slightly below, or just at, subsistence level. It seems that these experiences of his formative years awakened him to a basic awareness — even though not yet of a co-ordinated and systematic nature — of China's most pressing social problem, the backwardness of her villages and the plight of her peasantry. He must have made up his mind at this early stage — probably influenced by his uncle's memories of the Taiping rebellion — that the misery of the Chinese countryside and the injustice to which so many peasants were continually exposed could not be tolerated with the traditional apathy but were to be actively fought against. Thus he developed a spirit of rebellion, which soon brought him into conflict with those who held the local power in his home area. However, neither this general awareness of social problems, nor his rebellious spirit, was yet directed at even the most general political or social goal. And from the spring of 1916 onwards they were submerged by his second major formative experience: the drastic improvement in his material living conditions and the warmth of the comradeship which he found on joining the military. The army became a second home for P'eng, as it did for so many impoverished peasant boys in China during the early decades of this century. Since he was obviously an excellent soldier — a brave fighter well disciplined and full of initiative — he progressed from Private second-class to Colonel and regimental commander within the short space of twelve years. Such a career would have re-enforced his preference for the life of a professional soldier.

We have also seen that it was in the army that P'eng found his political direction. The young and fervently nationalist officers whom he met in the Hunan provincial military helped him to understand and accept, even though in very broad and crude terms, the platform of the KMT under Dr Sun Yat-sen. But within the ranks of the nationalist movement in 1926–7 it was members of the CCP who impressed him most with their dedication, their personal discipline, their obvious consciousness of social problems, and probably too because the answers they gave were simple and easily comprehensible. These experiences with cadres of the CCP gave him an increasing propensity towards Marxism-Leninism, but in his decision to join the communist movement, made during the second half of 1927 and carried into effect in the spring of 1928, Marxist-Leninist doctrines and ideological considerations played hardly any part. P'eng became a communist not because he was convinced that the concepts of Marx, Engels and Lenin were correct — he knew very little about them at the time of his acceptance as a Party member, and probably not much more later — but he was impressed by the attitudes of communists, among whom were some of his closest personal friends, like Huang Kung-lüeh.

So the Party now became his new home, even warmer and more reassuring than the army. Like so many other communists, he soon developed a great sense of belonging, comfort and security, in the ranks of the fighting CCP. And like many others too he repaid these psychological benefits with an unswerving loyalty to the Party, which apparently lasted to the very end. At several points in his career, P'eng was not in agreement with current CCP policies, and the plight of the Chinese peasantry which followed from the implementation of Mao's mobilisatory concept of development in 1958 probably gave him reason to doubt the wisdom of the Party leadership. Indeed it is hard to believe that such doubts did not increase when he was censured at the Lushan conference, isolated in his ramshackle house in the suburbs of Peking during the early 1960s, arrested, tortured, thrown into prison, and in the prison hospital sensing the approach of death. But these doubts never became strong enough to make him break with communism. Hence, as we know from Huang K'e-ch'eng's report, one of P'eng's last desires, if not his very last one, was for a 'fair judgement' of his career and of the political positions he had taken in 1958–9, by the Party whose leaders had been responsible for the agony of his persecution.

Non-communists, particularly those brought up in the critical, liberal and personalist traditions of the Western world — the traditions of Greece, Rome, Christianity, the enlightenment and humanitarianism —, cannot easily understand such an attitude. But it was by no means extraordinary to P'eng Te-huai. There was Bukharin who continued to protest that he had always been loyal to, and loved, the CPSU as he was being led out to execution. There was Laszlo Rajk who appears to have sincerely believed that it was necessary for the future good of the Party that he should confess to crimes which he had never committed during the show trial that preceded his execution.[1] And there was Imre Nagy who, while he sympathised with the demonstrating crowds in Budapest on October 23, 1956, did not take the side of the revolution on that day because he had not received an order from the Party Centre to do so.[2] These three examples stand for many others. History seems to tell us that communists who have joined the movement during its fight for power — with a few exceptions among the more intellectually sophisticated — are unable to break with the Party even if they have suffered severe persecution at its hands. This of course is especially true of those with comparatively simple natures: P'eng Te-huai was one such, since almost all accounts portray him as honest, straightforward, courageous, outspoken and hot-tempered. He was quite uninterested in a life of luxury or even one of modest comfort. Not even the most violent attacks on him during the Cultural Revolution accused him of corruption or high living as they did Teng Hsiao-p'ing, P'eng Chen or Ho Lung. P'eng's frugality was thus a reasonably well-established trait of his character.

Simplicity and courage were other traits which we may consider well-established. Roderick MacFarquhar reports an event which is characteristic of P'eng's temperament and mentality:

When the Soviet Leader Anastas Mikoyan led the CPSU delegation to China to attend the CCP's 8th Congress in 1956, P'eng asked him face to face why it was only now that the Soviet Party was criticising Stalin. Mikoyan apparently replied: 'We did not dare advance our opinions at that time. To have done so would have meant death.' To which P'eng retorted: 'What kind of a communist is it who fears death?'[3]

But was P'eng also influenced by personal warmth, kindness and humanitarian considerations? To this question the answer has been uncertain, because the record here is ambivalent. Even before 1959, which also means before he underwent his posthumous rehabilitation in December 1978 and was once again styled as a hero, a number of reports testified to his care for his subordinates, particularly simple rankers and their families, his tendency to help people in need, and his willingness to consider means of fighting injustices. On the other hand, already at the time of the P'ingchiang uprising in 1928, and even more during the civil war in southern Kiangsi in the early 1930s, he had no qualms about staging mass executions without any legal formalities. In 1948/9 his First Field Army obliterated whole families and even whole villages when faced with stiff resistance, especially in the Hui (Chinese Muslim) areas of Kansu and Ningsia. And it was P'eng who invented the 'human sea' tactic in the Korean war, ruthlessly driving thousands of his men without sufficient cover 'over the top' into the teeth of American firepower. And it was most probably his unwavering, almost religious belief in the cause of communism and the Party from which he derived his firm conviction that the end always justifies the means.

The 'human sea' tactic leads us on to the question of his qualities as a military leader, already discussed in some detail at the end of Chapter 3. Here I can only briefly recapitulate my earlier findings. P'eng was excellent as a rank-and-file soldier and as a campaigner, and a medium to good tactician. Yet it was never claimed for him that he was a good strategist. In terms of strategy, he showed considerable abilities in defence but his performance when on the attack tended to be rather poor. On the other hand, he had great organisational abilities, which he proved first in Korea when the PVA was being revamped after the spring of 1951, and again when he engineered the comparatively successful drive for the modernisation and professionalisation of the PLA between 1954 and 1959. The latter was probably his greatest contribution to the cause of communism in China after the establishment of the PRC. Thus in the military arena P'eng's performance showed courage, discipline and organisational aptitude rather than deliberation and sophistication.

This courage and simplicity, if not plain naivety, also determined the role he would play as a politician. Straightforward, loyal to the Party but poorly trained in ideology, P'eng rarely exerted a strong influence on the policy-making process within the ruling CCP élite. He had too great a distaste for the cult of personality to be definitely accepted by Mao as one of his innermost circle, but on the other hand he lacked the programmatic drive and the ability to rally his equals into a viable faction. He would have needed this in order to become a serious challenge to the Party Leader when he finally came to the conclusion that an attack on Mao and his policies had to be launched. He reached this conclusion late in the day, in the course of 1958, as the result of deep inner conflict. As he witnessed the dislocations caused by the Great Leap Forward and the establishment of the people's communes, P'eng increasingly realised that his first and greatest motive in becoming a Marxist-Leninist, concern for the plight of the Chinese peasantry, conflicted with his loyalty to the Party Leader, if not to the Party. He had fought for the victory of the CCP to help alleviate the misery of the countryside, not in order to push the peasants once more into need and even famine. It seems reasonably safe to suggest here that, together with his concern about the morale of the PLA rank-and-file, of whom approximately four-fifths came from the villages, P'eng's understanding of the peasantry's situation impelled him to the decision to 'speak up for the people'. When he did so, he ran — perhaps unintentionally — into headlong confrontation with Mao at the Lushan conference. Despite the few non-committal pleasantries which the Chairman uttered during his next and last meeting with P'eng on September 23, 1965, he could neither forget nor forgive the Lushan challenge. P'eng had to pay the price — a very high one — between December 25, 1966, and November 29, 1974.

The confrontation at Lushan may have had grave consequences for P'eng's career and personal life, but it had a radical effect of a different kind on his image among the 'old hundred names' (*Lao pai hsing*), i.e. the plain and simple people of China. For many of them the Marshal became the first Party man who had openly protested at their plight — who had dared to raise his voice in order to alleviate their misery. Rumours about the events at the Lushan conference began to trickle down in to the city alleyways and the villages between the autumn of 1959 and late 1962, and to this very day P'eng Te-huai remains one of the few CCP leaders genuinely respected by the common people, the 'masses' of Maoist verbiage. The present author can testify to this on the basis of numerous contacts with PRC Chinese since 1980, whenever and wherever he has told them of his intention to write this monograph. The image which P'eng, albeit unwillingly and without his instrumentality, projects among many inhabitants of the PRC appears greatly to exaggerate his political ideas and his abilities. But this image was already a force to be reckoned within the early 1960s, and it had to be destroyed by the planned projection of an entirely different image on behalf of Mao and his followers in order to win a political victory in the Cultural Revolution. P'eng's image among the common people may also have threatened that of other leaders after the death of Mao. But by then P'eng was already dead, and this image could be used for the political benefit of those leaders who had survived the storm. Thus since 1967 the CCP media have confronted the Chinese people and the world with two entirely different P'eng Te-huais: P'eng the villain and P'eng the hero.

P'eng Te-huai the villain

The systematic creation of the image of P'eng, the villain, began immediately after the open confrontation with Mao at the enlarged Politburo meeting in Lushan. However, it was meant only for internal consumption among the CCP élite who received the 'Resolution of the 8th Plenary Session of the Eighth CCP/CC concerning the Anti-Party-Clique headed by P'eng Te-huai', adopted on August 16, 1959. Only eight years later, on August 16, 1967, excerpts of this resolution were finally published in the CCP media.[4] The resolution already insinuated that there had been a conspiracy by a faction — or a 'clique' (*Chi-t'uan*) in the Party's Marxist-Leninist terminology — rather than an attempt by P'eng to persuade Mao to revise his policies through criticism of the communes and the Great Leap:

In the period before the Party Centre convened an enlarged session of the Politburo at Lushan in July 1959, and during the Lushan meeting, a fierce onslaught on the Party's general line, the Great Leap Forward, and the people's communes was made inside our Party by the right opportunist anti-Party clique which was headed by P'eng Te-huai and which included a handful of others, such as Huang K'e-ch'eng, Chang Wen-t'ien and Chou Hsiao-chou.[5]

This 'clique', so the resolution stated, had not just been formed at the Lushan conference:

The activities of the anti-Party clique headed by P'eng Te-huai aimed at splitting the Party have been going on for a long time. The letter of opinion which P'eng Te-huai wrote to Comrade Mao Tse-tung on July 14, 1959, . . . and his speeches and remarks in the course of the meeting represent the platform of the right opportunists in their attack on the Party. [. . .] P'eng Te-huai . . . in essence negates the victory of the general line and the achievements of the Great Leap Forward, and is opposed to the highspeed development of the national economy. [. . .] In his letter, he brazenly slandered as 'petty-bourgeois fanaticism' the revolutionary zeal of the Party and of hundreds of millions of people.[6]

Yet the allegation that P'eng and his supporters had formed a 'clique' was not a enough to explain why he should be criticised for making a deliberate attempt to split the Party. It had to be connected with the previous intra-Party dispute. So the resolution of August 1959 already created a link with the case of Kao Kang and Jao Shu-shih, both purged in 1955:

. . . the activities of the anti-Party clique headed by P'eng Te-huai prior to and during the Lushan meeting were purposeful, prepared, planned and organized. They represent a continuation and development of the case of the anti-Party alliance of Kao Kang and Jao Shu-shih. Investigation has now established that P'eng Te-huai and Huang K'e-ch'eng long ago formed an anti-Party alliance with Kao Kang, of which they were important members. Chang Wen-t'ien, too, participated in Kao Kang's factional activities.[7]

And because the members of the ruling CCP élite are Marxists, the reasons for P'eng's opposition to Mao had to be found in his socio-historical background, as it was presented in 1959:

P'eng Te-huai's present mistake is not accidental. It has deep social, historical and ideological roots. He and his accomplices and followers are essentially representatives of the bourgeoisie who joined our Party during the democratic revolution. P'eng Te-huai joined the Party and the revolutionary army led by the Party with the idea of 'investing in a share'. He only wants to lead others, to lead the collective, and does not want to be led by others, to be led by the collective. [. . .] Indeed, his anti-Party activities reflect the kind of class-struggle in which the Chinese bourgeoisie opposes the proletarian socialist revolution and attempts to remold the Party, and the army, and the world in its own bourgeois image. Since his world outlook is incompatible with revolutionary proletarian Marxism-Leninism, and runs directly counter to it, inside the Party he is naturally unwilling to accept the Marxist-Leninist leadership presented by Comrade Mao Tse-tung.[8]

Thus the resolution of the Lushan plenum had already delineated most of the principal features of P'eng's negative image, which was to be further developed during the Cultural Revolution: the idea of a conspiracy against Mao, the connection with Kao Kang and Jao Shu-shih, P'eng's alleged bourgeois ideology, and his character as a 'great ambitionist'.

One feature, however, was still missing in the 1959 image: the allegation that P'eng had co-operated with the Soviet Union to oppose Mao and the CCP leadership. At some time during the second half of 1962 — probably as part of Mao's successful attempt to prevent P'eng from being rehabilitated at the 10th plenum of the Eighth CCP/CC — an internal Party communication must have accused P'eng for the first time of 'clandestine connections with a foreign country' (*Li-t'ung wai-kuo*). Although such a document has not so far become available, we have evidence that he told his niece of this allegation, and at the same time refuted it, indicating that it particularly saddened him.[9] However, the image of P'eng projected by the Lushan plenum's resolution was not at that time, or until the summer of 1967, connected publicly with his name. In the autumn of 1959 the CCP media merely made general attacks on 'a number of rightist opportunist elements' who were said to 'oppose the general line of the Party, the tremendous leaps forward, and the people's communes'. But the connection with P'eng was still obvious. Only eleven days after the public announcement of his dismissal as Minister of National Defence on September 28, 1959, the alternate secretary of the CCP/CC Secretariat, Liu Lan-t'ao — who was himself to be purged and persecuted in the Cultural Revolution — attacked P'eng indirectly:

'Unity and unification are the lifeline of the Party. Absolutely no opportunist factions and absolutely no views and activities aimed at splitting or usurping the Party are allowed within the Party. To be sympathetic to and to connive in these anti-Party activities. . . . are, in fact, acts to help the bourgeoisie and to oppose the proletariat, regardless of the subjective desire. [. . .] There are persons who are determinedly opposed to placing politics in command, saying that as ideological and political work cannot yield grain or steel, this task is unable to solve any practical problems. This ideology, which tends to sever the political leadership of the Party from the practical work of the masses, . . . aims actually at weakening and even repudiating the leadership role of the Party'.[10]

While in 1959, and occasionally during the three years that followed, the attacks in the CCP media remained concealed, and direct condemnation was limited to internal Party documents, the full image of P'eng as villain was only revealed after the publication of the 1959 CCP/CC resolution in August 1967. At this point P'eng definitely became the 'great conspirator, great ambitionist, and great warlord', whose 'crimes' had their roots in the whole of his life. He had been born into a 'rich peasant's family';[11] the Hunan army which he joined in 1916 (1915, according to a source published in 1967) was not a provincial military

organisation but a 'KMT army'; and even his first personal
name — given him by his father — supposedly revealed his ambition:
'He was originally called P'eng Te-hua and, according to his own
confession, this name meant that all China should become his personal
possession.' In 1920, so it was now said, he 'fraternised with the local
bullies and bad gentry, accepting invitations to banquets, and he sent for
songstresses to keep his company. He led the dissolute and shameless life
of a parasite.'[13] This remained the only accusation of debauchery made
against him. Otherwise the attacks were mostly political, or were aimed
at establishing that he had a poor military record. Hence he 'wormed his
way' into the Party in 1928.[14] In 1967 the Red Guard publications
alleged that the P'ingchiang uprising was not staged by P'eng, but by
Huang Kung-lüeh and others, and P'eng only joined it hesitantly 'with
the ambition to advance [his career]'.[15] From then on P'eng's military
career was depicted as an almost incessant series of failures. He 'failed
miserably' in 1930, and in the 'Hundred Regiments Campaign, as well
as in the battle of Paochi in 1948'.[16] The victory of Shachiatien, on the
other hand, was not won by P'eng but 'personally directed by Chairman
Mao'. The same was said of the PVA successes at the beginning of the
Korean war: 'The first, second, third, and fourth campaigns were
fought by the PVA according to Chairman Mao's operational plans, and
a victory was won in each campaign.'[17] The fifth campaign, which ended
in failure, on the other hand, had been directed by P'eng in contraven-
tion of Mao's orders.[18]

Politically, P'eng was accused of 'faithfully implementing' the lines
proposed by Li Li-san in 1930, and by Ch'en Shao-yü (Wang Ming)
from 1932 to 1934 as well as in 1937–8.[19] Of course, following the
allegations in the resolution of the Lushan plenum, P'eng had also been
in 1953 'a ringleader of the Kao Kang/Jao Shu-shih anti-Party alliance.[20]
In his position as Minister of National Defence P'eng had implemented a
military line diametrically opposed to that of Mao. 'Seriously imbued
with the working style of a warlord', he copied everything wholesale
from Soviet revisionism;, particularly turning against the establishment
and promotion of the militia.[21] However, since 1957, he had developed
'clandestine connections' with the Soviet Union and was greatly
encouraged by Kruschev to attack Mao at the Lushan conference in
1959.[22]

Thus the image of P'eng Te-huai emerges as that of a great 'ambitionist' from a rich-peasant class background, who had joined the
communist movement only to advance his career and to achieve fame for

himself. His military achievements were mediocre and he had only been capable of winning victories under the direct leadership of Mao. He had co-operated with all the deviationists in the history of the Party since 1930, and had been an integral part of the alleged conspiracy of Kao Kang and Jao Shu-shih against Mao's leadership. At Lushan he had acted under the direct influence of the CPSU and Khrushchev (this accusation only came to the fore in 1962, and was not systematised till 1967, which leads one to doubt its reliability). Moreover, this warlord or KMT officer with a non-proletarian class background had never internalised the doctrine of the CCP:

P'eng Te-huai was never a Marxist. He is a great conspirator, a great ambitionist, a would-be gentleman. He is an old opportunist, he is a counter-revolutionary revisionist, he is the representative of the greatest capitalist-roader in power [Liu Shao-ch'i] within the army [. . .] When he joined the Party and the P'ingchiang uprising, he speculated with the revolution. The brain of this ambitionist is full of capitalist thoughts, full of revisionist thoughts. There is not the tiniest bit of Marxism-Leninism![23]

Given his non-proletarian background, P'eng had necessarily developed anti-Party thoughts throughout his whole life as a CCP member. There was nothing in his nature which could make him a loyal representative of the revolution led by Mao:

P'eng Te-huai always took a reactionary bourgeois viewpoint. He opposed Chairman Mao, he opposed the proletarian revolution and proletarian dictatorship. In all the historic struggles within our Party, he always stood at the side of the opportunists and opposed Chairman Mao's correct line.[24]

In the final Marxist-Leninist analysis, people like P'eng the villain, are not human. They have to be degraded to sub-human status, to be considered as animals that can be destroyed without qualms: 'These scoundrels like P'eng Te-huai are poisonous insects of Trotsky's and Khrushchev's ilk!'[25] They must be attacked and 'struggled' until they break down ('until they stink'). The CCP leadership and their supporters successfully meted this treatment out to P'eng from December 25, 1966, till his death eight years later.

P'eng Te-huai the hero

Immediately after his official posthumous rehabilitation by the 3rd plenum of the Eleventh CCP/CC on December 22, 1978, a new image of P'eng Te-huai began to emerge which had almost nothing in common with that promoted in 1959 and in 1967–8. However, some of its major elements had already been used to describe the Marshal in the late 1950s when he was still Minister of National Defence. At that time P'eng had been characterised in occasional media reports and war memoirs as extremely courageous and honest, and as a capable military leader who above all took great care of the ordinary soldiers under his command.[26]

Starting early in 1979 and continuing up to and past the publication of his 'autobiography' in December 1981, the personal image of P'eng the hero was systematically created. The CCP media started with a re-evaluation of his 'class background': now he was of 'poor origin',[27] even from a 'poor peasant's family'[28] or, as the editors of his 'autobiography' suggest, from a 'lower-middle peasant's family' — meaning that he originated from a proletarian or at least a semi-proletarian social group, according to the definition used by the CCP. The miseries of his child-hood and youth from 1905 to 1915 are now fully set forth, and his participation in the local uprising against speculating grain merchants in 1913 is emphasised. Of his career in the warlord armies and even in the KMT army as well, it is recounted that he excelled in battle, took great care of the men under his command and grew in political awareness, which led him finally to enter the CCP. It is pointed out that he joined the Party at a time when it was in a shambles, thus indirectly refuting previous allegations that he had joined the communist move-ment to advance his career. In July 1928 it was he himself who, together with some other CCP members, planned, started and led the P'ingchiang uprising.[30] Thereafter he had always shown the 'utmost loyalty to the Party and to the people'. Such loyalty had been the major reason why the Fut'ien rebellion against Mao failed: P'eng had refused to join the rebels, and at the Tsunyi conference in January 1935 it was he who turned the tide in favour of Mao by 'resolutely supporting the leadership position of Chairman Mao for the whole Party'.[31]

As for P'eng's military exploits, the CCP media have hardly ever again mentioned any of his defeats since January 1979, concentrating instead on his victories and insisting that the battle of Shachiatien was fought under his 'personal command and directives'.[32] So too were the battles of Yich'üan and Watzuchieh and the victorious campaign to conquer the Northwest of China.[33] No longer is it insisted that Mao himself planned the first four PVA campaigns in the Korean war; they are now described as having been planned and led entirely by P'eng.[34]

After his appointment as Minister of National Defence P'eng strove restlessly for the modernisation and professionalisation of the PLA, yet without neglecting the 'political work' which he had already strongly promoted during the Korean war.[35] On his inspection tours, which led him from the mountains in the western part of the country to naval bases in the far south, he incessantly called for greater efforts in training and to achieve the spread of technical knowledge.[36] At the same time he never forgot to look after the wellbeing of the common soldiers, caring for the quality of their food, their health and the environmental conditions of their barracks, and often for their personal problems. He helped his bodyguard to establish a family and to arrange a visit from his father, and cared for the families of old friends who had died in the Civil War.[37] A major element in the image of P'eng the hero is the emphasis on his simple life-style and his personal modesty, frugality and courage in dealing with the Party leaders. It is not denied that he was occasionally hot-tempered, but the new descriptions of P'eng after December 1978 stress that, while sometimes scolding his subordinates, he was always just and fair, and they did not resent his attacks because he was as strict and tough with his superiors as he was with them.[38] And P'eng is now reported as having neglected his personal wellbeing when he had to complete his self-imposed tasks.[39]

In discussing P'eng's political attitudes, his periods of leaning towards the concepts of Li Li-san in 1930, of Ch'en Shao-yü and the 'Twenty-eight Bolsheviks' in 1932-4, and of Ch'en Shao-yü and Chang Kuo-t'ao in 1937-8 are no longer mentioned. And of course there was no 'conspiracy', not even the formation of a group around P'eng before or at the Lushan conference. P'eng voiced his criticism of Mao because Mao had explicitly asked for such criticism at the beginning of the meeting; the Marshal had not the slightest intention of hurting the Chairman, and was somewhat astonished at the harshness of Mao's counter-attack.[40] Since December 1978 P'eng's military blunders have almost entirely disappeared from CCP media coverage. The battles of Kanchow and Kwangchang are no longer mentioned, nor are his defeats at Paochi and in the Kuangchung River valley. Thus he appears as an almost infallible military leader, an excellent tactician and — particularly in the many newly-published accounts of the battles of Shachiatien and Yich'üan-Watzuchieh — even at times an excellent strategist.

There have been five prominent features in the post-1978 evaluation of P'eng, which have become the major elements of his image as a hero of the CCP: 1. his humble origins, the misery of his youth, and his early compassion for the oppressed, which are presented as having finally led him into the communist movement; 2. his simplicity, frugality and personal honesty, which make him a 'shining example' of the virtues that a communist is supposed to display; 3. his great achievements not only as a campaigner and courageous soldier, but also now as an important and successful strategist (this feature of course requires his military blunders to become non-events in the history of the PLA and its forerunners); 4. his concern for the peasants, and his willingness to voice their complaints against the Three Red Banners policy which is now considered to have been a 'severe mistake' committed by Mao under the influence of evil advisers; and 5. his unswerving loyalty to the Party, and to the cause of communism, the climax of which occurred in his continuous quest for a 'fair judgement' by the Party during the agony of persecution.

We suggest here that the image of P'eng the hero was easier to create than that of P'eng the villain, because it could draw on more facts of his career and possibly even on genuine traits in his character and personality. But just as the image of P'eng the villain — particularly as constructed first by CCP media and then by Red Guard publications during the Cultural Revolution — finally reduced him to an almost sub-human status, so has his new image elevated him almost to superhuman heights. If our tentative evaluation of P'eng Te-huai's personality in the first part of this chapter comes close to the real P'eng — and the available sources suggest that it probably does — then both the images promoted at different times by the different circles that have formed the core of the CCP ruling élite bear remarkably little resemblance to the historical reality. This dissimilarity may be greater for the image of P'eng the villain but it is also noticeable in the case of P'eng the hero.

Does this mean that the CCP ruling élite, speaking through the media which it controls, have deliberately distorted the facts first to damage and later to enhance memories of P'eng the man? My research has led me to the conclusion that this question does not touch the essence of communist communications concerning persons. We should ask instead whether the CCP ruling élite was as interested in P'eng's personality as in the creation of symbols for the promotion of specific policies and the projection of specific Party leaders in power. We will now seek an answer to this question.

Personal images as an instrument of Party politics

Against the background of P'eng Te-huai's life, experience and political attitudes about which we have been able to grasp at least a few major aspects that can now be considered reasonably well-established, the two conflicting images of him projected within the PRC over the last twenty years have a certain unreality. This is definitely true of the image of P'eng the villain, but the image of P'eng the hero also shows a number of differences from historical fact. But it would seem that the two different cores of the CCP ruling élite who have projected these respective images — the Mao Tse-tung/Lin Piao/Ch'en Po-ta/K'ang Sheng/Chiang Ch'ing coalition in 1959 and, more intensively, after 1967, and the Teng Hsiao-p'ing/Ch'en Yün combine since 1978 — were not primarily interested in the destruction or the elevation of P'eng the man but in political ends for whose promotion he could serve as a communication symbol. This hypothesis takes on a clearer outline when we look at the political situation during the time when the two images of P'eng were first being projected on a large scale.

In the autumn of 1959, the negative evaluation of his personality in the resolution of the Lushan plenum was not projected beyond the confines of the élite itself, and the Chinese public were only informed of his dismissal from office and that some 'rightist opportunists', then still unnamed, had threatened Party unity. In August 1967, however, the man who had openly opposed Mao at the Lushan conference was publicly identified. Only twenty-seven days before the Party Centre finally published the eight-year-old Lushan resolution, the Commander-in-Chief of the Wuhan Military Area, General Ch'en Tsai-tao, had moved with his troops to support an *ad hoc* organisation which opposed the central leadership of the Cultural Revolutionary Left. When emissaries of the CRG came to Wuhan in order to throw the weight of the Party Centre behind the local enemies of this mass organisation, Ch'en had them arrested and brought before a 'struggle meeting'. Only after the central military leadership had employed parachutists, airborne units and a number of gunboats of the PLA navy's Yangtze flotilla to encircle Wuhan did Ch'en surrender, whereupon the arrested leaders from the capital were set free. The Wuhan events gave

Lin Piao and his supporters in the central military establishment reason to doubt whether the regional commanders would remain loyal to the centre. So an enlarged meeting of the CCP/CC's Military Commission was convened in Peking, at which on August 9 Lin pleaded with the regional military leaders for their support.[41] A few days later — probably on August 12 or 13 — this support was expressed and guaranteed, but by way of a compromise. The central leadership had, first, to agree to curtail the power and activities of the Maoist mass organisations with military help; secondly, to give the PLA a decisive share in the emerging new provincial leadership groups; and — last but by no means least! — to refrain from further attacks on generals and veteran cadres, with the exception of those whose names were included in a list jointly agreed by the regional commanders and the central authorities. This list, circulated by the centre on August 14, contained fifty-five names among which there was not even one of the regional military leaders. Yet prominent among those names was that of P'eng Te-huai, who was now singled out as the object of a major campaign of 'criticism and struggle' (*P'i-tou*). With his comparatively small following in the PLA — much smaller, at least, than that of Ho Lung, who had also been purged but was not attacked outside of Red Guard publications —, as a possible rival of Lin Piao, and as the first Party leader who had dared to oppose Mao openly since 1949, P'eng was an ideal target. The attacks on him and the projection of his image as that of a villain hurt none of the PLA leaders who were then still in positions of command. On the other hand they could serve as a warning to others to abstain from displaying undesirable attitudes in response to stimuli from the leadership, and they had the added value of placating the leading core of the Cultural Revolutionary Left.

P'eng's posthumous rehabilitation occurred at a time when Teng Hsiao-p'ing and his close associates had gathered enough strength to advance three major thrusts. The first of these, in internal élite politics, was an attempt to undercut and erode the power base of Hua Kuo-feng — who, since 1976, had tried to save as much as possible of Mao's concepts for the future of China — by means of a thoroughgoing re-evaluation of Mao as a person, and a revision of the policies which the Chairman had promoted in his later years. The second, in military politics, was a drive to move away from Mao's concepts of 'people's war', and back to the ideas of modernisation and professionalisation which had prevailed under the leadership of P'eng Te-huai in the 1950s. The third but not the least important, in rural societal politics, was a major offensive aiming at a total revision of the structures in the communes, with the ultimate goal of at least a partial de-collectivisation of agricultural production, while collective ownership of land would be preserved. For all these three thrusts P'eng Te-huai could serve as an extremely appropriate symbol. While basically loyal to the Party, he had dared to criticise Mao's mobilisatory policies which, in 1958–9, Hua Kuo-feng had obediently supported. P'eng's name stood for the first large-scale attempt to modernise the PRC's armed forces and to introduce into them traditional values of military professionalism. At the Lushan conference he had been the first to attack the organisational concept and the validity of the communes as well as of the Great Leap Forward. Moreover, he was no longer alive, which meant that his elevation to the status of a national hero could mobilise the sympathies which many Chinese harboured for him without threatening the political power of Teng and his close associates.

In each of the two cases, therefore, the image of P'eng projected by the CCP leadership group in the ascendant at the time was in fact a symbol of undesirable or desirable personal attitudes and political concepts. This symbol was used in political communication as a paradigm for the doctrine prevailing at that particular period of PRC history. P'eng Te-huai as an individual may have aroused the anger or the sympathy of members of these dominant leadership groups, and it may be that his life and personality provided more material for the hero image that has been propagated since December 1978 than for the villain image of the years after August 1967. Yet it was not the individual person who truly mattered in either case, but the positive or negative symbol into which his personal images could be manipulated.

From the way in which P'eng Te-huai was presented in the CCP media one can develop a number of reasonably well-founded assumptions concerning the techniques used by the Party in the manipulation of such personal images. The positive symbol must come from a proletarian or at least a semi-proletarian social background. He must be courageous, straightforward, honest and fair in his attitudes towards subordinates as well as superiors. He must be depicted as leading — or having led — a simple and frugal life, full of concern for the 'masses'. Moreover, he must have attained outstanding professional success. Most important, he must have an impeccable record of loyalty to the Party and the cause of communism. P'eng's life and personality provided a considerable amount of material for such an image, but even so, a number of his achievements and positive qualities were blown up out of all proportion in the propaganda depicting him as a symbol for the revisionist policies introduced in the PRC after 1978.

The negative symbol, for its part, must come from a social background which has imbued him with 'bourgeois' thoughts and attitudes. He must have adhered to all — or at least most — of the 'deviations' that had occurred in the history of the CCP since he joined it. He is depicted as utterly inept and to have had repeated failures in his professional career. He must have participated in conspiracies against the 'correct' leadership of the Party, even if he was not accused of such participation at the time when the respective 'conspiracies' were first discovered. And, if possible, he must have co-operated with 'foreign countries', preferably those considered as the 'major enemy' at the time when the negative symbol is developed, e.g. with the United States in the case of some intellectual leaders attacked after the Hundred Flowers Campaign, or with the Soviet Union in the case of P'eng Te-huai. Finally, at least some negative traits of character must be attributed to him, in P'eng's case mainly a persistent ambition.

Such positive or negative symbols, however, are not entirely artificial; some foundation in fact is always to be found in the symbol's real life and personality, even though — as in the case of P'eng the villain — it can be rather scanty. When the theory of 'people's war' and guerrilla ethics held a dominant place in CCP military doctrine, P'eng's propensity for professionalism and professional military ethics provided such a foundation, as did his temporary co-operation with Li Li-san in 1930, and with the pro-Comintern factions within the Party in 1932–4 and 1937–8. The foundation for the image of P'eng the hero appears much stronger. The projection of this image draws heavily on the true facts of his life-history, and it could incorporate some of his more obvious personal characteristics, although these had to be painted in somewhat stronger colours than a realistic evaluation would allow. Yet in order to develop the positive symbol, his numerous military blunders and his connection with some of the intra-élite groups which are still considered 'deviationist' had to be swept under the carpet. The CCP media did this with apparent success between 1979 and 1981.

After this brief description of the basic features of image manipulation, we have finally to ask how the mechanisms of image promotion appear to work in political communication in the PRC. Both positive and negative symbols are chosen by decisions of central leadership bodies, and the *leitmotiv* of their projection is given either by resolutions of central decision-making organs or by an initial statement of a major Party leader, or both. In the case of P'eng the villain it was a compromise decision by the enlarged meeting of the CCP/CC's Military

Commission in August 1967. The basis was the eight-year-old Lushan resolution, which was augmented and sharpened by Lin Piao's speech at the 'struggle meeting' against P'eng in late August 1967. It should be emphasised that the case of P'eng was different from those of many CCP leaders who were persecuted during the Cultural Revolution in that he was only attacked in a big way by Red Guard publications *after* the central CCP media had sounded the clarion call for the offensive against him. In the case of P'eng the hero, the decision was made by the 'Central Work Conference' preceding the 3rd plenum of the Eleventh CCP/CC, and ratified by this plenary meeting. The basis for the projection of the image itself was provided by Teng Hsiao-p'ing in his commemorative address at P'eng's belated obsequies on December 24, 1978.

Then both positive and negative symbols are first set forth in major articles, mostly editorials, in the central CCP media, which elaborate on the *leitmotiv* set by conference decisions and by the speeches of major leaders. After these initial signals, however, the methods of promoting positive and negative symbols develop along different lines. In the promotion of a positive symbol, newspapers and journals begin to publish memoirs by the symbolic person's former associates, subordinates or relatives, which bring out and strengthen the characteristics which form the major elements in the projected image. After some months these testimonies are concentrated in the form of commemorative literature, and symposium volumes or individual memoirs lauding the symbol will be published in large editions at very low prices. If the political goals for which the positive symbol has been employed are achieved, at least to a great extent, the image-promotion campaign comes to an end. P'eng Te-huai is still a positive hero in the PRC today, but the CCP media have seldom mentioned him since the end of 1981, and few, if any, publications about him have appeared since then.

Till the late 1970s if not later still, the 'wrath of the masses' was more important in the promotion of a negative symbol than memoirs or reminiscenses. It was instigated by a flood of newspaper articles and broadcasts degrading the person selected as the symbol, and had to be aired at large criticism and struggle meetings. At these meetings the language used to describe the negative symbol became ever more denunciatory. He was a 'scoundrel', an 'insect', a 'gangster', a 'black back-stage man', or — in the Maoist terminology much favoured in 1966–71 and again in 1976 — even a 'freak and monster'. If the undesirable attitudes represented by the negative symbol had been overcome, or if a new negative symbol had taken its place, the personal image of the villain simply disappeared from the public media. The person who had been developed into a negative symbol became a non-person, his name was no longer mentioned, and often — as in the case of P'eng — even his relatives and closest associates did not hear from him for years until or unless there was a major policy reversal and the former villain became a hero. However, since the 11th Party Congress of the CCP the handling of disgraced CCP leaders has undergone some changes. In spite of being criticised, the former Chairman Hua Kuo-feng and his purged supporters have, since 1980, not been as thoroughly degraded as P'eng and many others — including the leadership core of the Cultural Revolutionary Left — were till the late 1970s.

In all these techniques of political communication, the actual person concerned does not seem to play an important part. The symbols become thoroughly de-personalised: they are no longer individuals but images to be manipulated. However there are limits to the degree of manipulation possible, because at least some grains of fact have to remain for the symbols to be created. It is in this way that the man P'eng Te-huai, particularly since 1967 and again since late 1978, has been overlaid by his images. He was used, and because of his unswerving loyalty to the Party we cannot even be sure whether he would have resented his de-personalisation for political ends.

NOTES

1. Cf Emilio Vasari, *Die ungarische Revolution 1956: Ursachen, Verlauf, Folgen* (The Hungarian revolution of 1956: Origins, progress, consequences) (Stuttgart: Seewald, 1981), p. 165 f.
2. Sándor Kopácsi, *Die ungarische Tragödie* (The Hungarian tragedy), (Stuttgart: DVA, 1979), p. 109.
3. MacFarquhar, *Origins 2, op. cit.*, p. 194.
4. *JMJP*, Aug. 16, 1967. The English translation of the excerpts from the resolution here was taken from URI, *Peng*, pp. 39–44.
5. *ibid.*, p. 39.
6. *ibid.*, p. 40.
7. *ibid.*, p. 41.
8. *ibid.*, p. 42.
9. Jung, *loc. cit.*, p. 70; and Lung, *loc. cit.*, p. 63.
10. *JMJP*, Sept. 28, 1959.
11. *Canton collection*, p. 5.
12. Ssuma Lu, *op. cit.*, p. 118. Author's emphasis. '*Te-hua*' means 'to be awarded splendour', also 'to be awarded China'.
13. *ibid.*

14. *Canton collection*, *ibid*.
15. Ssuma Lu, *ibid*.
16. *Canton collection*, *ibid*.
17. Ssuma Lu, *op. cit.*, p. 128.
18. *ibid*., p. 129.
19. *Canton collection*, *ibid*.; and Ssuma Lu, *op. cit.*, pp. 120–3.
20. *ibid*., p. 132.
21. *ibid*., p. 131.
22. *ibid*., pp. 134 f. and 137.
23. *JMJP*, August 17, 1967.
24. *HC*, no. 13, Aug. 17, 1967, p. 22.
25. *ibid*., p. 21.
26. So, e.g., *HCPP*, vol. X (1959), pp. 49–52.
27. Huang K'e-ch'eng in *HC*, no. 1, Jan. 1979, p. 38.
28. *CNP*, unpaginated.
29. *PTHTS*, p. 1.
30. *PCC*, pp. 7 and 27 f.
31. *ibid*., p. 8 f.
32. *ibid*., p. 13.
33. *ibid*., pp. 97–107.
34. *ibid*., p. 125 f.
35. *ibid*., p. 127.
36. Ching/Ting, *op. cit.*, pp. 40–3.
37. *ibid*., pp. 38 f. and 57 f.; and *Ke-ming wen-wu* (*Revolutionary Heritage*), Peking, no. 5, Sept. 1979, pp. 26–30.
38. Ching/Ting, *op. cit.*, p. 47.
39. *ibid*., p. 16 f.
40. Huang, *Letter*, p. 4 f.
41. Cf. Domes, *Politics*, *op. cit.*, p. 190 f.

BIBLIOGRAPHY

SOURCE MATERIALS

Braun, Otto, *A Comintern Agent in China, 1932–1939* (London: Hurst; Stanford University Press, 1982), transl. by Jeanne Moore from *Chinesische Aufzeichnungen, 1932–1939*, Berlin (East): Dietz, 1973.

Canton Area Workers Revolutionary Committee (ed.), *Fan-ke-ming hsiu-cheng-chu-yi fen-tzu 'jen-wu-chi'* (Collected biographies of counter-revolutionary revisionists), Canton, March 1968.

Capital Red Guard Congress, Chinghua University Chingkangshan Corps (ed.), *Ta yin-mou-chia, ta yeh-hsin-chin, ta chün-fa P'eng Te-huai tsui-e shih* (The wicked history of the big plotter, big ambitionist, big warlord P'eng Te-huai), Peking, November 1967.

Central Publishers, *Ke-ming wen-hsien* (Revolutionary Documents), vol. VII; XXV, Taipei: Central Publishers, 1955.

Chang Kuo-t'ao, *Wo-te hui-yi* (My memoirs), 3 vols, Hong Kong: Ming-pao Monthly Press, 1972–4.

Chih-yüan-chün i jih (One day with the PVA), 4 vols, Peking: People's Publishing House, 1956.

Ching Hsi-chen with Ting Lu-yen (eds), *Tsai P'eng-tsung shen-pien: Ching-wei ts'an-mo-te hui-yi* (At the side of Commander P'eng: Memoirs of a body-guard), Chengtu: Szechwan People's Publishing House, 1979.

Chou En-lai, *Report on the Question of Intellectuals,* Peking: Foreign Languages Press, 1956.

Chu Te, P'eng Te-huai, *How the Eighth Route Army Fights in Northern China,* Hong Kong: New China Information Committee, 1939.

Editorial Bureau For Revolutionary Heritage (ed.), *Chi-nien P'eng Te-huai T'ung-chih* (Remember Comrade P'eng Te-huai), Peking: Chinese Revolutionary Museum, 1980.

Haik'ou tsao-fan pao (Haik'ou Rebel News).

Ho K'e-hsieh *et al.*, *Chiang-chia wang-ch'ao-te fu-mieh* (The downfall of the Chiang dynasty), Peking: PLA Cultural Publishing House, 1961.

Hsing-huo liao-yüan (A single spark can start a prairie fire), 10 vols., Peking: People's Literature Publishing House, 1958–63.

Huang K'e-ch'eng, 'Please give Comrade P'eng Te-huai his reputation back', Letter to the Organization Department of the CCP/CC, Nov. 19 1978.

Huang-ch'i p'iao-p'iao (The Red Flag waves) 20 vols., Peking: People's Publishing House, 1957–80.

Mao Tse-tung, 'On coalition government', *Chieh-fang jih-pao* (Liberation Daily), Yenan May 2, 1945.

——, 'On New Democracy' in *Mao Tse-tung hsüan-chi* (Selected Works of Mao Tse-tung), vol. 2, 2nd edn, Peking: People's Publishing House, 1969.

Mao Tse-tung t'ung-chih shih tang-tai tsui wei-ta-te Ma-k'e-ssu-Lieh-ning-chu-yi-che

(Comrade Mao Tse-tung is the greatest Marxist/Leninist of the present), no place, no publisher (cf. note XX, chap X).

New China Publishing House (ed.), *Cheng-feng ts'an-k'ao wen-chien* (Reference Documents of the 'Cheng-feng'). Yenan: New China Publishing House, 1944.

P'eng Te-huai, *Cheng-ch'ü t'e-chiu k'ang-chan sheng-li-te hsien-chüeh wen-t'i* (Grasp the problems of securing victory in the protracted war of resistance), Yenan: no publisher, November 1937.

——, *San nien K'ang-chan yü pa-lu-chün* (Three years' war of resistance and the 8th Route Army), Yenan: New China Publishing House, 1940.

——, *Wo-men tsen-yang chien-ch'ih Huapei liu nien-te k'ang-chan* (How did we stand through six years' war of resistance in Northern China?), Yenan: New China Publishing House, 1943.

People's Publishing House (ed.), *Heng-tao li-ma P'eng chiang-chün* (General P'eng, efficient and courageous in battle), Peking: People's Publishing House, December 1979.

——, *K'ang-jih chan-cheng shih-ch'i-te Chung-kuo jen-min chieh-fang-chün* (The Chinese PLA in the period of the anti-Japanese war), Peking: People's Publishing House, July 1953.

——, *P'eng Te-huai tzu-shu* (Autobiography of P'eng Te-huai), Peking: People's Publishing House, December 1981.

——, *Stories of the Long March,* Peking: Foreign Languages Press, 1958.

Political Department of PLA Unit 51034 (ed.), *Wei hsin Chung-kuo fen-tou* (Fighting for a new China), Shenyang: Ch'un-feng Literature and Arts Publishing House, 1981.

Resist-America Aid-Korea Association General Chapter (ed.), *Wei-ta-te k'ang-Mei yüan-Ch'ao yün-tung* (The Great Resist-America Aid-Korea Movement), Peking: People's Publishing House, 1954.

Shanghai People's Publishing House (ed.), *Jen-min-te hao tsung-li* (The good Premier of the people), vol. 1. Shanghai: People's Publishing House, 1977.

Ssuma Lu (ed.), *P'eng Te-huai,* Hong Kong: Research Institute on Chinese Problems, 1969.

Teng Chung-hsia, *Chung-kuo chih-kung yün-tung chien-shih* (Short history of the Chinese labour movement), Yenan: New China Publishing House, 1943.

Union Research Institute (ed.), *Collected Works of Liu Shao-ch'i, 1958–1967,* Hong Kong: URI, 1968.

CHINESE NEWSPAPERS, JOURNALS AND PERIODICALS

Ch'angchiang jih-pao (Yangtze River Daily), Wuhan.
Cheng-ming (Debate), Hong Kong.
Chieh-fang-chün pao (Liberation Army Daily), Peking.
Chieh-fang jih-pao (Liberation Daily), Yenan.
Chieh-fang jih-pao (Liberation Daily), Shanghai
Ch'ien-hsien (Front), Yenan.
Chin-tai-shih yen-chiu (Studies of Modern History), Peking.
Ching-chi kuan-li (Economic Management), Peking.
Ching-chi yen-chiu (Economic Studies), Peking.
Ch'inghai jih-pao (Ch'inghai Daily), Hsining.
Ch'ün-chung chou-pao (The Masses Weekly), Yenan.
Chung-kung yen-chiu (Studies on Chinese Communism), Taipei.
Chung-kuo ch'ing-nien pao (China Youth Daily), Peking.
Chung-yang jih-pao/Central Daily News, Taipei.
Honan jih-pao (Honan Daily), Chengchow.
Hsin chien-ch'a (New Investigation), Peking.
Hsin-hua jih-pao (New China Daily), Yenan.
Hsin-hua wen-chai (New China Digest), Peking.
Hsin-hua yüeh-pao (New China Monthly), Peking.
Hsin-hua yüeh-pao wen-chai-pan (New China Monthly Digest), Peking.
Hsin Hunan jih-pao (New Hunan Daily), Changsha.
Hung-ch'i (Red Flag), Peking.
Hung-ch'i t'ung-hsün (Red Flag Bulletin), Chiangmen, Kwangtung.
Hupei jih-pao (Hupei Daily), Wuhan.
Jen-min jih-pao (People's Daily), Peking.
Ke-ming wen-wu (Revolutionary Heritage), Peking.
Kuang-ming jih-pao (The Light Daily), Peking.
Kung-jen p'ing-lun (Workers' Review), Canton.
Min-kuo jih-pao (Republican Daily), Wuhan.
Nan-fang jih-pao (Southern Daily), Canton.
Nei-meng-ku jih-pao (Inner Mongolian Daily), Huhehot.
New China News Agency, Peking.
Nung-ts'un kung-tso t'ung-hsün (Rural Work Bulletin), Peking.
Pai-k'e chih-shih (Encyclopaedic Knowledge), Peking.
Ssuch'uan jih-pao (Szechwan Daily), Chengtu.
Ta-p'i-p'an t'ung-hsün (Great Criticism Bulletin), Canton.
Tung-fang-hung (The East is Red), Peking.
Tung-hsi-fang/East and West, Hong Kong.
Wen-ke feng-yün (Storm Clouds of the Cultural Revolution), Peking.
Wuhan kang-erh-ssu (Second Steel Headquarters of Wuhan), Wuhan.

LITERATURE

Abegg, Lily, *Chinas Erneuerung: Der Raum als Waffe* (China's Renewal: Territory as a Weapon), Frankfurt/Main: S. Fischer, 1940.

Ahn Byung-Joon, *Chinese Politics and the Cultural Revolution: Dynamics of Policy Processes,* Seattle: University of Washington Press, 1976.

Barnett, Doak A. (ed.), *Chinese Communist Politics in Action,* Seattle: University of Washington Press, 1969.

Baum, Richard/Frederick C., Teiwes, *Ssu-ch'ing: The Socialist Education Movement, 1962–1966,* Berkeley. Calif.: University of California Press, 1968.

Belden, Jack, *China shakes the World,* New York: Random House, 1949.

Bradbury, William C., *Mass Behaviour in Battle and Captivity: The Communist Soldier in the Korean War,* Chicago University Press, 1968.

Brandt, Conrad, *The French Returned Elite in the CCP,* Hong Kong University Press, 1961.

Chang, Carsun, *The Third Force in China,* New York: Bookman Associates, 1952.

Chang Chia-ao (Chang Kia-ngau), *The Inflationary Spiral: The Experience of China, 1939–1950,* Cambridge, Mass.: Harvard University Press 1958.

Ch'en Chih-hua (Chi Hwa Chen), 'Verkehrsentwicklung and Verkehrsplanung in China and ihre Auswirkungen auf die Volkswirtschaft' (Communication development and communication planning in China and their implications for the economy), unpubl. doct. diss., University of Vienna, 1941.

Ch'en Kung-po, *The Communist Movement in China,* ed. Martin Wilbur from MA thesis, Columbia University, 1924, New York: Columbia University Press, 1960.

Cheng Chu-yüan, *The People's Communes,* Hong Kong: URI, 1959.

Cheng Hsüeh-chia, *Chung-kung Fut'ien shih-pien chen-hsiang* (The real story of the Chinese Communist Fut'ien incident), Taipei: Institute for the Study of International Communism, October 1976.

Chow Tse-tsung, *The May Fourth Movement: Intellectual Revolution in Modern China,* Cambridge, Mass.: Harvard University Press, 1960.

Clark, Ann B., *Selected Biographies of Chinese Communist Military Leaders,* Cambridge, Mass.: Harvard University Press 1964.

Compton, Boyd, *Mao's China: Party Reform Documents,* Seattle: University of Washington Press, 1952.

Domes, Jürgen, *China after the Cultural Revolution: Politics between Two Party Congresses,* London: C. Hurst & Co., 1976.

——, *The Internal Politics of China, 1949–1972,* London: C. Hurst & Co., 1973.

——, *Socialism in the Chinese Countryside: Rural societal policies in the People's Republic of China, 1949–1979,* London: C. Hurst & Co., 1980.

——, *Vertagte Revolution: Die Politik der Kuomintang in China, 1923–1937*

(Adjourned revolution: Kuomintang politics in China, 1923–1937), Berlin: De Gruyter, 1969.

——, *Von der Volkskommune zur Krise in China* (China from the commune to crisis), Duisdorf: Studiengesellschaft für Zeitprobleme, 1964.

Dutt, Vidya Prakash (ed.), *East Asia: China, Korea, Japan, 1947–1950,* Oxford University Press 1958.

Fokkema, Douwe W., *Literary Doctrine in China and Soviet Influence, 1956–60,* The Hague, Mouton, 1965.

Gittings, John, *The Role of the Chinese Army,* Oxford University Press, 1967.

Glaubitz, Joachim, *Opposition gegen Mao: Abendgespräche am Yenshan und andere politische Dokumente* (Opposition against Mao: Yenshan evening chats and other political documents), Olten/Freiburg i. Br.: Waltern, 1969.

Goldman, Merle, *Literary Dissent in Communist China,* Cambridge, Mass.: Harvard Univesity Press, 1967.

Goodman, David S.G. (ed.), *Groups and Politics in the People's Republic of China,* Cardiff: University College Press, 1984.

Griffith, Samuel B. II, *The Chinese People's Liberation Army,* New York: McGraw-Hill 1967.

Groeling, Erik van, *Der Fraktionskampf in China* (Factional Fight in China), Cologne: Bundesinstitut für Ostwissenschaftliche und Internationale Studien, 1970.

Guillermaz, Jacques, *A History of the Chinese Communist Party 1921–1949* (New York: Random House, 1972), transl. from *Histoire du parti communiste chinois, 1921–1949* (Paris: Payot 1968).

Harrison, James Pinckney, *The Long March to Power,* New York: Praeger, 1973.

Heinzig, Dieter, *Mao Tse-tungs Weg zur Macht und die Otto-Braun-Memoiren* (Mao Tse-tung's road to power and Otto Braun's memoirs), Cologne: Berichte des Bundesinstituts für Ostwissenschaftliche und Internationale Studien, no. 52, 1970.

Heller, J., 'The Labour Movement in China', *Communist International,* Moscow, November 1925, pp. 3–5.

Hollington, K. Tong, *Chiang Kai-shek,* 2nd edn, Taipei: China Publishing Co., 1953.

Hsiao Tseng, *T'u-ti kai-ke chih li-lun yü shih-chien* (Theory and Practice of Land Reform), Taipei: Land Bank Press, 1953.

Hsiao Tso-liang, *Power Relations within the Chinese Communist Movement, 1930–1934: A Study of Documents,* Seattle: University of Washington Press, 1961.

Huang Chen-hsia, *Chung-kung chün-jen chih/Mao's Generals,* Hong Kong: Research Institute of Contemporary History, 1968.

I-chiu-liu-chiu fei.ch'ing nien-pao/1969 Yearbook on Chinese Communism, Taipei: Intelligence Bureau, MND, 1969.

Isaacs, Harold J., *The Tragedy of the Chinese Revolution*, 2nd edn, Stanford University Press, 1951.

Joffe, Ellis, *Between Two Plenums: China's Intraleadership Conflict, 1959–1962,* Ann Arbor, Mich.: Center for Chinese Studies, University of Michigan, 1975.

——, *Party and Army: Professionalism and Political Control in the Chinese Officer Corps,* Cambridge, Mass.: East Asian Research Center, Harvard University, 1965.

Johnson, Chalmers A., *Peasant Nationalism and Communist Power: The Emergence of Revolutionary China, 1937–1945,* Stanford University Press, 1962.

Joy, C. Turner, *How Communists Negotiate,* Net York: Macmillan, 1955.

Kindermann, Gottfried-Karl, *Der Ferne Osten in der Weltpolitik des industriellen Zeitalters* (The Far East in World Politics in the Industrial Age), Munich: DTV, 1970.

Klatt, Werner (ed.), *The Chinese Model,* Hong Kong University Press, 1965.

Kraus, Willy, *Economic Development and Social Change in the People's Republic of China,* New York: Springer, 1982.

Leckie, Robert, *Conflict: The History of the Korean War,* New York: G. P. Putnam's Sons, 1962.

Leng Shao-ch'uan/Norman D., Palmer, *Sun Yat-sen and Communism,* New York: Praeger 1960.

Lethbridge, Henry J., *The Peasant and the Communes,* Hong Kong: Dragonfly Press, 1963.

Lucas, Christopher, *Women of China,* Hong Kong: Dragonfly Press, 1965.

MacFarquhar, Roderick, *The Origins of the Cultural Revolution:* vol. 1, *Contradictions among the People, 1956–57,* Oxford University Press, 1974; vol. 2, *The Great Leap Forward, 1958–60,* Oxford University Press, 1983.

McLane, Charles B., *Soviet Policy and the Chinese Communists, 1932–1946,* New York: Columbia University Press, 1958.

Michael, Franz, *Mao and the Perpetual Revolution,* New York: Barron's/Woodbury, 1977.

Moody, Peter R., *The Politics of the Eighth Central Committee of the Communist Party of China,* Hamden, Conn.: Shoe String Press, 1973.

Nee, Victor/James Peck (eds), *China's Uninterrupted Revolution: From 1840 to the Present,* 2nd edn, New York: Random House, 1975.

North, Robert C., *Moscow and Chinese Communists*, 2nd edn, Stanford University Press, 1968.

Office of the Vice-Chief-of-General-Staff For Intelligence Republic of China (ed.), *Kung-fei chün-ch'iu: T'an chih P'eng Te-huai che-ke jen.* (Military Chieftains of the Communist Rebels: What do we known about that man P'eng Te-huai?), Taipei: MND, October 1968.

Paloczi-Horvath, Georg, *Mao Tse-tung,* Frankfurt/Main: S. Fischer 1962.

Parish, William L./Martin King Whyte, *Village and Family in Contemporary China,* University of Chicago Press, 1978.

Rue, John A., *Mao Tse-tung in Opposition, 1927–1935,* Stanford University Press, 1966.

Schurmann, Franz, *Ideology and Organization in Communist China,* 2nd edn, Berkeley, Calif.: University of California Press, 1968.

Schwartz, Benjamin, *Chinese Communism and the Rise of Mao,* Cambridge, Mass.: Harvard University Press 1958.

Shabad, Theodore, *China's Changing Map: National and Regional Development, 1949–1971,* 2nd edn, New York, 1972.

Snow, Edgar, *Red Star over China,* rev. edn, New York: Grove Press, 1956.

Tang, Peter S.H./Joan M. Maloney, *Communist China: The Domestic Scene, 1949–1967,* South Orange, NJ: Seton Hall University Press, 1967.

T'ang Leang-li, *The Inner History of the Chinese Revolution,* London: publisher unknown, 1930.

——, *Wang Ching-wei: A Political Biography,* Peking: China Publishing House 1931.

Teiwes, Frederick C., *Politics and Purges in China.* White Plains, NY: M.E. Sharpe, 1979.

Thornton, Richard C., *China: A Political History, 1917–1980,* Boulder/Colo.: Westview Press, 1982.

Tsou Tang, *America's Failure in China, 1941–1950,* University of Chicago Press, 1963.

Union Research Institute (ed.), *The case of P'eng Te-huai,* Hong Kong: URI, 1968.

—— (ed.), *Communist China, 1949–1959,* Hong Kong: URI, 1961.

US Government Printing Office, *United States Relations with China: With Special Reference to the Period 1944–1949,* Washington, DC: US Government Printing Office, 1949.

Van Slyke, Lyman P., *Enemies and Friends: The United Front in Chinese Communist History,* Stanford University Press, 1967.

Vasari, Emilio, *Die ungarische Revolution 1956. Ursachen, Verlauf, Folgen* (The Hungarian Revolution of 1956: Origins, Progress, Consequences), Stuttgart: Seewald, 1981.

Wang Chien-kuo, *Jen-hai ta tsui-hsi* (The Criminal Game of the Human Ocean), Hong Kong: Asia Publishing House, 1956.

Wang Chien-min, *Chung-kuo kung-ch'an-tang shih-kao* (Draft History of the ·CCP), Taipei: Reprint Institute on Mainland Problems, Chinese Cultural University, 1983.

War History Bureau, Ministry of National Defense, RoC (ed.), *K'an-luan chiang-lieh chan-shih: Yich'uan chan-tou* (History of heroic generals of the Civil war: The battle of Yich'uan), Taipei: MND, 1959.

Whiting, Allan S., *China crosses the Yalu,* New York: Macmillan, 1960.

——, *Soviet Policies in China,* New York: Columbia University Press, 1954.

Whitson, William W./Hùang Chen-hsia, *The Chinese High Command: A*

History of Communist Military Politics, 1927–1971, New York: Praeger, 1973.

Wilbur, Martin/Julie L. How, *Documents on Communism, Nationalism, and Soviet Advisers in China,* New York: Columbia University Press, 1959.

Wladimirow, P.P., *Das Sondergebiet Chinas, 1942–1945* (The Special Area of China, 1942–1945), Berlin (East): Dietz, 1976.

Wu Hsiang-shuang (ed.), *Chung-kuo kung-ch'an-tang chih t'ou-shih* (Behind-the-scenes History of the CCP), 2nd edn, Taipei: Wen-hsin Publishers, 1962.

NON-CHINESE JOURNALS AND PERIODICALS

China Digest, Hong Kong.
China News Analysis, Hong Kong.
China Quarterly, London.
Current Background, Hong Kong.
Current Scene, Hong Kong.
Facts and Features, Taipei.
International Press Correspondence (Inprecor), Moscow.
Issues and Studies, Taipei.
Kraznia Sviezda (Red Star), Moscow.
Quatrième International, Paris.
Der Spiegel, Hamburg.
Union Research Service, Hong Kong.
Worldview, New York.

INDEX